ABOUT THE AUTHOR

Mary Anne Fitzgerald is the author of *Nomad*, a bestselling account of African adventures. Born in South Africa, she has been a regional correspondent for the *Financial Times*, *Independent* and *Sunday Times* based in Nairobi. She now divides her time between Africa, Europe and the United States.

MY WARRIOR SON

Mary Anne Fitzgerald

PENGUIN BOOKS

PENGUIN BOOKS

Published by the Penguin Group
Penguin Books Ltd, 27 Wrights Lane, London W8 5TZ, England
Penguin Putnam Inc., 375 Hudson Street, New York, New York 10014, USA
Penguin Books Australia Ltd, Ringwood, Victoria, Australia
Penguin Books Canada Ltd, 10 Alcorn Avenue, Toronto, Ontario, Canada M4V 3B2
Penguin Books (NZ) Ltd, Private Bag 102902, NSMC, Auckland, New Zealand

Penguin Books Ltd, Registered Offices: Harmondsworth, Middlesex, England

First published by Michael Joseph 1998
Published in Penguin Books 1999
1 3 5 7 9 10 8 6 4 2

Copyright © Mary Anne Fitzgerald, 1998
All rights reserved

The moral right of the author has been asserted

Set in Monotype Sabon
Printed in England by Clays Ltd, St Ives plc

For my loyal and loving parents,
Mary and Gordon Richdale

LIST OF CHARACTERS

Peter Lekerian – Mary Anne's adopted Maasai son
Aunt Naserian – a Samburu woman and distant relative who brought Peter
  up as her son
Mary Richdale – Mary Anne's mother
Gordon Richdale – Mary Anne's father
Nursie Pursie – Mary Anne's nanny when she was a child
Anthony Fitzgerald – Mary Anne's husband
Tara Fitzgerald – Mary Anne's elder daughter
Petra Fitzgerald – Mary Anne's younger daughter
John – Petra's boyfriend
Amina –Tara and Petra's nanny
Sintahui – the nightwatchman at the Fitzgerald's house in Nairobi
Russi – Sintahui's wife
Kyengo – the cook
Esta – the gardener
Kate Macintyre – a friend who lived with the Fitzgeralds in Nairobi
Kathy Eldon – an American friend who shared an office with Mary Anne in
  Nairobi
Mike Eldon – Peter's parent figure after Mary Anne left Kenya
Gabriel Lochgen – a Samburu who ran the aid organisation SAIDIA
Godfrey – a boy whom Mary Anne put through school
Chege – another boy whom Mary Anne put through school
Peris – Chege's sister
Kipenget – a Maasai woman who lived on the slopes of the Ngong Hills
Kili – Kipenget's husband
Meriape – Kipenget's eldest son
Narasha – Kipenget's second son
Lepapa – Kipenget's third son
Segenun – one of Kipenget's many daughters
Joseph Simel – a Maasai activist and Peter's best friend
Anastasia – Joseph's wife
Rosina – Peter's girlfriend
Grace Wagaki – the girl who momentarily vied for Peter's affections
Kashoi – Peter's friend at Oloolaiser High School
Gachuka – a bully at Oloolaiser High School
Njenga – another bully at Oloolaiser High School
Nnee – Peter's real mother
Mebikie ole Kepaeka – Peter's father

Mama Safi – Mebikie's sister

Lankisa – Peter's eldest 'one stomach' brother

Nalotu-esha – Lankisa's wife whose name means she who was married during the rainy season

Salaiyo – Nalotu-esha's baby

Mure, Medien, Ntangenoi, Mbele – some of Peter's siblings

Tumpeni – Peter's youngest 'one stomach' brother

Lori Grinker – a photographer who went to the Plain of the Blue Trees with Peter and Mary Anne

Mereso – a wealthy Maasai man whose *boma* was on the Plain of the Blue Trees

Noonkepa – one of Mereso's young wives whose name means The Breaking of Water at Birth

Mama New York – the nickname Mary Anne gave to another of Mereso's young wives

Ololokidomo – Noonkepa's lover whose name means he who comes from the *boma* with too much cow dung

Nanyokie – Mereso's beautiful young daughter whose name means red

Ole Materr – Nanyokie's husband

Pashet Sengeruan — Mereso's brother and chairman of lower Engaruka

Mary – Pashet's wife

Jekleen – Mary's daughter

Cecilia – the young Maasai girl who was circumcised at Engaruka

Moses Lekor – chairman of upper Engaruka

Paul – a Maasai at Engaruka who spoke English with an Oxford accent

Bill Forse – an English dairy farmer

Alan and Leslie Mowlem – goat farmers in Somerset

Mr Mash – an English farmer who raised Limousin cattle

Mr Boughton – a retired pig farmer who lived next to the Mash farm

Fiston – the prize Limousin bull which Peter looked after when he was in England

Chris Marshall – Mary Anne's friend who drove her and Peter to Engaruka

Tariq el Gamal – owner of the Ostrich Park and Peter's employer

Nasaroni – the most sought-after doctor in Kiserian

Miti – the Kikuyu mechanic who rescued Mary Anne

CHAPTER I

Peter's squat image was caught by the thin winter light on the bowl. It lengthened and vanished as I turned it, rubbing the wad of silver cleaner along its curves. He was leaning against the kitchen counter with feet crossed at the ankle like a farmer taking the sun against a stone wall. Or a warrior loitering on a *duka*'s shaded verandah. I smiled and said, 'It's a bit dark still. It gets lighter.'

Though there were no curtains to shut out the sky, jellyfish grey that day, it was too early for the morning to capture the sheen of the saucepans at his elbow or to tease the blues and reds of the Ethiopian enamel dishes ranked above the stove.

I stood up and crossed from kitchen to living room. The Tibetan knives needed cleaning as well. I paused in front of them longer than necessary, to take in the books arranged along the shelves, for a moment forgetting he was with me. Their presence filled the room, brought it to life. I still felt a frisson of pleasure every time I looked at their covers. Some were dog-eared, some in remarkably pristine condition considering how hastily they had been thrown into cardboard boxes and the long years they had lain mouldering in an attic. Each one spoke of history. It was good to have them around again.

Despite my blonde complexion and British passport, I am an African. The heat of Africa's blood runs through me. I celebrate the rustle of the grasses on the plains, the wind drifting across mountains millions of years old. Yet Africa is unpredictable. Decisions can be reversed before the ink has dried and lives shattered by entrenched power. Six years ago, I was expelled overnight from my home in Kenya for an article I had written for the London *Sunday Times*. It criticized the government for its human rights abuse. In the years that followed I was forced to acknowledge a difficult truth. When you are wrenched from the soil where you are born, new territory holds scant appeal. To amputate the past is to invite the exile's pain of loss.

Before the books arrived, only a month ago, I would stand at the window of the small living room, staring across the street at the seagulls lined up on the ridge of the church roof, and reach out to a landscape that wasn't choked by buildings and traffic. I hated falling asleep to the grunting of the trucks as they changed down a gear to round the corner. I longed for the familiar banshee whoops of hyena calling to an inky night sky, the resounding thump of a moth's wings against the bedside lamp.

Now, with my possessions around me, a sense of home began to banish the restlessness. I admired the arrangements of artefact and photograph, the goatskin rugs that covered the floor. I picked up a dirt-encrusted gourd and passed it beneath my nostrils to capture the ghostly smell of charcoal and curdled milk. The living room had taken on a personality. I behaved as if it was a lover.

Peter took one of the sausages from the plate beside him and held it between finger and thumb while he peeled off the skin. He did this slowly and with great care as if all his future lay before him, which it did. Before, I had not been able to offer him a home. But now he was here. It was his first full day in England.

He lifted back the browned skin as tenderly as if it was the petal of a flower and talked as he did so. I listened, watching him from the corner of my eye.

'Did you hear all that noise last night?'

'Noise?'

'I woke up. I was very frightened. I thought it must be thieves. I thought, they are breaking into M. A.'s room.'

'I didn't hear a thing.'

'There was banging and crashing.' His mouth formed a big O. 'Whooooeee. It was such a big noise.'

'Wind. Blowing the chairs around on the roof garden. It gets very windy at night.'

'I looked at my watch. It was 1 a.m.' He put the sausage back on the plate and raised his hands palms outwards giving them hard little flicks. 'The windows were shaking. I thought someone was trying to get in.'

'The wind makes them rattle. Don't worry. It's not like Nairobi. We're safe here.'

'I brought my *rungu*. It's under my pillow. I didn't bring my sword because of the immigration people. They would have said, "And why are you coming to England with a machete? Who do you want to cut?" And I am not even a British person who would be bringing a *soovenah*.' He pronounced it as someone who knows the word through reading not speech, embalming it with lilting vowels.

'Are you warm enough?' I said.

He was eating breakfast in a knee-length waterproof coat. A diaphanous white Somali shawl was draped over his head and tucked under the collar. It looked like a tea towel and lent a faintly androgynous air to the outfit. He had taken off his woollen gloves to peel the sausage.

'Why aren't you wearing that sweater I gave you?'

He drew his mouth into a tight circle as if he was going to blow the down off a dandelion. 'I can't. It's not good for my skin. The wool will give me a rash.'

I said nothing. He would learn soon enough.

When he had finished the sausages, he turned to the sink and opened the tap. He wet the plate with a trickle of water. Then he shut the tap and made slow circles on the plate with a dishwipe while I rubbed away at the Tibetan knife. He talked all the time he was doing it about his friends at home and what they would think of him when he went back. When the plate had been put to dry on the draining board, he slumped back against the counter and fixed me in his stare. A thin reef of white had appeared in the sky. The muted voices of the mothers and children walking to school rose to meet it. 'Is it cold now?' he asked.

He said it in an eager, innocent sort of way.

I gave him a lopsided smile. 'I don't think it's cold in the kitchen. But it's cold outside. Go and stick your head out the window. See what it feels like.'

He went into the living room and came back shaking his head. 'It's too much. It's too much.'

I picked up the silver and put it on the tablecloth and threw the

3

used newspaper into the bin. 'Come and sit down for a minute. I want to ask you something.'

There are things that a mother should know about her son. When he was born, for instance. And, if you are not his *tumbo moja* mother, where and how he was born. I wanted to dispel African approximation and replace it with Aristotelian fact. So I started at the beginning.

'How old are you?'

'Twenty-three.'

'You're twenty-two.'

'I was born in 1972, the year of *pee elak Irkololik enkeene*. When the Irkololik age group untied the traditional rope.'

'So you're twenty-two.'

'Tomorrow is 1995. I'll be twenty-three.'

'No you won't. You have to calculate from the day you were born. Not from the beginning of the year.'

He was determined. 'Then I was born in 1971.'

'Well, in that case you're twenty-three.'

Having found the means to arrive at the age he wanted to be, he bent and rested his head on my shoulder. It was a gesture of affection that I remembered well. 'Thank you M. A. for helping me to know how old I am!'

He grinned and I grinned back, finding pleasure in the easy compromise. The year ahead was certain to be stitched with far more difficult ones. Was there sufficient love to bridge the cultural chasm that yawned between us and to bond us as mother and son?

My adopted son, Peter Lekerian, is a Maasai. This Galahad with dream-laden eyes doesn't evoke the postcard image of the proud nomad standing on one leg, sunlight reflecting off his spear and cattle photogenically positioned behind his right shoulder. Peter wears slacks bought in the downtown bazaar and trendy, second-hand jackets that arrive in tattered brown parcels from overseas. Peter is gregarious and likes making new friends. If he stood watching cattle all day without someone to talk to, he would be lonely.

There is a photo of him in his red *shuka*, the traditional garb of his age group. It is propped on the windowsill beside my desk where

I can see it while I work at the computer. He is aglow with finery. The friends I show it to cannot tell if his smile is one of pride or laughter. I know it is both. Peter is convinced that Maasai chic is the apogee of African fashion.

Strands of beads are heaped about his neck. Slivers of bead-encrusted leather encircle his ankles and wrists. A large triangle of ochre has been smeared onto his shoulders and chest and tapers towards his belly button. The ochre is a mineral ground to powder and mixed with animal fat. The warriors use it as bodypaint. They sit on the ground and etch the designs of their clan onto each other's cheeks with twigs. It is fastidious work that takes many hours.

Lying against the dark concave flesh of Peter's knee is a lion's tail. This particular bit of frippery confirms he is in the make-believe realm of dressing up. The tassel of salt-and-pepper hair is a medal for bravery, exclusive to warriors who have killed a lion with a spear.

The watery London light has mellowed the African reds to russet. But I imagine that on the day the photo was taken the ochre glistened, catching the soft tunnels of morning sun falling through the trees outside the window. From my vantage point behind the desk I look at the photo and the trapdoor of memory snaps open to send me tumbling through time. The odours of the *boma* sing in my nostrils: goat urine, udders swollen with milk, great pats of cow dung, and wood smoke from the cooking fires. This trick of recall never fails to make me homesick.

I think of photos of other Kenyans, standing in Trafalgar Square amongst the pigeons, which are hopefully dispatched to a sunnier clime. They wear overcoats that are too big for them and smile into the lens. Like Peter, they stand divided between stardust and confusion, straddled between the culture which is their birthright and the one they have adopted. Peter wants to be the lion-killer, but he also wants to be the man about town. He would like to commute between a mundane world and a heroic one.

My maternal impulses are rooted in pragmatism. I want the best for him, but it is difficult to determine just what that is. Perhaps it is to be at home in two worlds: Africa and the West. Right now, at the cusp of the centuries, Maasai culture, like that of the American

Indians a hundred years ago, is fragile. It needs intensive care if it is to survive the transition to modern times. I would like Peter to be aware of land legislation and water tables, to know about dam construction and how democracies function. I would like him to surf the Internet so that he can ride his future on the crest of a wave. Lion hunts have very little to do with all this.

Peter aspires to clothes, music and cars. He wants security and status: an office job and money, marriage to a girl who speaks good English. In the overcrowded, decaying confines of urban Africa, to have these things is to be very lucky indeed.

Yet with ancestral yearning he also desires the life he has never truly been part of. His *rungu* is an icon for a world where his hair is braided and long and flaps against the belt at his waist as he dances. And in his dance he spirals towards the sky, chanting a song that rumbles from the depths of his belly, and the girl he has beaded for his own throws out her chin and tight breasts, and her collars of beads rise and fall as she ululates her love with shut eyes. The warriors sweep forward, spears aloft, passing across the parched wasteland like some sort of frenzied serpent. Touching his *rungu*, Peter is among them. His dreaming is tempered by an ache for the steadfast, transient society of animals and grass, ritual and ceremony that is not his.

Peter wants the kudos of being a warrior without having to live in the arid land of his relatives where he would trudge miles for a drink of water. Who can blame him for that? Why do I, regarded as an incurable romantic by the rest of the family, strive to ground fantasy in fact where he is concerned? What does it matter that he conjures up for my friends the slap of his thorn-scratched feet as he runs over the stones, the whoosh of his spear arcing towards its target and the soft thunk as it finds the lion's flesh. Peter moulds the truth into different shapes as it suits him. That is the African way. I think. In any case, it's Peter's way.

He was about twelve years old by the time I met him. The cultural dichotomy had already set in. What is taken for granted elsewhere is deemed a privilege in Kenya. Not all parents can afford schools or even understand the need for them. This is particularly true among the Maasai. Once launched along the path of formal education, it was inevitable that Peter would struggle with a split identity.

Yet, as his mother, I have presented him with even greater opportunities which otherwise would not have come his way. Now that the family has a home in England, I want him to be a part of it and more. He says he wants to be in tourism and that he wants to raise cattle. I hope that he can get work experience with a tour company and on a farm. I know very little about office life and nothing at all about ranching, but I will learn from him. He will explain the ins and outs of marketing holiday destinations to the English and how to fatten many cattle on a few acres of land. Computerized tourism. Intensive animal husbandry. Understanding these things will put Peter on a course to becoming rich and successful. When he returns to Kenya, they will call him the Big Man. I imagine Peter's future and feel proud of him already. I worry too. Am I opening a Pandora's box? The chimeric monster of disappointment has always been lying in wait, ready to entrap us both. Now that Peter is in London and we can spend time together, perhaps we will come to subdue it.

CHAPTER 2

Anthony and I had been husband and wife for four years when the big drought of 1974 settled on the land. At first we ignored it. We were too new to married life to be excited by disaster, too involved in our doll's-house life to be disturbed by misfortune that struck beyond our nuclear family. For by that time we had two lovely daughters – Petra the baby, and Tara, who was three.

Anthony owned an advertising agency. I ran a public relations consultancy. We lived ten miles outside Nairobi, an easy commute into town. We had finished building our new home a year before and were still settling in. It was a lovely house hidden from the rest of the world amongst native vegetation at the end of a winding dirt driveway. Before marrying Anthony I'd worked as an assistant to a professional hunter. After the wedding, I told him I wanted to live in a tent. So we constructed an A-frame with mahogany and cedar from the forests of the Mau escarpment. We put the living room and dining room beneath these honeyed beams that smelt of loam. The bedrooms were on the ground floor. When you sleep you travel other spaces. You don't need a view.

Our property stood on a ridge which fell away to the Mbagathi River. On the far side of the river were the Athi Plains. They were contained by the gently rolling Mua Hills to the east, the silvery snow-capped peak of Mt. Kilimanjaro to the south, and to the west, the Ngong Hills. It was 125 miles to the horizon, and the plains looked empty to the naked eye. In fact, they were filled with lion and cheetah, large herds of zebra, giraffe, wildebeest, antelope and gazelle. And the Maasai.

In the late afternoons we sat on the upstairs verandah and gazed on the rise and fall of the Ngongs' knuckled summits. Their green slopes sucked the parched plains to them, damming all those miles and miles of sun-becalmed space. The savannah was only five miles away yet an unbridgeable chasm lay between us and this timeless other Africa inhabited by the Maasai. They had no electricity to defy the dusk, no running water or telephone, no doctor to ease the bronchial coughs brought on by sleeping in smoke-filled huts. Our property had once belonged to the Maasai. We were living on ancestral land.

After we had decided where to build, we employed a man to cut a clearing in the bush. In the day, when he was hacking and scything away with his machete, it was his domain. At night he retired to his corrugated-iron shack and the animals took over: a couple of lions, a leopard, several giraffe and sometimes a herd of eland. The builders, who lived on site too, were mostly tolerant of the bush conditions but given to occasional complaint. They said the lions stopped them from stepping outside for a pee in the middle of the night. Now it was I who griped about the wildlife. The giraffe browsed on the hibiscus and the passionflower vines I had planted against the bedroom walls.

'Look, Petra, *twiga*,' said Tara, standing on her bed and pressing her nose against the window. *Twiga*, giraffe. It was one of the first words she learned.

Engagement, wedding, nesting, babies . . . one phase had flowed on from the other. It had happened effortlessly, confirming my conviction that nothing could violate our conjugal domesticity. Hardship wasn't factored into my expectations.

I had met Anthony the day he arrived in Nairobi. He had flown out from London overnight, worked all day at his new job as creative director for an ad agency and then found himself at the raucous, whiskey-drinking end of a duck shoot. I was less than friendly, perhaps because I mistrusted Englishmen or maybe because I realized that I fancied him. 'Don't think it's all parties and elephant hunts. We work hard too. And when we do go hunting, we carry our own meat,' I harrumphed. It was an inauspicious start.

We didn't meet again for several months until our hostess asked Anthony to be my escort at her New Year's party. We saw the dawn in, sitting on the doorstep of my one-room cottage. Three weeks later I took him to spend the weekend on a friend's ranch. One of the men shot an eland, and I insisted on staying behind to help the tracker. I needed practice at skinning and butchering, I announced.

That night Anthony proposed even though my behaviour did nothing to paint me as a homemaker. We served eland curry at the engagement party.

I behaved like a white African, but my family's roots in the continent were only a generation deep. My parents, Mary and Gordon Richdale, had departed the suburbs of London for Johannesburg immediately after their honeymoon in early 1939. I was born in the wake of World War Two, the second of their two children. Not long after that, my father quit his job as head of a mining house to accept a position as president of a large company which supplied precious metals to American industry. He, my mother, my elder brother Jeremy and I set sail from South Africa to London on the *Capetown Castle*. My eighth birthday was celebrated as we crossed the equator. When we docked in New York on yet another ocean liner, the *United States*, it was as immigrants. Nursie Pursie, our South African nanny, was with us, too. She was white, of course. This was in the 1950s.

A limousine took us to our new home, a thirty-room mansion set atop a hill in the New Jersey woods. Another chauffeur-driven car had followed behind carrying the steamer trunks and my mother's hat boxes and vanity cases. It was my first intimation of our changed lifestyle. From then on we always travelled with an entourage of friends, hangers-on and luggage.

Nature had soon captured my soul. I spent hours, the whole day if possible, wandering through the countryside accompanied by imaginary playmates. They were the comic-book heroes of the day: Robin Hood, Prince Valiant, the Lone Ranger riding his stallion Silver. I was dreamier, more solitary than Jeremy, who was soon sent to boarding school. My father was too busy working to be around much. My mother spent a lot of the time being sad because, she said, she did not fit into the American way of life as we did. Only Nursie Pursie noticed my absences, but said nothing as long as I returned in daylight. I took this to be a conspiracy but thought nothing more of it. In my child's heart, I accepted her unconditional love as my birthright.

When I was fourteen, my mother sat me down and said we were leaving the States. There was no explanation. A cross-examination of my brother failed to shed further light on the matter. He was halfway through seventeen, had a crewcut and wore dark glasses – 'shades' – even at night. He looked like he was interning with the FBI. We spent a year in London living in an expensive hotel overlooking Hyde Park. Then my father announced that we were going back to South Africa.

Ensconced once again in the country they loved, my parents shed the trauma of their sudden departure. My father found status as chairman of a merchant bank which he ran from an office in downtown Johannesburg. My mother became giggly and girlish, which was the hallmark of her charm, and looked svelte and beautiful in her long evening gowns. They were living out the heyday of their marriage. My father bought a thirty-acre estate in the veld and transformed a run-of-the-mill farmhouse into a Spanish-style mansion. My mother covered it with pink and green chintz. My father filled it with the antique glass paperweights and furniture he loved to collect. There was a floodlit tennis court, a swimming pool and stables. On the weekend a dozen or more sat down to meals in the poolhouse. We were a small family but we were never lonely. My father had metamorphosed as a patron of sport. He financed aspiring golfers, tennis players and racing drivers. None of them hit the big time, but we got to know some star athletes. Jackie Stewart showed me how to roll a car and I discovered Ken Rosewall, the Wimbledon champion, ate steaks for breakfast. One of our houseguests, whose six-month stay set a record even by our stand-ards of hospitality, reckoned that the servant population was one per acre. I don't know if this included the prisoners who came once a week to do the heavy gardening work. They wore baggy white uniforms and were to be found in the further reaches of the property weeding and trundling wheelbarrows under the bored gaze of a warden.

The prisoners' silent presence was discomforting. I watched them and wondered if they had broken into a house like ours to steal silver, money, things that could be carried easily through the night on foot. Had they done it to feed their families? What did their homes look like? Perhaps they had caught a bus into the city from a distant place where the rains failed and crops shrivelled on the stalk. Perhaps they had walked from back door to back door looking for work and had been turned away as they stood with eyes fixed on the fedora clasped in their hands. Most likely they had been picked up for being in a white suburb without a pass. It was the apartheid days of the 1960s.

After boarding school in England for two years, I begged my father to let me attend Georgetown University in Washington, DC. I passed all the exams even though I partied a lot. Then I dropped out without a thought to how I had wasted his money. Academia was too confining. By then nineteen, I became a scriptwriter for a radio production house. I drove to the office in the Alfa Romeo my father had bought me, which meant that I wasn't around when the anonymous prisoners arrived once a week standing in the back of a truck. While I was living this life, I detected a schism in my articles of faith. I basked in the love and security provided by my parents. I had everything anyone could ever want. Yet it wasn't enough. The opulence of Johannesburg's smug white suburbs was unsettling.

The journey towards self-knowledge can set us on paths undreamed of. Mine was triggered by the realization that all around me were people mired in a dead-end poverty that had been sanctioned by the state's cornerstone policy of segregation. I knew that if I stayed in South Africa, I would become involved in political protest which in turn might land me in jail. I opted instead for a road trip through thousands of miles of African bush. When I reached Kenya, having turned twenty-one while camping by the railroad tracks at Victoria Falls, I unpacked my duffel bag and stayed.

The big drought of 1974 was my first intimation of how Africa can punish those who live there. A fierce light scalded the sky and made it transparent. It impaled us with its brightness, leaving us exposed, with no place to hide. The heat stifled our will to do anything and suffocated the land. In Nairobi the sun glared from the shop windows and ricocheted off cars sitting in traffic jams. It turned the tarmac into an oozing glue that stuck to the tyres. Not even the shadows could withstand it. They were no longer deep pools of soothing darkness but brittle and glassy and hot.

We all suffered that year. Out on the plains the waterholes shrank to puddles, then dried up completely. The earth became shrivelled and cracked, as certain a presentiment of death as looking upon the face of an octogenarian. Then the wind appeared, snatching up the bare soil and carrying plumes of it into the gardens and through the windows onto the tables. It coated our skin and even seemed to impregnate our brains. It was a time when we shouted at our neighbours and argued over nothing.

We waited for the rains month after month. When they didn't come and it was finally agreed that they had failed altogether, we commuted to the office alongside Maasai herders seeking grazing on the outskirts of town. They had walked long miles in sandals made of car tyres and wore faded red *shukas* or shabby macs that were buttoned up to the collar and didn't reach their knees. Their eyes stared straight through us.

The cattle's coats were lank and smelled musty, as if they were stuffed. In time hunger made the animals angular and concave. Then they had no stuffing at all. They were just bones in a leather pouch. Soon after that there were carcasses by the side of the road.

Anthony and I continued as normal: going to work, coming home and playing with the children, eating supper, discussing what we'd done during the day.

Tara's bedroom was by the front door and her eager little face was usually there to greet us when we drove up in a cloud of dust. But not on this particular day during the big drought. I knew the moment the house hove into sight that something was dreadfully wrong.

'Why are the curtains drawn?' I asked Anthony.

'Beats me. Maybe Amina's throwing a party.'

'And these flies. Look at all these flies around the place. What on earth's going on?'

We tried the front door. It was locked. Neither of us had a key. We never locked it, didn't see the need to. So we banged on the door, calling out the *ayah*'s name. 'Amina! Amina!'

There was no answer. We turned aside, puzzled and not a little alarmed.

A flowerbed ran beneath Tara's window and extended further to the left. It was backed by a fence of split bamboo poles which blocked the view of the lawn at the front of the house. We called it the garden although the foraging giraffe ate most of the flowers that tried to grow there. There was an entranceway in the fence which gave access to the servants' quarters and the stairs which led to the kitchen on the upper storey. It was through this which we now walked.

It is a feature of owning a home, particularly one that you love, that you know it so well you automatically picture each aspect in your mind before turning the corner and coming upon it. I knew that when I passed through the entranceway I would see the herb garden with its yellowed parsley and dying fennel and on the left a continuation of the bamboo fence enclosing the servants' compound. There would be the struggling pawpaw trees, the wilting granadilla vine, perhaps a dog bowl or two licked clean. Beyond that, the sweep of the lawn down to the thick tangle of bushes and trees. It wasn't a huge garden, but neither was it small. An acre or so.

On other days there would have been Petra asleep in her pram beneath a tree. Beside it, sitting with her legs stretched out in front of her, the comforting bulk of Amina in her gingham dress and white apron. And Tara, engrossed in playing some game with her nanny. But on this day, because the house was shuttered and still, I expected the garden to be deserted, abandoned to the blistering sun. So I was momentarily confused when I saw something else.

It was a Maasai encampment.

A thin trail of grey smoke spiralled up into the leaves of a tree. It came from a cooking fire which smouldered where Amina was accustomed to park Petra's pram for her afternoon nap. Two warriors were crouched over it making tea in a battered tin saucepan. They squatted on their haunches with their backs to us. The wild, bright light glistened on the ochred plaits which tapered down their spines. As they stretched and stirred, their minimalist movements traced the understated strength of their muscles. By their side, where sometimes Amina and Tara played pretend supper with Tara's dolls, two spears had been thrust into the ground. They stood tall and straight, were composed almost entirely of metal with just a hand's

14

breadth of wood separating the throwing and stabbing ends. They glinted and sparkled. Fighting spears to protect the livestock.

There were certainly enough cattle around. They were foraging in the bushes, trampling the flowerbeds, spread out across the lawn. All over Africa cattle stood like this, heads down, tails swishing at the flies, steadfast teeth grinding and munching the cud. But never before had they done it on our carefully laid Kikuyu grass.

Instinctively I looked back to the house. The curtains were drawn across the plate-glass doors of our bedroom. So were the curtains in Anthony's dressing room. On the bedroom doorstep sat a third warrior. His spear was planted between his feet and he touched it loosely with one hand. His stare appeared insolent, but it was an affectation which masked something else. I sensed defiance born of desperation. We had to tread gently. We had stumbled onto a powder keg.

'Looks like we've got visitors,' said Anthony.

'Yes, but have we still got a family?'

My question was answered as soon as I'd said it. There came the impatient rattle of a key in the door, a creak as it was opened. Standing above us on the kitchen balcony was Amina. She had a protective arm around Petra, who was riding on her hip. Tara, clutching her other hand, gave a happy shout. 'Mummy! Daddy!' Petra blinked in the sunlight and looked around with bland curiosity. But Amina was Boadicea incarnate. She was a Nandi, had worn skins as a young girl. Her forefathers had routed the weakling Maasai before the British came. In short, fighting blood ran in her veins. She surveyed the scene with a fierce stare.

'You'd better come inside,' she told us in Swahili.

It had started in the morning, Amina said. The warriors drove their cattle before them and with them came the flies. When Amina heard the soft plopping sound of hoof on dust, she went to the dining-room window and saw the cattle fanning out, the warriors leaning against their spears with their feet crossed at the ankles, cleaning their teeth with sticks. She ordered them to leave at once. There was a heated exchange. Amina could tell the warriors were very angry because they advanced on her, holding their spears stiffly and away from their bodies. They threatened to burn the house down if she tried to stop their cattle from grazing on the lawn. She retreated inside, locked the doors and closed the curtains. She had to protect the children. She harrumphed as she said it.

'But why didn't you phone us?'

She folded her arms across her ample bosom and gave me a look which implied I was particularly stupid. 'I cannot read. And I don't know how to use a phone.'

'What are we going to do?' asked Anthony.

What do you do for any visitor who has come to stay? I didn't give it a second thought. 'Make some *posho*. They must be starving.'

The atmosphere changed after the peace offering of a meal. The warriors remained aloof and self-contained but they were friendly enough. Even Amina's obdurate heart softened. After a day or two she once more wheeled Petra's pram into the shade of a tree on the lawn although she made an ostentatious show of covering it with mosquito netting against the flies. She even gave in to Tara's pleas to go and play with the warriors. Tara would hunker down next to the fire while they were brewing tea, or stand by their side in her flowered dungarees and watch the cattle, little fingers firmly clutching a spear shaft. Tara loved everyone.

Our visitors were a subject of conversation in the neighbourhood. We were a close-knit community. We might not have sought each other out in other circumstances yet the shared difficulties of living in a comparatively remote area had linked us together. But yielding right of way to the Maasai made our family different and set us apart. It was not because the incident was considered unusual. Other neighbours, who had turned them away, had later had rocks hurled through their windows in the middle of the night. Nor were we criticized for putting the girls in danger. We all left our children in the care of *ayahs* and trusted them completely. It was because we had made the Maasai feel welcome. This was frowned upon. The cattle brought unspecified disease which would spread to the horses and the dairy cows. There was a subtext to this. Despite living in the heart of Africa, the neighbourhood cosmos was almost exclusively white. We had opened the borders to the barbarian horde.

The big drought was a watershed. It was as if the Maasai had made a chink in my life and inserted a wedge in the chink. I'd been in *bomas* in my hunting days. It was usually on business: to take on a local tracker when we'd lost a wounded buffalo or to show the clients 'a real Maasai home'. After the warriors' visitation, I began spending more time with them. Not immediately or frequently but in the capricious and random manner in which life unfolds. Friends of mine took me along to visit Maasai friends of theirs. We set off for two, three, four days and lived with them as they lived. We took presents of sugar and tea, helped to collect water, ate and talked together, went on excursions to look at cattle and game. Sometimes we drove to the nearest wood-fronted general store to buy things. For a good part of the time we were left to mooch around on our own. And when there was a party, by way of a ceremony, we joined in and had a good time. I formed friendships with families which have endured to this day.

Very often I took Tara and Petra too. They accepted everything with equanimity except the food, which they hated. *Posho*, the staple, is ground maizemeal cooked up into a sort of tasteless white blob which you knead with your fingers. That wasn't too bad. But the *maziwa lala*, they said, was 'yukky'. They didn't like curdled milk the consistency of lumpy yoghurt. The Maasai keep it in a calabash which has been rinsed out with goat's urine. After the milk has been poured in, it is stirred with embers from the fire. The smoky flavour overlays an acrid bouquet of urine. It's an acquired taste.

Sometimes when the land was fat with rain, they slaughtered a goat for us. Our hosts led it into the bush, where it was suffocated with a cloth clamped to its nostrils. The animal paddled its legs and twitched in an ever more feeble way as life ebbed from it. Its eyes were always wide open.

The legs flexed and straightened and the men crowded round. With their knives they sliced along the line of the brisket through the clam-white layers of fat. Then they used the ball of their fists to carefully punch the hide away from the carcass and free a flap of skin. It formed a basin beneath the jugular. Someone pierced the vein with his knife and blood spurted and bubbled into the flayed hide.

'Come, Mary Anne. Drink.' The guest must be first. They were kneeling and looked up, excited and pleased. I knelt too and dipped my head towards the pool of redness. They were watching me closely. I took a few prim sips. It was warm and essentially devoid of taste. I sat back on my haunches, ran the back of my hand across my lips and smiled. We all laughed.

Supping from the jugular put me into a state of free fall. It was an atavistic act which cut me loose from the endorsement and condemnation of the Western value system. I was open to everyone's truths. The Maasai believe that the blood which courses through the veins of their herds is a gift from God. They slaughter by suffocation so that not a sacred drop is spilled. I could assimilate that easily enough. It held resonances of the Catholic mass.

The Maasai prayed to Nkai, who was the unknown, embodying those things beyond their influence: the telegraph, railway engines, thunderstorms and rain. They had two gods because they said opposites kept the world in balance. The light and the dark. Nkai Narok, the Black God, was the same colour as them. He was good, benevolent. The Red God, Nkai Nanyokie, was the angry avenger with tongues made of lightning, who chased away the rain and brought famine and death.

Often, they repeated the prayer four times. Four was a potent number. The life source came from four-legged animals, and life's cycle was reflected in the four colours of black, green, red and white. The Black God, Nkai Narok, produced black children, who were protected by green, the colour of regeneration. Green symbolized nutrition, growth and survival. Mothers tied green plants or green grass at their babies' necks and waists to invoke robust health. When the boys matured, they became warriors and painted themselves with red ochre. Red blood flowed from the animals slaughtered for the ritual ceremonies that marked their passage into manhood. Finally, they became old and their hair turned white. They died and their white bones were left to bleach in the sun.

Nkai, intamelono nintorropil too naleng e kishu o tunglana.

O God, bring sweet and fragrant blessing to the best of cow and man.

I began to feel more and more at home in this other milieu,

looked forward to the excursions in the bush. By the time Tara was six and Petra three, we were attending ceremonies to which few *wazungu* were invited. It was the year of the *eunoto*, the rite of passage when warriors become elders and settle down to married life.

Maasai society revolves around a patriarchal hierarchy that is rigidly compartmentalized into age groups. After boys have been circumcised, usually sometime between the ages of sixteen and twenty, they form an age set and become warriors. This creates a special bond amongst agemates which lasts for the rest of their lives. The old-boy network is called into play, time and time again, as men move up together from one age group to the next: junior warrior to senior warrior, then junior elder, firestick elder and, finally, senior elder. From youth to senility, a man who has been circumcised with another man is expected to share his wife with him, save his life in battle, help him out when the going gets tough. Age bonding is a survival mechanism to ensure that a community is mutually supportive.

Each change in a man's status is couched in ritual. The *eunoto*, which closes the chapter on the halcyon days of warriorhood, is the finest ceremony of them all. Warriors are the Maasai military. They adhere to the hard-charging Spartan philosophy of discipline, deprivation and facing the enemy head on. They are arrogant and brave to the point of being foolhardy. If a lion comes near the *boma* or steals a cow, they regard its insolence as a personal affront and hunt it down at once. When the clans are threatened by an enemy tribe, they blow the sacred kudu horn to muster a war party armed with spears and buffalo-hide shields.

Because they protect the clans, warriors are privileged and indulged. A blind eye is turned when they rustle cattle from neighbouring tribes. They eat apart and make much of their sexual rowess. In the language of Maa, warrior – *imurani* – is almost synonymous with penis – *imura*. Uncircumcised girls start to take warrior lovers by the time they are twelve and sometimes when they are as young as nine.

Warriors are wonderfully vain: painted faces and beaded necklaces, bracelets, anklets and earrings. They braid their hair into long plaits and dye it red with a mixture of ochre and fat. At the time of the *eunoto*, this glory is reluctantly traded in for the dull domesticity of the newlywed.

The ceremonial *emanyata* of forty-nine huts was set in a sprawling oval. It was not encircled by the usual thorn fence. That would have been an insult to the warriors' courage. We arrived for the last day, in time for the climactic moment when the warriors' heads would be shaved and they would be blessed by the elders.

They had painted white zebra stripes on their bodies. They wore headdresses: lion manes and ostrich plumes which shimmied and quivered in the sun. They emanated a wild, primordial energy. It was a palpable current charged with excitement and anticipation. We plunged into the throng. I carried Petra on my back while Tara held my hand. There were hundreds of young men in full regalia, and every one of them seemed to be fascinated by the girls' pale blonde locks. They wouldn't stop fingering them. They touched our faces and bodies too. We were covered in ochre smudges. I sensed the danger. For once I was ill at ease, on my guard.

Tara and Petra at first were calm, enjoying the spectacle. It wasn't long before they became irritable. 'Tell them to leave us alone,' Tara complained. I couldn't. The slightest provocation would have unleashed that rampant testosterone.

In some parts of the *emanyata* there were so many people you had to press your way through the crowd. We edged between the bodies. The three *wazungu* were the cynosure of many eyes. A firm hand gripped my crotch. It was impossible to make out which of the ogling men it belonged to. I peeled the hand from between my legs and pumped it up and down. '*Habari*? How are you?'

Suddenly the crowd exploded. It was a warrior on the rampage. He hurtled towards us and fell at our feet writhing and groaning. Two other warriors quickly moved in and grabbed his outstretched arms. He struggled against them, half-raised off the ground. His body jerked and went rigid again and again. Froth dribbled from his mouth. Deep whoofing noises burst from his throat. His bulging eyes were huge. No one paid any attention. His two friends held his wrists and gazed into the distance. It was nothing unusual. Warriors were expected to have fits when they got excited.

We moved on and the mauling started up again. The warriors towered above Tara and Petra. They twisted and turned the girls' silky strands of hair with eager delight. Even at that age, Petra had a well defined concept of personal boundaries. She'd had enough. A warrior advanced on her with an outstretched finger. Petra opened her mouth. Very wide. The finger drew nearer. She lunged and clamped her teeth round it. Extremely hard. The warrior leapt back, surprised. A shocked silence fell. My pulse raced. The warrior snorted through his nose. His shoulders shook. He was laughing.

The next day we jolted up the escarpment back to Nairobi. The Land Rover heaved and creaked as it negotiated the obstacle course of rocks and gullies. Safe in the car we were limp and relaxed. I was extemporizing the latest episode in the Little Lulu series. Little Lulu was a make-believe girl who just happened to be rather like Tara. That day's story was about Little Lulu at the *eunoto*.

The girls were particularly happy because they had been presented with a nanny goat. She was brown with white speckles. They had already given her a name, Wairimu. She was swaying unsteadily on her hooves at the back of the car, depositing nervous little pellets of dung on the sleeping bags and camping gear.

Just before we reached the house, we saw Anthony coming the other way in his car. He drew abreast of us and stopped. He didn't bother to lean across and roll down the window. He was mouthing something at me and pointing at Wairimu. His face was contorted and indignant. I mouthed back that I couldn't make out what he was saying and that I'd see him at home. Then I drove on. We didn't have a pen to put Wairimu in so we left her tethered for the night on the lawn by the pawpaw tree.

The girls were in a state at breakfast the next morning. Tara glared at me. She was red-faced. 'Why do you always kill our pets?'

Puzzled, I looked at Anthony for a lead. He was smug, very pleased with himself. I went to the window. Wairimu was still there beneath the pawpaws. Or at least, part of her. Her brown and white hide was stretched out, pegged to the grass.

We had transported a wondrous, living Maasai creature to our home and almost immediately it had ceased to exist. It was a troubling thought. No matter that Anthony had instructed the gardener to slit Wairimu's throat. Her method of death was incidental. Crossing the invisible fault line between the modern and traditional worlds was a perilous business. Knowing that I was launched on a less travelled road, I wondered if I would be instrumental in the withering of other things too. The premonition vanished the moment it came into my head.

CHAPTER 3

When Tara was six and Petra three, Anthony and I decided to separate. I stayed on in the A-frame house with my daughters. He returned to England. It was hardly an opportune moment to abandon the financial security of public relations and break into the much tougher world of being a foreign correspondent. Yet this was what I'd been longing to do for some time. It happened slowly, over a couple of years, and I loved it. Most of the reporting was routine and carried out from Nairobi, which meant I could be around for the girls as well as earn a living to support them. As I got better established, there were trips out of town, mainly to Uganda. The wires would carry reports of a coup or heavy fighting, and I'd get into my car and drive north through the night to the border.

My first foreign assignment was to cover the fall of Idi Amin, the brutal buffoon who never failed to make good copy, even when he had already fled town. Kampala, the capital, was in shambles. There were corpses in the gutters by the side of the road and more corpses in the cellars of the State Research Bureau, headquarters for the secret police. The prisoners had been forced to bludgeon each other to death with sledge hammers. There was no transport so I walked everywhere, along streets lined with palm trees that drooped in the soggy heat. It made them look sad, like the buildings pockmarked by heavy weapons fire. I scoured Amin's deserted house and found a hand grenade in the drawer of his bedside table and some medals bearing his likeness. He'd commissioned them from Spink's of London, royal medallists to Her Majesty the Queen.

Uganda had been stormed by Tanzanian troops and Amin had fled to Libya in a helicopter. The Tanzanians were young conscripts from the bush, away from their villages for the first time. They were high on adrenaline and power and as bewildered as I was. The press and the TV crews stayed at the only operational hotel. So did some of the Tanzanian military. They helped themselves to our whiskey and sat down to eat at our tables. They took our cigarettes too. The hand grenades at their belts dipped into the gravy as they leaned forward to cadge a light.

The band at the hotel's disco played throughout the fighting. They entertained Amin's soldiers one night and the Tanzanians the next, concerned more about survival than politics. I partnered the Tanzanians. They bowed before asking me to dance and escorted me back to my seat afterwards, just as we had been taught in dancing class in New Jersey when I was eleven. Most had assault rifles or rocket-propelled grenades slung over their shoulders. Quite often they were so drunk they fell over. Sometimes this triggered a round of bullets through the floor of the bedroom above.

I brushed my teeth in whiskey because there was no running water. The phone in my bedroom had been ripped off the wall. The sheets looked very well used. The lock on the door didn't work. I seem to remember I was the only woman amongst the press corps. The previous week soldiers had raped the widow of one of four journalists who had been shot by Amin's men. It had happened on my floor. I slept like a baby. In those days, when the chaos was someone else's and not mine, I had an astounding capacity for injudicious optimism.

In this way I got to know the A team of Ugandan mayhem: dictators, politicians, disgruntled exiles. This may have been why the *Financial Times* decided to give me a career break and appoint me as their stringer for East Africa. Sometimes I disappeared into the bush for a day or two to make contact with the guerrillas. Those sort of trips, which made the front page, were good for my career but put a strain on family life.

Mostly, I kept what I'd seen to myself. I came back dirty and sleepless and my movements were quick and sure. To help me unwind, I made tomato soup and while I stirred, I gazed out the window at the tree where the hyrax lived.

Tara envied her schoolfriends' ordinary lives. They swam in the pool at the country club while their mothers played golf. Their mothers wore pumps and slacks and gold-chain necklaces with their names written in Arabic. Her mother wore tribal bracelets which clanked loudly when she came to talk to the teachers. It made Tara want to hide under the desk. 'Your mum's really pretty,' whispered the girl next to her. 'No, she's not. She's all wrinkly,' Tara hissed back. I was in my early thirties.

Tara never impugned my lifestyle to my face, but I knew she wanted me at home every night to tuck her into bed and read her stories. She hated the fact I looked different from the other mothers. If she had thought she could get away with it, she would have burned my Afghan waistcoat.

She came into the kitchen and stood beside me. 'I was worried about you.'

'Were you? I was fine.'

'I didn't know where you were.'

'I told you I was going to see the rebels,' I said. And I thought, *But not that the road was mined and a priest warned me there was only a fifty-fifty chance of survival if I went down it.*

'I was so worried. When you didn't ring, I cried all through class the next day.'

'But why? I told you I might be out of touch for a night or so. And you knew the High Commission would phone if anything went wrong.'

I kept on stirring. I didn't know how to handle these conversations. They made me defensive. Maybe I shouldn't have been so frank. Maybe I should have lied and said I was going to visit a missionary who wasn't on the phone. What I refused to acknowledge to Tara was that I too had been apprehensive about the risk I was taking. What if things had gone wrong and I'd been abducted or shot by a drunk soldier at a roadblock? I hadn't spelt it out, but I'd made my plans known to Tara and Kate Macintyre, a friend of twenty-three who was living with us, so they would know where to turn if they didn't hear from me again. But those were the rules that adults played by, not little girls.

Tara thrust clenched fists at the floor and said, 'I rang them from school. They said they didn't know where you were.'

'Oh?'

'I got that colonel. He said you looked like you could look after yourself.'

'Pompous git. What does he know?'

'Why do I have to miss games just to find out if my mother's dead or not? I didn't know if you were dead.'

The best of intentions had gone horribly wrong. I was filled with remorse. I turned to the hyrax tree, then looked at Tara. She blinked rapidly as if she had just come out of the water.

'You funny little thing. You mustn't worry so much. You mustn't. See? We're all right. It's okay. It's all okay.' I dipped the spoon and proffered it, 'Mmmmm . . . Try this. Bit bland? What do you think?' I stroked her head then reached past her to get the salt. No one ever said freedom was easy.

The girls and I viewed my reporting forays through different prisms. I recall that period in our lives as one of huge compromise. The school run versus coups. It seemed to me that my trips were not that frequent or long: a few days or a week at the most. I did my utmost to disturb their routine as little as possible. They stayed in the neighbourhood with one or other of their friends. Amina walked over after school to be with them, and they could run back to the house to fetch their toys and clothes whenever they wanted.

They were children of Africa: at home with the Maasai, the bush and wild animals. They knew no fear. Yet Tara felt insecure when I went away. Perhaps it was the violence she sensed, fearing it might infiltrate her cloistered childhood. Probably it was more straightforward than that. Mothers should be there.

I carried the guilt of the single working parent and it made me doubt my maternal instincts. Unable to do the right thing by my own children, it astounded me that I should put myself up as a candidate for more. The fact is, I didn't. There are a lot of things in life that just sneak up behind you and shove you onto a different course before you know where you are. Heather was responsible for one of those interludes which, at first seemingly banal, swivels your life in a different direction.

She was one of my oldest friends, a pilot who flew light aircraft for a charter company. She possessed a singular beauty that had something to do with her blondeness and her snub nose and square chin. Many admirers had floundered on her sex appeal because her inner essence refused to be caged. She was one of the finest and bravest pilots on the airfield. As soon as she climbed into the cockpit, some strange alchemy fossilized her nervous system into stone. This disregard for danger made her the darling of some unlikely clients, most of whom operated in the war zones of the Horn of Africa: aid organizations, guerrillas, missionaries and smugglers.

She had asked me to dinner because there was somebody she wanted me to meet. He was being brought by a priest who worked at a mission station. Heather was in an ecclesiastic phase.

I was late as usual and they had been sitting on her leather sofa for half an hour by the time I walked into the living room. Her friend looked to be in his sixties. He had white hair and craggy features. The other man must have been a good forty years his junior. They were both wearing the cloth and dog collar. But while the older man was shy and self-effacing, the younger one spoke at length with fiery animation. He had that fey Irish colouring: a wild halo of hair as black as a witch's cloak and parchment-pale skin. What with the beard and the unwavering gaze of his pale blue eyes, the effect was quite messianic. So was his conversation.

'Majesty lies within us all. Deep within our hearts there are a thousand hidden dreams, countless hopes and burning ambitions. Inside us, too, there is a sense of what is precious.'

The two men had driven or flown that day from a place in the desert near the border with southern Sudan. The older one worked there. The younger one was from Ireland. Or was it Liverpool in England? He was on a visit. Or perhaps he had come to work at a mission. From the way he talked, he gave the impression he was a priest, perhaps a doctor too. It was unclear to me. Having arrived late, I presumed that these details had been gone over before I arrived. So I kept my mouth shut and asked fewer questions than I would have under normal circumstances.

The young man produced a thick Kodak envelope of photos and passed them first to Heather, then to me. He bent his head over the pile, pointing to each one as he talked. They were of poor quality – bad lighting, the tops of heads cropped – but moving for all of that. Most of them were of Turkana, a tribe which lived in the far north of Kenya. None of them looked very well. The pictures appeared to have been taken at a clinic.

His ghostly hands framed a boy of wraithlike proportions being cradled in someone's arms. You couldn't tell who was holding the child as the adult had been rudely guillotined at the shoulders. The child's head lolled backwards and his eyes rolled in the direction of the camera. Was he sick or was he starving? And where was he anyway?

I shook my head in sympathy. 'This was taken . . .?'

'Our age is an age of violence and indifference, a time when dog eats dog. Pain and insecurity give birth to loneliness and emptiness . . .'

' . . . at a mission?'

'These children are dying. Yet despite their poverty they can show us the way. The quality of our lives is not about the comforts that we surround ourselves with. It is about our capacity to love, our vision of reality, our sensitivity and empathy with each other. We have been put on this earth to serve others. But how many of us are selfless in our giving? How many of us can truly say we are helping those less fortunate than ourselves?'

I kept quiet. I didn't want him to think I didn't care about the poor. So I abandoned a basic journalistic imperative: never trust someone whose explanations leave you confused. Clearly he enjoyed a metaphysical ecstasy that eluded the rest of us. I was intrigued.

He must have seen this for I was to hear more from him. He phoned two days later to ask where he could buy a car on the cheap. I said I had a friend who sold cars and who would always do me a favour. What model did he have in mind exactly? Two days after that it was a drill to cobble together some boards for a bookcase. He didn't want to buy a drill just for a one-off job. I thought I could help him on that too. The following week he was in search of low-cost housing. Well, as it so happened, I had another friend who erected houses made of compacted straw bricks. I said I'd talk to him and see if he would do it at cost.

Soon he was wandering in and out of the office almost on a daily basis and coming home for tea too. Did I have connections in the government? Did I know people who donated to charitable causes?

Could I tell him more about Maasai culture? I always could. And I always did.

Brian had been so moved by the children he had seen in Turkana District that he decided to build a health clinic outside Nairobi. He had the financial backing of an Irish organization. Its structure and funding was not exactly clear to me nor was the rationale for siting his charitable work near Nairobi when he confessed to be concerned about the Turkana. I let it go. Me, the *Financial Times* correspondent who critiqued national budgets and censured finance ministers for their shoddy fiscal policies. Me, the journalist who pilloried anyone who claimed grey was white. I sat in the anteroom of Brian's great goodness and was content. In Africa, strangers appear amongst us and we take them at face value. So I never queried his credentials, never bothered to check if he really was a priest or a doctor. His actions were validated by my own feelings of vocational inadequacy.

CHAPTER 4

One day Brian invited me to join him for lunch with a World Bank official who was visiting from Washington. I had introduced the two to each other the previous week. I presumed the purpose was to canvass for money for the clinic so I accepted.

The World Bank and I both had offices in Nairobi's only sky-scraper, which was a thrusting twenty storeys. We stood on the pavement at its entrance waiting for Brian. He pulled in to the curb a few minutes late in the beat-up four-wheel-drive Toyota I had found for him. There were two passengers inside: Maasai boys wearing greased black leather cloaks and giraffe-hide sandals. They each had an extravagant headdress of dead birds fanning out around their heads. Whorled copper hung from their ears.

We all greeted each other with great joviality. I climbed into the back with the boys while the pin-striped World Bank man settled gingerly into the front passenger seat. He swivelled his shoulders around and threw the boys a cocktail party smile. 'Are you guys on holiday from school?'

They hung their heads demurely and stared at their knees. They were nestling against each other like puppies, seeking comfort from this barrage of foreignness. One had the broad shoulders and inner-tube lips of a Nuba wrestler; the other, the moist, wide-set eyes of a gazelle. I wondered what the American made of them.

Brian, who had recently begun lessons in Maa, said a few words without turning round. The boys laughed delightedly, teeth and eyes gleaming white against the black.

'Meriape and Isaac have been circumcised. It's a ritual that is very important to the Maasai. They are like a mirror for us. Look at these two and you can see how beautiful we really are,' Brian intoned.

'Well, they're certainly different from my two sons,' said the World Bank official with polite admiration.

'Many people would be ashamed to eat in an expensive restaurant with these boys, because of their dirt and poverty. But the Maasai bask in splendour. We can learn a lesson from them and be humbled.'

Our lunch guest grunted as if to counter some point in an argument. He had assumed a glazed expression. I wondered if his thoughts were running along the same course as mine. I was hoping we were going somewhere you didn't need a tie.

Shortly after that, Brian rang the office in a state of excitement. He had found the land for the clinic. God worked in mysterious ways. It belonged to Meriape's father.

A thought occurred to me, 'Brian, where on earth did you find Meriape?'

'Standing by the side of the road with Isaac. They were so beautiful I picked them up.' He said it blithely, as if this was a routine way to acquire real estate.

He wanted just a little wedge of their land, five acres or so, to site the clinic on. If they were good people, which he was sure they were, they would give it to him outright. I interjected that this was very unlikely. In Africa, land is more precious than life itself. I suggested he rent it from them instead. Brian didn't seem happy with that solution. He thought they should at least let him have free use of the land in perpetuity.

'They're poor people. You're asking them to hand over their only asset.'

'It's the poor who know best how to give. Their suffering breeds compassion.'

'Well, you're in for some lengthy negotiations. The Maasai can talk the ears off a goat. Good luck to you.'

'No. Good luck to us. You know how they think and you're fluent in Swahili. I want you to come with me.'

We left Nairobi after I had filed to the paper. By the time we reached the Ngongs it was twilight. The *boma* clung to a deep slope, pincered between the lip of the Rift escarpment and the knuckled summits of the hills. Meriape was waiting for us by the side of the road for there was no track to indicate the way. The place was called Oldonyati.

The Toyota bumped downhill and Meriape walked beside us

with a hand resting on Brian's window. Insects swarmed in the headlights like falling snow. There was no noise in the emptiness save the growling of the engine as the car dipped and rose across channels of black earth, and the scrunch of dry grass beneath Meriape's feet. Every once in a while he turned his head and gave a shy grin of reassurance. He was leading us to the home of his mother.

Kipenget was a tall figure in the shadows. A length of dirty material was knotted at her shoulder. There were oval hoops of beads anchored to her ears. '*Sopa! Sopa!*' She said it in a way that was breathy and forceful. Most Maasai women greet *wazungu* without touching. Kipenget pinned my arms with her hands and kissed me on the lips. Then she stepped back and her round face dimpled. '*Karibu!*' She turned and we followed her into the hut. It was tiny and cramped. Kipenget pulled forward low round stools and straightened her arm in their direction. We sat.

Children scuffled like mice in the gloom; there appeared to be about eight of them. They were barely visible in the darkness, but Kipenget's face picked up the red glow from the fire – no more than a few twigs – as she bent to pour sugar from a brown paper packet into the tea that was brewing.

The negotiations were generous and uncharacteristically brief for a Maasai affair. Brian seemed unaware of how extraordinary it was for Kipenget to be the family representative in this discussion. Maasai society is fiercely patriarchal. The *wazee* sit in the shade of a tree and chew endlessly over matters of import. Women have no say in what transpires. Despite this, Kipenget had evidently usurped the role of decision maker in the family.

She said she would allow Brian to build the clinic on the land. She was happy to contribute towards the welfare of the community, she explained. In return Brian agreed to help the family financially. This part of the deal was founded on goodwill and left open to interpretation. It was a magnanimously trusting gesture on Kipenget's part. Brian had won her over when he offered to pay Meriape's school fees.

We concluded the agreement rapidly. Soon she and I had moved on to other things: children and the rigours of being a hard-working mother. We were of a similar age, middle thirties.

Before we knew it, we were lambasting the ways of men and drunken husbands, a subject on which Kipenget had a rich repertoire. Her husband Kili haunted the bars while she struggled to eke out a living selling beadwork. She made no reference to the daily trek to fetch water, bent by the weight of the round metal drum on her back. That was a woman's duty. But she took umbrage at Kili's schemes to lay his hands on her cash. He had a habit of taking her hard-earned shillings and beating her when she hid them too well.

He was trying to sell a portion of their land while she battled to reverse the transaction. It was a betrayal which particularly irked her. In the telling, we could see that she was a spirited woman, at once bountiful and obstinate. The conversation flowed strong, swirling around riptides of laughter. On that day the seeds of my enduring friendship with Kipenget were sown.

It was not long before Brian asked me to keep an eye on the place and disappeared to Ireland. The weeks turned into months, and his cheery, badly typed letters continued to land on my desk. They were a mix of his news – bouts of malaria, talks to raise money for the project – and things to do for the clinic. He made considerable extracurricular demands, too.

By the time he left, Brian was supporting several teenage boys who had run away from home to find their fortune on the streets. Some of them went to school. Others didn't. They all lived with Meriape at the clinic. Brian seemed to think it was my job to buy their food, make sure they studied properly and to take them to the movies in Nairobi on the weekend. Isaac was smoking and must be disciplined. Meriape wasn't doing too well at school and must be encouraged.

Looking back on it, I suppose this was my first taste of looking after other people's children. I was the person to whom they addressed their daily needs. It meant a lot of responsibility, with my non-existent authority exercised through the powers of persuasion. In the domain of parenting, it was a frustrating no-man's-land.

'I can't say how much your love and understanding has meant to me. Never once have you got annoyed or angry. Above all I miss your smile and your faith that little efforts do work,' Brian wrote.

Despite the sugary compliments, his requests were in reality directives. They were like a leaking tap, dripping away without let-up. Sometimes I wondered if I was going to drown in them. Yet I must have been keeping some sort of faith because I was achieving quite a lot. Against all probability hope was triumphing over ignorance.

The construction of the clinic had been completed, and I was installing gutters along the roof and a barrel to catch what little rain fell during the year. Brian wanted to start another clinic in Samburu District and I had made the day's drive north to the tiny village of Lesirikan to negotiate with the local county council. This had been very successful. There was a dispensary standing empty which we could move into straight away. Everything was ready to roll, we just needed Brian's signature on a contract.

When he wrote, Brian failed to address my urgent queries about terms of leave for the clinic staff or how to excavate a pit latrine on a three-in-one slope. The clay soil regularly turned to mud in the rains and I had premonitions of a patient disappearing into a pile of excrement as soon as the heavens opened. Neither did he respond to my plea to allow me to make decisions on the Samburu dispensary. I didn't know what I was doing, but I tackled everything as best I could.

I gradually got into the swing of my new life with all its respons-ibilities. It was a question of commuting between the office in Nairobi ten miles in one direction and the clinic on the slopes of the Ngongs fifteen miles in the other direction.

My office was a Stygian cell in the Press Centre. I shared it with Kathy Eldon, a redheaded American who possessed a primal energy I envied. She was a restaurant critic and feature writer for the local *Nation* newspaper. Somehow we squashed in Francis the messenger and a large Indian bed with coconut fibre woven between its ornate wooden frame. Francis used it to spread out his papers and do the filing. Along the opposite wall two black leatherette armchairs stood like sentries beneath a poster-sized cartoon of a woman astride a charging bull. She was virtually naked save for boots and a Viking helmet of rampant horns and shining steel. In her left hand she held a spear aloft ready to do battle. Kathy told everyone it was me doing the school run.

Kathy's dedication to networking, together with the demands of her job, ensured an unletting flow of visitors passed beneath this alter ego Boadicea. There were chefs, politicians, magicians, safari guides. Even Nelson Rockefeller. I was so engrossed in my writing I paid him the scantest attention when we were introduced. Kathy couldn't believe it and said as much afterwards.

'Nelson Rockefeller? Why didn't you say?'

Kathy rolled her eyes up to the ceiling. 'I *did*. Why don't you listen?'

I didn't listen because there were too many people talking at me already. By then the office was a political surgery for the Maasai and the Samburu. Oblivious to the workplace ethic of appointments, their arrival was heralded by the sound of jingling jewelry as they strode down the corridor. They threw themselves into the armchairs with a rattle of sticks and swords and sat with their legs thrown wide. '*Sopa, Merienna. Habari?*' prefaced a woeful litany of dead cows, unpaid school fees, brothers looking for work as factory watchmen.

I stuffed my ears with balls of wax and worked facing the wall in self-imposed isolation. Cows may come and cows may go, but the *Financial Times* wanted 800 words on the fighting in Uganda by 4:30. While they waited, the visitors turned their attention to Francis. It was a chance to give their laments and conspiracy theories a final embellishment or two before pitching them to me. He listened patiently, his turbaned head nodding above the morass of papers on the Indian bed.

These men had no need to hurry. Life's leisurely pace was regulated by the rise of the sun above one mountain and its eventual disappearance behind another. They greeted strangers with instant interest and under ordinary circumstances would have thought my manners appalling. But they came to realize people in towns behaved in an odd way, so they waited until I swivelled my chair round to face them and listened to their worries.

Isaac and his family seemed to have more problems than most.

35

Isaac was about the same age as Meriape and wanted to hang out with him. But whereas Meriape was tall and dark and broad-shouldered, Isaac was short and brown and thin. Meriape's physique had the well proportioned aspects of a classical sculpture. Isaac's limbs were cobbled together with angular negligence, protruding wilfully from his tattered khaki shorts and torn T-shirt. He had a slight limp.

Isaac's family were the poorest of the poor. They were landless and lived across the road from Kipenget. Mama Isaac freeloaded off Kipenget, who in turn relied on me to help feed her brood. Baba Isaac was no better. He was an examplar of cultural erosion. His *shuka*, red and white checks like a bistro tablecloth, was encrusted with dirt. When he walked, it flapped open to reveal great purses of sagging, wrinkled elephant skin at his buttocks. His gnarled and knotted knees looked as if they belonged to an ancient tree.

Baba Isaac often asked me for money with a cunning smile. When I refused, his face darkened. Isaac bore an uncanny resemblance to his father. This was a cruel thing for it foreshadowed a manhood as bereft of love as his childhood had been.

In the West, Isaac and his family would have been regarded as dysfunctional. It is a term that has no currency in Africa because, if it did, the entire continent would have had to go into therapy. Africa cannot look after its own. It is battered by corrupt government and civil war, eroded by drought and recession. Its people are infinitely more fertile than the land.

Half of Africa's population was born after 1980. These youngsters flowed into the towns looking for work. They walked the streets expectantly until they discovered that hope is the forerunner to despair. Disillusioned, they turned to crime or joined a rebel move-ment and rooted for a future with the snout of an AK47. Some, like Mama Isaac, lapsed into fatalism and clasped any outstretched hand. Others were smarter. Like Isaac, they knew that survival required Artful Dodger tactics.

Kipenget handed out the food I brought her to Daniel and Peter, Isaac's younger brothers. I used the money my parents had given me for my birthday to buy Isaac a bed. It was promptly appropriated by his father. This diversion of my charity bred worms of resentment.

In those early days my goodwill was structured around the misplaced notion that my gifts were to be used as I had intended. How foolish of me to try and hold on to what I had given away. I had still to understand that the expectation of gratitude is even more insidious than gratitude itself. Isaac's family usurped my intentions yet I continued to give: in response to the still eyes of the baby glued to Mama Isaac's back and to ease Kipenget's burden. I gave because it seemed the right thing to do, but my affection for this blunt-edged boy was elusive.

I paid for Isaac's school fees. Every day he walked with Meriape down the steep, twisting footpaths to Kisamis at the bottom of the escarpment. The village edged a wilderness of hundreds of square miles that was speckled with thorn trees and where journeys were made on foot and marked against the brooding goblin presence of extinct volcanoes. The primary school was a row of classrooms constructed from wood offcuts and set back from the road. I had often driven past them on my way to Lake Magadi for picnics. I'd never stopped in Kisamis, hardly noticed the dusty shacks and the men promenading at a ponderous pace in their wool bobbin caps, tyre sandals and raincoats. I might have thought, *How on earth do people survive here?* That's all. The war zones of Uganda were interesting. Not Kisamis.

The school consisted of two small buildings constructed from wood offcuts. Paul Wagucu was the headmaster. He was an avuncular man whose stomach was not as prosperous as he would have wished. Paul had to make do on his skimpy teacher's salary. To redress this lack of stature he always wore a tie and a hand-knitted cardigan which buttoned snugly over his teapot belly. His office was a miniature of the classrooms, dirt-floored and basic. It contained a desk and two straight-backed wooden chairs. Shelves ran along one of the walls. They were cluttered with notebooks, a crude wooden carving of a giraffe, and the cups won by the school soccer team in district tournaments. An umbrella hung from a roof beam.

I remember the office because I was in there quite often. Paul summoned me regularly, to take the flak when Isaac stepped out of line. He didn't study. Even worse, he stole from the other boys, Paul complained. The headmaster's tolerance was being sorely tried by the boy's miscreant ways.

When I talked to Isaac about this, his face became shuttered and he looked like his father. I felt that his soul had retreated to an inner redoubt beyond the reach of kindness. In his defence, I attributed his behaviour to a lack of love and discipline at home. Paul was more censorious. Isaac was hopeless, not worth the money I spent on him, he said. He was enough to try anyone's patience and he didn't know why I put up with him.

'You are wasting your time. You lecture him about stealing. He does it again. He is not a good boy.' Paul and I had reached an impasse over Isaac. Each hoped the other would do something to ring a miraculous change in his ways.

'Are you sure it was him?' I said lamely.

'Twenty shillings. The boys confirm that. I'm sure.' He kept moving his head from side to side, not to refute his words but in sorrow. 'He makes too many problems. And he refuses to work. I can't have him in the school anymore.'

I put an elbow on my knee and fingered my forehead, staring at the dirt floor. It had been compacted smooth over the years by agitated feet and chairs being scraped back from the desk in preface to audiences such as this. Paul was waiting for me to speak.

I was accustomed to dealing with the ebb and flow of political regimes. I performed well as the inquisitor, setting the pace of an interview, closing my notebook with an authoritative snap when I chose to end it. But coming to grips with the mundane drama of other people's lives left me flummoxed. It was worse than digging latrines. I said nothing.

'I have a boy you can sponsor instead of Isaac. He studies very hard and gets good marks,' Paul offered.

What happened next came in one fluid choreographed movement. The headmaster suddenly stood up. He stepped back, opened the door behind him and spoke a low command. On cue a skinny twelve-year-old took a few tentative steps into the room. He wore the school uniform of grey shorts and green sweater.

'Come, come.' Paul put a hand in the small of his back and

pushed him forward. 'This boy is an orphan,' he announced. 'His name is Peter Lekerian.'

Peter was different to Isaac even though, as an orphan, he too must have been deprived of parental love. I could tell that the minute I saw him. He had an air of shy reticence about him as he stood by the open door, but in retrospect there was more to it than that. Some inner, unspoken instinct held him in check. He longed to be taken care of, but he didn't want anyone to know.

'Good morning, sir. Good morning, madam.' Peter's head bobbed up and down twice, then came to rest cocked to one side, parrot fashion. He crossed his hands and placed them palms down in front of his crotch. It was a gesture I came to know well. He looked like Adam leaving the Garden of Eden.

Paul told me that he let Peter sleep at his house. He didn't mind because the boy was such a good student, but it was difficult on his salary. Peter was nearly thirteen. He would be starting secondary school next year, he went on. What would he do with him then?

You didn't need a crystal ball to tell where this was leading.

'Mary Anne, can you please look after him?'

'You mean, pay his fees?'

'Yes.'

'What about food?'

'He will have to eat. But only in the holidays if you find him a boarding school.'

'And clothing?'

'He won't need much. The school uniform. Some trousers and shoes.'

I was beginning to fidget. 'Where's he going to live?'

Paul brightened. 'He has an aunt called Naserian. She is a very old lady and very poor. She lives here in Kisamis. He can stay with her in the holidays.'

Peter's still, expectant face looked from me to Paul and back to me during this exchange. He reminded me of a glistening jellyfish stranded on the beach at low tide. I shifted uneasily in my chair. His vulnerability was transparent.

'All right, I'll do the fees and clothes and things.' Then I said, too abruptly, 'As long as he can live with his aunt.'

39

Paul's relief was obvious. He beamed first at me, then at Peter. 'That will be all,' he said.

Peter inclined his head in a solemn bow. 'Thank you, madam.' He turned on his heels and took a hand from his crotch to shut the door behind him.

'I don't earn that much either, you know,' I said ungraciously, then added, 'I suppose I'll have to find another school that will take Isaac.'

'Yes, you will. I can't have him here any longer. He causes too many problems. But Peter's very good. He's no trouble at all.' Paul said this as if he was talking about a second-hand car that did good mileage.

As adoptions go, it certainly lacked formality. In England I would have been subjected to rigorous screening and found gravely wanting as a desirable parent for Peter. It was virtually impossible under any circumstances to adopt across racial lines. In addition to that, I was a single working mother rising forty. And compounding it all was the fact that I had no particular desire to take on the responsibility of another child. The awkward coupling between Peter and myself which Paul had engineered would have been impossible if I had been living in London. But in Africa, where crisis is routine, we couldn't afford the luxury of being politically correct.

I should have felt elated. The truth was I didn't. I was filled with dread because I saw in Peter the shadow of my own needs. I too was searching for arms to enfold me, the haven of another to love me and be loved. I wanted a man. God had chosen to give me a boy instead.

CHAPTER 5

The wind picked up the dust at the side of the road and chased it between the feet of factory workers trudging home from work. A suffocating heat rose from the floor of the car. I rolled down the window and tapped my fingers on the door. We were stuck in a traffic jam on Uhuru Highway. It was the Christmas holidays. Peter was fourteen and had just completed his first year at Oloolaiser High School. He was still living with his Aunt Naserian, but he often came home for weekends and during the holidays.

'It is an issue of finding a place whereby I won't be bullied,' he said.

We had been running errands in the industrial area all afternoon. Until now the conversation had been confined to shopping. I was equipping the Lesirikan clinic in Samburu District. Having done it all once before at Oldonyati, it was proving to be a less daunting task this time round. I had fallen out with the elusive Brian. He had turned out to be neither priest nor doctor. I could have stomached the deception if it hadn't been for his erratic management style. He was absent much of the time and incapable of making a decision when he was around. So there had been a palace coup. I was now running the Samburu dispensary with two friends. They were Kate Macintyre, the Cambridge graduate who lived with us and looked after the girls while I was on assignment, and Gabriel Lochgen, a Samburu whose family lived at Lesirikan.

We were an unlikely threesome to oversee the health requirements of an area the size of a county. Amongst Gabriel's previous incarnations he had been a mechanic in the air force and the chauffeur to the military attaché at the United States Embassy. Kate had an honours degree in history to offer. With my tuppenceworth of experience at Oldonyati clinic, I was the old hand. We didn't know what we were doing, but we were committed to setting this particularly remote little part of the world on fire. In Africa, where your best shot amounts to no more than compromise, anything is possible.

'Survivalwise, I must find a school that will be kind to me,' Peter reiterated.

Becalmed in the morass of gleaming vehicles and hooting drivers, it seemed as good a time as any to discuss his latest problem. At one level it was simple enough. He was a poor, orphaned boy from the bush. His classmates were the rich middle-class sons of Kikuyu businessmen and civil servants. The Kikuyu have always looked down on the Maasai, regarded them as having two oars out of the water. It was probably inevitable from the outset that Peter would become a target for their bullying. But I had no idea what to do about it. This sort of thing never happened to Tara and Petra.

A blanket of despondency sat on my shoulders. Competition for places in secondary schools was fierce. It was unlikely I would be able to get him in anywhere else. Even if I did, who could guarantee the bullying wouldn't start all over again? There was only one thing for it.

'Can't you sort it out somehow with those other boys? Wallop them back?' I looked across at him. He was rather short for his age and still startlingly thin. The odds were long on that particular solution.

Peter must have secretly agreed because he said, 'They are too big. And too fat. They will kill me.'

He had a point.

I didn't know how to handle this so I launched into a philosophical monologue on life. It was emerging as a mangled version of Konrad Lorenz's theory of parental bonding.

' . . . and so if you take the mother duck away and put a paper bag in her place, the baby duck will think that's its mum and behave like the paper bag. Follow it everywhere it goes.'

Peter's eyes widened several apertures. He was listening intently. I was painfully aware that I wasn't making sense and changed tack. 'The point is, we all do what our parents do because that's the only example we have to learn from. Take lions. They teach their cubs how to hunt. When the cubs grow big enough, they hunt on their own without their mother's help. Then it's up to them whether they bring down a wildebeest and get to eat. If they don't, they go hungry. Their mother can't do anything about it.'

'So you are a lioness and I'm a cub. You must teach me everything you know.'

Suddenly we were both enjoying the conversation.

'I can't hunt for you. I can't stop the bullying. It's only fun for the other boys if you react to it. They want to hurt you. If you show them you can't be hurt, they'll stop doing it.'

His face was fired with zeal. 'I won't let them steal my food. I'll learn to hunt like a lion, Mum. You'll see.'

Sometimes I resented Peter. He was an added responsibility on top of the other four children I kept an eye on. I'd placed Isaac in a boarding school where he continued to tax the patience of the teachers. There were also Godfrey, Chege and his sister Peris. Godfrey and Chege were the best of friends. I knew them because they were altar boys at our local Catholic church. All three children came to the house at weekends. We went to the movies, visited Kipenget at Oldonyati and drove down into the hot Maasai country in my Land Rover, where we shared our sandwiches with barefoot herdsboys.

One memorable Saturday, Godfrey, Chege and I accompanied a vet and game rangers on an expedition to capture a rhino on the plains near the house. It was to be translocated to a game park. The vet, a friend of mine, said he needed the boys' help. He explained that he was going to dart the rhino with a tranquillizer to make it woozy. Then, he said, he would lasso its horn with a rope and hold on tight while two of the rangers grabbed its tail and pulled hard. That way it couldn't run off. But, he continued, looking thoughtful, while the rhino was swaying on its feet like a felled redwood, who was going to take the rope and hogtie its legs? His brow wrinkled and he tapped his lip with a stubby finger. Then his gaze fell on Godfrey and Chege. 'Aah!' he exclaimed, looking relieved. 'That's where you boys come in. Mary Anne can help you.' We didn't, of course, but the prospect stoked the boys' excitement to fever pitch. Their faces were like sun shining on a mirror.

Our time together was an *ad interim* way of parenting, but they were pragmatic enough to embrace it wholeheartedly. I was the only security they had. Godfrey's father drank too much and worked too little. Chege's and Peris's father, a dedicated alcoholic, was in and out of jail for petty theft and disturbing the peace. Their mother had long since moved to the other side of town, where she set out pyramids of tomatoes – three to a pile – and waited for customers. Not many people bought her tomatoes so she moonlighted as a prostitute. The three children counted their blessings in the momentary happiness that brought them to another day. Tomorrow was in the lap of the gods.

It was two years since Peter and I had been thrown together in the office of Paul the headmaster. Right from the start it had been obvious Peter wasn't going to settle for the sponsorship at one remove which Paul had dangled as bait. He was hesitant, cautious with me but invasive none the less, silently demanding to be loved. His hunger was ravenous, couldn't be satisfied with the sort of attention which put a smile on the faces of the other children.

As we chatted together on his visits, Peter offered up his childhood, piece by piece. Thus the jigsaw began to take shape. While the overall picture remained elusive, there were periods of his life in which I could envisage what it had been like for him.

He could remember back to when he was three or four and lived with his Aunt Naserian and a Maasai man on a *mzungu* ranch in the Rift Valley. The ranch was called Ndabibi and stood on the shores of Lake Naivasha. I knew the place. It was owned by Lady Diana Delamere, one of Kenya's more infamous British settlers, the protagonist for *White Mischief*, the film directed by my friend Mike Radford. Yellow-barked fever trees rimmed the lake shore, from which came the barks of colobus monkeys and the chirrups and twitters of scores of brightly coloured birds. At night buffalo and hippo grazed there.

I had even walked past the place where the cattle herders still lived. It was called The Lines because their one-roomed huts were laid out in rows with military precision. Pepper trees grew near by, but they cast little shade. It was burnt away by prisms of blinding light dancing off the lake and reflected in the cloudless sky. The dust smelt like powdered chalk.

Peter used to play hide-and-seek around those huts with the other herders' children. He liked to dig into the earth with his fingers and mix it with warm pats of cow dung so that it was malleable, like Plasticine. Then he shaped miniature enclosures with his fingers and when they had dried, he filled them with stones and berries. These were his cattle and his sheep and his goats.

Peter said he was happy then. He thought Naserian was his mother, and the man she lived with, his father. He loved Naserian. Her hands were rough from years of chopping wood. The sun had lined her forehead. She was old – forty or even older – but she was gentle.

One day as Naserian passed him with a plastic *debe* of water balanced on her head, she told him to stop his play and follow her into the hut. '*Ou, osotua lai*. Come here, My Umbilical Cord. I have something to tell you.' She took his wrist and pulled him towards her. 'We are leaving here and going to a place far away at the foot of the Ngongs. Your father has important business there.' She often addressed him with pet endearments instead of his baptismal name of Peter. His other name, Lekerian, was a derivative of her own name. It meant peace.

'Why are we going?' he asked.

'Your father's father was killed in a war. There has been a council of the elders. The murderer must pay a fine of cattle to your father and his brothers, My Fragile Bones. Your father is the eldest so he must go to Kisamis to see that the cattle are shared out fairly. We will be rich. We will have cattle of our own.'

His father appeared as she was talking and his bulky frame filled the doorway. 'Why are you telling the child these things? *Loikop* is a grave matter. He is so small he cannot even help with the herds. He is too young to understand,' he said.

But Peter did come to understand. He knew that this grown-up, serious thing called *loikop* had made everything different. It made his father go away from them and leave him and his mother in a mud hut in the town called Kisamis that was so big it had as many buildings as he had toes and fingers. The most important change in his life was that he wore a green sweater and green checked shirt, and shorts and shoes, and went to school. Naserian insisted on walking with him each morning and held his hand to cross the

45

road. She said the cars were dangerous even though none ever drove by.

He sat on a bench, squashed between other boys and girls and made patterns on the dirt floor with his shoe. The corrugated-iron roof was never silent, and when he got bored with lessons, he liked to listen to it. In the heat of the dry season it expanded and creaked. When it rained for just a few minutes, in its usual halfhearted way, it sounded as if chickens were pecking for worms above his head. But when it thundered and the rain rattled and drummed against the roof, which was seldom, it made such a racket he imagined he was standing on a platform and a train was rushing through the station.

His teacher had a floppy bosom and a string of plastic pearls at her neck. She wrote on the blackboard with a stubby piece of white chalk and taught everyone how to read the words out loud. She was Maasai but she was called Mrs Williams because her husband's baptismal name was William.

Mr Chege taught him maths, which he found very hard to understand. Mr Chege always appeared in the classroom in the same rumpled pin-stripe jacket and grey flannels. Mr Chege was his favourite teacher because he coached the boys in soccer after school. Peter was far too small and skinny to try out for the team, but in a few years' time he would be bigger. Then he'd be on the team, for sure.

In some ways the school had been a happy place for him. Yet it also held disturbing memories. In Peter's mind, he had been sent to the school in Kisamis because the man he thought was his father had inexplicably abandoned him. And at some stage during the years between his arrival there and the time I met him, he had learned that Naserian was not his mother but his aunt. He didn't tell me how this had happened.

I'd looked on Oloolaiser High as a fresh start, an arena where he could gain confidence. The school intimated a certain melancholy, but it was kept at bay by the boisterous energy of the students – all boys, all wearing frayed maroon sweaters. Perched on one of the lower ridges of the Ngong Hills, it attracted fronds of mist which licked at the wattles lining the dirt driveway and obscured the distant red roofs of Nairobi's suburbs. Crows swooped over the playing field and gave hoarse caws from the trees. The one-storey cinder-block buildings were as grey as the clouds that swirled above their corrugated-iron roofs.

Peter was full of stories of his prowess at sport and the parts he had in the school plays. He played number nine on the soccer team, whatever position that was. They had fixtures all over the district and seemed to be hot property judging by the hard-fought victories he related to me in numbing detail. He was a keen member of the Drama Club – lots more prizes won there too, apparently – and enjoyed an active social life centred around the local church.

He had even gone on a school trip to Ndabibi. He described at length his visit to the little walled cemetery Diana Delamere had created for her husbands. Tom Delamere lay alongside Gilbert Colvile. Diana had reserved a space for herself between them. Peter related how 'a dog pet' had been interred at the foot of each grave. It amazed him but he didn't query the sense of it. The souls of important Maasai elders returned to earth as snakes. They slithered onto the chair where the man had once sat, or basked by the water where his cattle used to drink. People took care not to kill the spirit snakes. The totem for the Delamere lord, who was also a big man, was obviously a dead dog. It illustrated what he already knew. *Wazungu* had different customs from the Maasai.

Peter failed to mention that he had lived at Ndabibi until he was five or six. Just as he never said that when he was small he thought his aunt was his mother. As for the man whom he had believed to be his father, I didn't know he existed. In my Western way, I took Peter at face value. I was too preoccupied with other things to reflect that he might be holding something back.

I imagined his life was happy and fulfilled, but he kept on popping up like a jack-in-the-box. He would appear at the office in the middle of the afternoon, knock on the door and walk straight across to my desk. There was no question of behaving like the other Maasai and sitting on the black leatherette chair while I finished what I was doing. He'd come right over and stand so close I could feel the soft cloth of his shorts on my elbow. Then he'd lean round and peer at me with the contained urgency of someone about to warn of impending catastrophe.

'Peter, I can't hear you. I have my earplugs in. Why aren't you in school?'

His hands would grip the edge of the desk. 'I need textbooks and a ruler and pencils and a rubber and a bag to carry them in. And a sweater because it's cold in the dormitory. And my shoes are too small.'

'Can't you see I'm busy? You'll have to wait until I've finished this.' Then I'd note the blind snap down on his anxious face and relent. 'All right. But make it quick. I've got to get this story filed.'

It was hard to reconcile this earnest boy reciting his shopping list in a barely audible monotone with the picture he painted of himself. Where was the carefree star of stage and soccer pitch who was so popular at Oloolaiser High?

Peter didn't hold back when it came to itemizing his needs: a paraffin lamp so he could read his textbooks at night during the holidays, a new roof for his aunt's home and a cupboard so he could keep his books dry during the rainy season. Other Maasai children who went to school kept their textbooks in a tin trunk. Soon I was helping to support his aunt as well. I gave her money for food and, at Peter's suggestion, provided the capital for beads and wire. 'Mum, while I'm at school, she can make Maasai jewelry to sell to the tourists.'

Poor Peter, he so badly wanted to grab everything that came his way in life as well as a lot that, it was obvious to me, was patently beyond his reach. I was drowning in his sea of unswerving aspiration.

The financial drain triggered by all this activity bothered me less than my refusal to give him the emotional support he needed. Even though he insisted on calling me Mum, I did little to deserve it. He came to stay with us on and off during the holidays, but most of the time he lived with his wizened aunt in her mud hut at Kisamis. In term-time, I was never the soccer mom who cheered from the sidelines or the stage mom who unconsciously mouthed his lines while he delivered them. Driven by guilt, it escaped my notice that he never invited me to watch him perform. I had too much on my plate: Tara and Petra, the other children, running a bush clinic a twelve-hour drive away. And, in case we forgot what financed all this activity, my job as a reporter. Peter's neediness frightened me. I was determined to keep him at arm's length.

There is always much discussion about whether genes or environment will out when raising a child who is not of your own blood. As far as I was concerned, there was a strong bias towards genes. Peter was hot-headed, irrational, superstitious, gentle and gregarious. Yet even though I knew these things, I found his behaviour mystifying. It was no easy task to muster I'll-die-for-you devotion to this stranger whose temperament was of a different genetic make-up from mine. He thought and acted in ways I didn't understand. He had a different sense of humour from the Fitzgeralds. I couldn't second-guess him as I could Tara and Petra. I ended up asking too many questions in an attempt to understand him.

Peter was the same age group as Meriape and Isaac, which meant that if tradition had been followed, they would have been circumcised and become warriors together. Their age group was called Irkipali. Each group was believed to take on a common personality, like classes at college and school. The elders said the Irkipali were rebellious troublemakers. 'It means we are clever and strong in our views. You can't rule us so leave us alone,' said Peter with pride.

He was good at role-dreaming. He was going to join the army, be a farmer, a tour guide, a lawyer. He was going to write detective stories and be famous. He was going to trade cattle and be rich. Yet he had no concept of who he actually was as a person.

The Maasai social system functions as a collective unit. They are one mass organism divided up into lots of smaller organisms: the clan, the age group, the *boma*. The Maasai don't celebrate the individual as we do. In fact, they have the scantest notion of exercising individual will. Even if they had known an inner self existed, they don't have the power of introspection to communicate with it. Peter's description of Irkipali, when I'd asked him what it meant, was the closest he got to explaining himself.

I stumbled often in my attempts to shape my association with Peter into a relationship. But as time went by I learned that love is an idiosyncratic realm of misty grey: ill defined and smudged at the edges. I began to realize I couldn't love Peter automatically, that there was no obligation to do so. My love for him was an amorphous feeling which existed independently of genes or environment. It just wobbled along, growing, shrinking, expanding. But mainly it expanded in tandem with our mutual history.

One Friday afternoon he arrived in the office looking extraordinarily pleased with himself. We had arranged to meet just before five o'clock. But there was more to his barely contained satisfaction than the prospect of a weekend at home. He looked older, more confident, as if he had just walked off the pitch after scoring the saving goal. We hadn't reached the lift before the story came pouring out.

Peter kept his school tuck in a tin box shoved under his bed. It was fastened with a small bronze padlock. Not that this stopped the older boys from stealing his food. They made him get out the key and open it. The first time it happened, he had refused and they had beaten him with *rungus*, sticks with knobs on the end. After that, he didn't resist.

A lot of the boys disappeared into the bushes after lunch to have a cigarette. Peter and his friend Kashoi took a dim view of this. Cigarettes were bad for athletes. But sometimes they hung out in the dorms. It was the first term of their second year, and at this particular lunchtime they had set a trap.

The door burst open; Gachuka and Njenga were silent silhouettes against the dim sky. The Kikuyu boys were two classes above Peter and Kashoi and big for their age, well fed. They advanced towards where Peter and Kashoi were sitting on the bed.

'Eating again, are you?' said Njenga.

'You boys are too greedy,' remarked Gachuka. He said it casually, but there was a menacing tone in his voice.

Peter and Kashoi stared up at them. They said nothing.

'You'd better give us your food,' said Njenga with a smirk. 'Open your box so we can see what you've got for us.'

'No.'

The Kikuyus exchanged sly grins. 'You're cheeky as well as greedy.' Gachuka fondled the *rungu* he was carrying and tapped his palm with its knobbed end. 'We'll have to teach you a lesson.'

'Keep away from my box.'

Kashoi felt the mattress quiver as Peter said it.

'Fuck you, Lekerian.'

'Fuck you.' Kashoi never swore. His nerves were getting to him.

'Fuck. You.' Gachuka took a step forward yet something restrained him from lifting his *rungu*. He couldn't put his finger on it, but he sensed the atmosphere was different. Lekerian was a sissy Maasai who always capitulated. Why was he regarding his hands so thoughtfully when he should have been scrambling to his feet and fishing the key out of his pocket? 'Fuck you,' he said again.

Suddenly Peter stormed to his feet with a howl and headbutted Gachuka in the stomach. Before the older boy could recover, Peter began to rain down blows on his head and shoulders and chest. And as his fists windmilled he kept right on howling. He was obeying the streetfighter's golden rule. Never miss a beat.

Cued by the hullabaloo, several of Peter's friends rushed into the dormitory. They leaped on Njenga and manhandled him to the floor. Gachuka they left to Peter until he was down. Then they crowded round. They stood on his arms and legs and panted in his face.

The wild, demented look in Peter's eyes subsided. He stepped back, took a gulp of air and straightened his shoulders.

'Don't ever try to take my food again,' he said and walked off.

The lift pinged to announce its arrival and the doors creaked open. Peter stepped out into the lobby. 'Don't worry, Mum. They don't come near me now.'

It spread, like a faint blush, from his eyes to mine. We smiled at each other. I was proud of him and he knew it. The bullying episode was a turning-point in our relationship. After solving the problem the way he had, by himself, his self-esteem blossomed. So did my affection for him.

He must have felt the world was a very unsafe place. The people who were most important to him – his parents – had died when he was a baby. It had taught him that anyone he might get close to would probably disappear. So he clung very hard. He made himself indispensable, like all 'good' children who don't want to be abandoned.

As time went by, Peter took it upon himself to act as the elder

51

brother towards the other boys. Isaac was managing at school, but Meriape, no natural scholar, had dropped out twice. He spent his time cruising Kiserian. It was a scrofulous little market town in the lee of the Ngong Hills, where one-storey buildings advertised misplaced optimism – My Secret Drycleaner, Survival Photo Shop, Eureka Retreat Centre Hotel.

Meriape's new life made him louche. He had grown a wispy moustache and his shirt tails flapped free of his ragged trousers. Peter said he looked like a Rasta and called him Bob after Bob Marley.

Meriape had become a denizen of Kiserian's bars. Kipenget moaned he was like his father Kili and wanted to slaughter her goats to sell the meat for beer money. She had taken to hiding them at someone else's *boma*. When I bumped into Meriape weaving along Kiserian's mud alleys, his face was loose and he regarded me with hostile eyes.

'He is a tragedy waiting to die,' Peter observed. He said it evenly without inflection.

Kipenget summoned me often, instructing me to talk Meriape out of his errant ways. We lay in the grass beneath the thorn tree by her house while she berated her son for his shortcomings. He flunked his exams. He spent her money on ganja and girls, she said, clicking her tongue against the back of her teeth and staring sternly at the distant volcanoes. I listened and watched the weaver birds as they chattered in the branches above. The drone of propellers hovered on the periphery of Kipenget's tirade. She relaxed moment-arily and squinted up at the light aircraft that seemed to be floating through the air. 'If *I'd* gone to school, I'd be flying that plane,' she said.

I let Peter be the caretaker of my concern. He was Meriape's age-mate, a diligent student, a man freighted with ambition. Who better to be the envoy of my displeasure? Peter stood with a hand on his hip, releasing a steady torrent of Maa just as an elder would. He was good at that sort of thing.

Meriape was the eldest son. He must work to support his brothers and sisters. It was the theme song of Kipenget's despair. In time, she hatched a plan for salvation. Meriape would become a taxi driver. She lobbied for a loan to bribe the examiner so he could get a driving licence. Although this was accepted practice, Meriape at the wheel of a *matatu* would have been an accident waiting to happen. I refused to underwrite this scheme and told Meriape he was shiftless and irresponsible. He, in turn, plucked a blade of grass and, pulling it between his fingers over and over again, wept crocodile tears of self-pity.

The others were being buffeted by their teenage years, too. Chege would be leaving school in a year or so and wanted to become a mechanic. Peris was showing considerably less interest in Petra's china doll which blinked when you rocked it and far more in braiding her hair in corn rows. She was about to start secondary school. Gentle Godfrey with the soft smile and luminous eyes dreamed about going to teachers' training college.

Godfrey was a fish-eating Luo from the shores of Lake Victoria. Neither Chege, a Kikuyu, nor Peter would deign to eat that slippery white stuff that came out of the water. Given the chance, they would have hunkered down by a goat carcass – Wairimu, for instance – and stayed put until every ounce of red meat had been filleted off the skeleton and gobbled down. The agricultural Kikuyu might secretly think the Maasai were savages while the Maasai called the Kikuyu potato-eaters behind their backs, but they had two things in common. They were as carnivorous as their cavemen ancestors and their manhood was ritually put to the test by having their foreskins cut. For the Maasai, circumcision was still carried out without anaesthetic when the boys were well into their teens. The Kikuyu, who were more Westernized, tended to do it younger and in hospitals. Godfrey, on the other hand, was . . . *uncircumcised*.

Having the three boys sit down at meals together was the ideological equivalent of dining with an Israeli, a Palestinian and, say, a Taliban fundamentalist from Afghanistan. Tara and Petra were more like the United Nations, a non-partisan presence who were unaware of the finer nuances of birthrights. Their chief concern was to create a *cordon sanitaire* around their possessions.

'Godfrey bent the pedal when he took the bike out,' grumbled Tara.

'So? It's a thing not a person. What matters is he had fun.' I bent and fiddled with the pedal as I talked. 'Here . . . look, I've fixed it.'

'Where's my red sweater?' demanded Petra.

'I gave it to Chege. It's cold and he hasn't got any.'

'It's my favourite,' she fumed.

'Good. Giving him a favourite thing is a way of letting him know you think he's special.'

The girls very rapidly latched onto this concept of giving selflessly. To this day they are two of the most generous people I know. Is it genetic? Or did Chege and Godfrey provide the right environment for learning about compassion?

The boys got on well and looked out for each other. It suited Peter to be protective and caring. It made him feel wanted and necessary. A smidgen of cultural superiority was in evidence, too. I could tell from the way he talked about Godfrey.

'In age we might be the same but the difference is Godfrey is a country boy. He is mild and too lean for a competition. The spirit of country boys at times is wishes, visions and unrealities. I will boost his morale in current affairs so that he may not remain behind on any aspect of life,' Peter volunteered, wishing to take his Luo friend's uncertain future in hand. He said these things with great gravitas. He was the Samaritan who was going to pick everyone up out of the gutter.

But then, we were all going to save a little bit of the world. The dispensary at Lesirikan had metamorphosed into an integrated rural development programme. As a result Kate, Gabriel and I had to bone up on all manner of arcane subjects relevant to the progressive pastoralist: immunization methods, co-operative marketing for hides and skins, water tables, maintenance-free pumps. We'd called the organization Samburu Aid in Africa so that we could use the acronym SAIDIA, which means 'help' in Kiswahili.

The A-frame house built by Anthony and I for a nuclear family of four became exponentially more crowded in relation to SAIDIA's success. Kate had taken up permanent residence long ago. Gabriel lived there, too, when he was in town, as did other Samburus. They appeared in the driveway, usually around breakfast time. They had travelled by bus or in the back of a cattle truck for a day or so and walked the last five, ten, fifteen miles to stretch their legs. They expected to doss down on the floor of the living room or the dining room or the study. In other words, to receive the same unquestioning hospitality they extended to us. They never entertained the possibility I would turn them away and I never did. The house was their Samburu outpost.

Sintahui, our Maasai night-watchman, was the first to greet the men from the northern savannah as they strode into sight at the end of the road. They swapped stories about married life. Sintahui had acquired his first wife, Russi, when she was thirteen. She played dolls with Petra until she gave birth a year later. Sintahui was shocked to discover Samburu women were circumcised the day before or even the morning of their marriage and that they lost their virginity to their husbands on the wedding night. The Maasai allowed their women a month to heal before they married them.

The house was a focal point of hospitality in the best Kenyan tradition. People drifted in from all over Africa, Europe, the States and stayed a night or two, several weeks or longer. As if this wasn't sufficient, Kate was a compulsive hunter and gatherer of people. I often returned from covering a story on ethnic fighting or national elections to find an intriguing new houseguest ensconced in one of the bedrooms. It was in this way that I made friends with Mike Radford, the award-winning director of *Il Postino*. Kate had invited him to stay for three weeks while he was on a recce for the film *White Mischief*. Johnny Gems, a playwright who billed himself as London's first punk rocker, struck up a special friendship with ten-year-old Petra and gave her a necklace made of goat's teeth to remember him by. When Meryl Streep moved in next door during the making of *Out of Africa*, Kate immediately hopped over the fence to welcome her to the neighbourhood and borrow a cup of sugar. We invited Meryl to supper, and she arrived on the doorstep barefoot, without make-up and carrying a baby on her hip.

Few formal invitations were issued, but no one was ever turned away. It was take pot luck with whomever was there. Government ministers rubbed shoulders with alleged Mafia, white farmers with Mossad agents. When a British general and his aide, a colonel, dropped in for supper, I added dessert to the modest meal I had laid on for Tara and Petra. The only banana in the kitchen was flambéed at the table over our kerosene camping stove, cut into five portions and served up with cream and brandy. The girls glared at me, but the general was delighted by this culinary eccentricity. A Maasai and his sister, two Kikuyu businessmen, an American artist and an environmentalist converged on the house at sunset. At ten that evening I offered the only food left in the larder – half a loaf of bread and two eggs, which I fried. Hunger did nothing to dampen the party mood. We danced until after midnight, then everyone spent the night, sleeping where they could. I found the Maasai woman, who had been bored by the *mzungu* dancing, asleep in my bed. The next morning, while she sat beside me under the duvet adjusting a series of bead necklaces, Kyengo the cook brought us tea. For the family, he always brewed up spiced tea in a saucepan which he ladled into tin mugs. But for the guest, there was Earl Grey served on a tray in the Spode blue-bird pattern teapot with matching cup and saucer, sugar bowl and milk jug. The tea service had been a wedding present.

Some of the guests knew me as the *Financial Times* correspondent and some as *lokop naibor*, the white Samburu. University professors in tweed jackets, best-selling authors, and socialites sat at the same table as men who ate with their fingers. Both groups were masters of sang-froid. The Samburu showed no surprise that the *wazungu* ate frozen cow's milk – ice cream – with a spoon. The *wazungu* men refrained from wincing when the Samburu women breastfed their babies at the table.

Peter, Godfrey, Chege and Peris mixed in well enough. I felt maternal towards them but never considered myself their mother. If I had paused to define the relationship, I might have said they were part of the shifting household tribe. But I never did. Life was too hectic to reflect on these matters.

The non-stop demands made upon me by teenagers and nomadic communities coincided with pressure at work. By this time I had left the *Financial Times* to become the *Sunday Times* correspondent for the region. I was busier than ever. There had been a crackdown on an underground opposition movement called Mwakenya. Detainees were being tortured and denied access to lawyers. The local papers failed to report the full story. They had been cowed into self-censorship by government intimidation.

Inevitably, writing on the rampant corruption and human rights abuse led me into a journalistic minefield. I was arrested and jailed briefly on spurious charges of currency smuggling. I got bail, was tried, convicted and fined. The court case was accompanied by a blaze of publicity in the media. Politicians blackened my name in public forums. The state machinery intended to crush me.

Then a few days before Christmas, as I was sitting at my desk in the office, the phone rang. It was Petra. 'Hello, Petal. What you doing? Having a good time?'

'I'm not at home, Mummy. I'm next door. There are men standing outside the house. They're looking for you.'

CHAPTER 6

'Where are you from?' they ask me in Dakar, Djibouti, Timbuktu.
'Kenya.'
'But you're not African. You're white,' they reply.
'It's my home,' I insist.

Protest as we might, white Africans are different from other Africans. When the going gets tough, we can get going. It's only the missionaries who batten down with the populace during Ethiopia-type famines and Somalia-type civil wars. Neither are whites usually imprisoned for their political beliefs. Nor are they forced into refugee camps. Being white means having options, although in the decades following independence, the tide of political events has swept away much of the privilege once accorded us. For the most part we are still tolerated – until we fall foul of authority. Then there is no recourse to legislation.

We survive by distilling the complicated facts of our life into something digestible, a sort of living epitaph. Even though I carried a British passport, I thought of myself as a white African. I cared passionately about the continent and was prepared to jeopardize personal security for speaking out on Africa's behalf. That belief came with a codicil attached. One day it might be put to the test.

There was another contemporary truth at large which held sway over my own plumped-up imaginings. The Kenyan administration was continuing to crack down on Mwakenya, the underground political opposition movement. As this cheeky British woman had been writing about it, she would have to be silenced too.

This is the conundrum of the whites who are the jetsam of the colonial era. We are dispensable. I had planted saplings in the belief that my children would sit in the shade of their branches. Yet I was a visitor in my own house.

In reality, I wasn't even that.

'What do the men look like?' I asked. I had called Petra back from another office. I was pretty sure my phone was tapped.

'There are five of them. Wearing suits and ties. I didn't see their socks. One has a walkie-talkie. I said you might have gone to town, but I didn't know when you'd be back. They're parked at the end of the road. The car's got ordinary licence plates.'

For a fifteen-year-old she had a cool head. As she and Tara grew up, I had taught them to observe, to look for the unusual. The entrance to the Special Branch office, next to a carpet shop, is barely noticeable. Lift your eyes and its existence is betrayed by the jumble of antennae on the roof. The Special Branch plainclothesmen don't wear badges proclaiming who they are, but a glance at their feet gives the game away. They have a penchant for red or brown socks. It's a lesson in urban awareness just as Maasai herdsboys learn to decipher the presence of lion from the warning bark of a zebra. Until now untested by crisis, I had sometimes wondered if I was exposing my children to pseudo-CIA paranoia.

'Stay right where you are. I'll ring Tara at Karen's and tell her what's happened. None of us must go home tonight. Let them stew in the driveway.'

'What about you?'

'I've got Peter with me. We'll find somewhere to sleep.'

'Love you.' There was a quiver in her voice.

'Love you too, baby. Don't worry. I'll get it sorted.'

Empty words, of course. You can't take on the state single-handed.

Back at the office a friend asked, 'Bad call?'

'Yes, very bad call. I might be going on a protracted holiday.'

'What do you mean? What's happened?' Peter looked as if he was standing in a cold wind.

I explained, touched on the looming deportation, but skirted round the implications. His face became frozen. How do you tell a sixteen-year-old boy who has been abandoned at birth that he is about to be deserted again? How do you tell him five days before Christmas that he is going to lose another mother? To regret my firebrand behaviour would have been self-indulgent. After all, I had done the best I could for Peter. His life had been easier for knowing the Fitzgerald family, and ours had been enriched since knowing him. If you fear imperfection in your actions, very little will come to pass.

Peter and I drove around looking for somewhere to hide, and as we followed roads aimlessly, recent events and imminent possibilities tumbled round in my head. My method of departure was the only choice remaining. If I turned myself in, the immigration authorities would put a stamp in my passport to show I was a prohibited immigrant. That route meant I would never be able to go home again. I considered taking a train to the coast. They would be watching the airport and the road exits but not the station. Then I could catch a fishing boat to Tanzania. On one level I was trying to formulate a plan, but in my mind I had already left home.

Home. Godfrey, Chege, Peris and Gabriel were arriving tomorrow. The turkey had been ordered. It was the gathering of the clan. How would the staff ever find new jobs? Thank goodness both girls had bases of a sort in England. Tara had finished school that summer and was working. Petra had started at Tara's old boarding school the previous year. At least they had somewhere to go to. But how could we spend Christmas together? Would they want to come with me or stay behind?

Peter was having none of the surrender theory. He was fired with gallantry and a desperate sort of optimism. He was in the throes of writing a detective novel. He'd called it *Spy Hunters*. Now things were taking an exciting turn. The chase scenes he had invented were springing to life from the pages of his notebook.

'I'll save you,' he said.

'You're a better man than most if you can. How?'

'I know a cave in the plains where you can hide. I'll bring you food and we can all have Christmas together. You can stay there for months. No one will find you.'

My life was unravelling too fast to daydream. Uncertainty seemed preferable to some distant cave. Witch hunts frighten bystanders, and several friends had made it clear their house wasn't available to us. Eventually, as night drew in, a girlfriend of twenty years' standing gave us refuge. It was a courageous offer, made against her better judgment. I had already attained pariah status.

While we tucked into supper, the plainclothesmen who had staked out the road leading to my house were having a bad time of it. They had been told to look out for a blonde white woman. My neighbours were throwing a Christmas party and had invited about 150 guests. Several dozen women with blonde hair drove by them that night.

The following morning they closed in, knocking at the neighbours' door and asking for Petra. She had been smuggled over the fence to another house. They found out which one and followed her there. Those neighbours, meanwhile, had hidden her under a blanket on the floor of the car and driven her to a third house. The men followed her there too. Thoughts of escaping in a dhow to Tanzania evaporated. As they hoped, I was unnerved by the fact that my baby girl was being harassed and I couldn't reach her.

I rang the chief immigration officer and told him I would be paying a visit. He and I discussed where in the world I would go to next with such amicable informality we might have been seated round the kitchen table mulling over a family problem. It's not easy to decide in fifteen minutes where you are going to live. I settled on England. I hardly knew the place, hated its small skies and grey rain, but it held a certain logic. We had friends and family in London. I spoke the language. I even worked for an English paper.

I was handed a deportation order, as I had feared. But I extracted a concession. The chief immigration officer agreed to turn a deaf ear to the instructions he had received saying that I was to be driven straight to the airport. He said I could have a night at home before leaving the country. As deals go, I could hardly lay claim to having struck a hard bargain. The Samburu would have said: Your plate is upside down.

The girls were stoic and uncomplaining. We decided Petra and I would cross the border to Tanzania so that we could be near by during the school holidays. Tara said she would stay and pack up the house. She was going to be eighteen on New Year's Eve. For Peter, Chege, Peris and Godfrey there was no choice. They had to remain behind.

We had invited friends to dinner and because there wasn't enough time to do anything very useful, we told them to come anyway. I had already lost everything so I had no immediate worries. Kyengo served the meal just as he always did. He was a safari cook who had learned to bake by shoving a tin box into the coals of the campfire. For over a decade he had made Tara and Petra brown Kyengo bread for breakfast and golden Kyengo cake for tea. He had six toes on one foot and if the girls pestered him enough, he would take his shoe off and let them look.

We chatted and laughed, uncorked a bottle of wine. It may have been the eye of a hurricane, but it was important to etch happiness onto our last day.

We took photos that night seated at the dining room table. We've moved round so we can all be in the picture. Peter's head is tipped to one side in his cockatoo pose. He has a hand at his mouth and the other is holding a piece of toast. I am sitting very close, leaning into him. Kyengo is standing behind us in his green apron. We are all smiling, smiling too much, as if facing some tribunal examining the sum of our existence as a family.

Petra went to work with the camera, too. There are several portraits of the dogs, tilted at inept angles. Bruce the black mongrel is lying on a fluffy white sheepskin by her bed. He is rolling his eyes and looking abashed as dogs do when they see suitcases.

Tara snapped Petra and I standing in a line with Kyengo, Sintahui and Esta the gardener. Petra has her arm linked through Esta's. Esta's other arm is wrapped around my shoulder and my hand is raised so that I can hold her hand. This time we are not smiling. Even then I refrained from crying in front of the children.

The ghost of Amina the nanny was with us in that photo. She had died suddenly and inexplicably Petra's first term away. She was in her seventies so it was reasonable to believe it was old age, but I thought her timing was suspect. She had come to work for us a few days before Tara was born and loved the girls as her own. Her relatives – bosomy women who worked in offices – came to help with the funeral. They told me things about Amina which made me think I hadn't known her at all. Amina's husband had thrown her out because she was barren. So her sister gave her one of her children for Amina to raise as her own. Everyone in the village knew that Esta was adopted except for the girl herself, the relatives said. It was their custom to do it that way.

This story fascinated me. In the West, the children are the first to know they are adopted. In Africa, it was the other way round. An entire community would be aware of the adoption before the child was. It was as if Amina had lived her life on two levels. The village life with its different values and superstitions was a separate world which could not overlap her town life amongst the *wazungu*. At the time, it didn't occur to me that this might be true for Peter as well.

When everyone had gone to bed, I roamed the corridors and rooms until the small hours of the morning. Still too young for retrospectives, I couldn't comprehend that the present was the past and I was stalking it. Just as well. The unbearable emptiness of exile comes of being stripped of your friends, your achievements, your local culture; in other words, the history that gives you meaning as a person.

The next day the neighbourhood wives congregated to empty drawers and pack the contents into suitcases that would one day join us somewhere. My personal preparations for the journey that would launch me on the next stage of my life took no more than five minutes. I stuffed a change of clothing into Tara's old school satchel and stood it in the hall beside a sleeping bag, a vintage portable typewriter and a judicious bottle of whiskey. When at last the time came to leave, everyone lined up outside the front door, standing in the dust beneath the kei apple hedge. Gabriel had driven down from Samburu. He'd had a presentiment of what had come to pass, he said, dreaming a few nights earlier that the house stood empty. Meriape had heard the news on the bush telegraph and arrived by *matatu*. Peter, Chege, Godfrey, Kyengo. They were all there. Esta, my sister. Sintahui, who had carried his spear around the periphery of the garden for thousands of nights, cocooned in gumboots, greatcoat and balaclava. Russi, his plump wife, who used to play dolls with Petra. My family. The neighbours. Their servants. My friends. I hugged and kissed each one. Then Petra and I walked to the waiting car and threw our things onto the back seat. We climbed in, shut the doors and did not turn to wave. The car slipped past the cactuses in the rock garden, nudged round the bush where the wild roses bloomed, distanced itself from the tadpole pond where the children used to wade, slid through the shadow cast by the casuarina at the end of the driveway and grunted into third gear on the tarmac road. Petra and I neither cried nor looked back.

Many years later when the pain of departure had subsided and lay obediently quiescent deep inside me, I wondered if Peter, too, had experienced some sort of internal exile, rudely amputated as he had been from the blood of his clan and the traditions which were his birthright.

After Petra and I had walked out the front door for the last time, Peter took Tara's bicycle and disappeared down the drive. He came back covered in mud. Tara, now the mistress of the house, fussed over him. 'What happened? You look terrible.'

'My mind went black. I fell into a puddle.'

The glasses, plates and books, the silver and paintings and records – the material accumulation of twenty years – were to be stored in the long-suffering neighbours' attic. The boys helped Tara to pack it all into boxes. They had discovered several pairs of dark glasses in a drawer and wore them as they worked. It gave their faces, already darkened with sadness, a strange funereal air. The toys and mementoes of Tara's childhood were contained in two small cardboard boxes. Gabriel wrote on them: Tara's World. She didn't see them for another seven years.

When term started in January, Peter returned to Oloolaiser High. He had two years to go to graduation. He struggled to come to grips with maths and physics, but he was pretty sure that if he studied hard he would pass. Under other circumstances he would have been happy, but he wasn't. He was miserable. He sat in the dorm on his bed hunched over a school notebook and wrote and wrote.

'Aren't you coming out for soccer practice?' asked Kashoi.

'No, I'm busy.'

'You're always writing.'

'You go on. I'll join you later.'

Peter got 'a prolonged stomach ache' and couldn't concentrate.

He was solitary in his grief. The other boys didn't have white foster mums. No one understood his anguish. He was determined to keep his family together even though we were separated by thousands of miles and an indefinite government ban on my return. His letters were bulging with sorrow. They plopped onto the mat in London and I read them over a mug of tea and cried.

> I really miss you. Your absence in Kenya brings me fear and I feel unloved. I became a son to you, who has lost a loving and caring mother. These days tears just drop off my eyes when I remember you and your loving parental love. What I would like you to know is that whenever you are in a sorrowful state, I am sharing your sorrowfulness state with you. Whenever I am tired in school and refuse to sleep early, I revive my former days with you in Nairobi. Restaurants, friends' houses, every-where as you have made me part of your robe. You are very much in my veins, heart and in my thoughts. Goodbye my Mum but not for a long time. God will give us time to meet.
>   Yours,
>   Peter Lekerian.

My friend and old office-mate Kathy Eldon had separated from her husband Mike and moved to London. She had a spare room in her flat and was putting me up. It was an act of true friendship. Those first months I talked little and cried a lot. No longer in danger, I didn't know how to cope with the void. I was more than homesick. It was a profound desolation. The grief gnawed at my vitals and soured my heart. I felt as if the marrow had been drained from my bones. A foul poison seeped into my brain and clouded it with melancholy. This unhappiness haemorrhaged my will to exist so that I became a shade, a walking zombie. I was convinced no one understood what I was going through. I looked the same as any other Englishwoman so they didn't know I was an exile. They simply presumed I'd had a bad experience and come home to lick my wounds.

I knew Africa for what it was yet still I missed it. I had long ago stopped subscribing to the postcard Africa of tented safaris and school holidays on palm-fringed beaches. My Africa was one of hardship, as my previous year's conviction for alleged currency smuggling had demonstrated. The charges had less to do with the dollars the customs official found in my handbag at the airport – the travel allowance the *Sunday Times* had sent me – than with the fact that for three years my reporting had managed to rile the KANU administration. While waiting for my court appearance I was held in one of the dungeonlike cells beneath the law courts. It smelt of urine so stale it must have seeped into the walls when the courts were built by the British in the 1940s. It was my fellow inmates – thieves and murderers – who kept my spirits up. They instructed me in burglary and fraud. I asked a prostitute what remand prison would be like. 'Not so bad. They let us out once a week, and we bask in the sun.' It was a lesson in reality. Life is what we perceive it to be.

I wanted to go home. Yet I couldn't. To set foot on Kenyan soil bearing the label of 'prohibited immigrant' was a criminal offence. Another stint behind bars would have smacked of carelessness.

'What have you got in there?' David, a friend from Kenya, had come to cheer me up.

'Clothes. I think. I don't know. Who cares?'

'Clothes? In a *bin liner*?'

I sniffed into a Kleenex and stared at the window. It framed a black rectangle of night which chilled and darkened the room.

'Shall I pull the blind down?'

'No. I can't stand to be shut in.' The bedroom felt like a prison. I wanted to scream and hammer on the walls with my fists until the room exploded and I could soar into the coal-black sky. Unable to conduct a proper conversation, David walked over to the cupboard and pulled the door open. It was empty. He made a face.

'You could hang them up in here.'

'What for? There's no point in unpacking.'

He crossed the room, sat on the bed beside me, his hands in his lap. I didn't look at him.

'You're here whether you like it or not. Is this the way you want to live?'

A wet sob burst through my nose, and I thought, *I'm going mad and I'm not going to do anything to stop it.*

I hated England – the way you drove through the countryside and saw no one walking in the fields; the way people got out of their cars at petrol stations to fill up and pay at the till, then got back in again and drove off. It was as if it was an elaborate board game where the only safe place to move forward was along gleaming black snakes. I longed to stride for hours through savannah or forest or desert and in the solitude of that sameness replenish my spirit. When I went outside, I crouched down and touched the damp grass – it had to be with all ten fingers, the palms pushing down amongst the wet leaves – to say, *Hello, I'm here. Talk to me.* People stared. I didn't care. The earth was my totem, a tenuous connection with Africa, and it consoled me.

The places where other people in London relaxed – the restaurants and shopping malls and art galleries – gave me no pleasure. But I liked what they hated. The clammy grey afternoons and soupy skies the colour of dirty dishwater, the wind which tore at the tree branches and the rain which left snail trails of water on the window-panes were a reason not to go out onto the streets and be a part of this alien cityscape.

One of the many things I disliked was the underground. It was my chosen method of transport because I couldn't read the city's topography, how the streets connected one with the other. So I travelled like a mole, disappearing into the ground and popping up again on the other side of the city. The underground had a metallic smell of soot and cold sweat. It was another snake and you travelled in its belly. Everyone hurried and had grim faces. They didn't look at anyone else, even when someone was in trouble. I did as they did. I spoke to no one and pretended I was alone.

Then one day I made a friend. It was early evening, the lull after the rush hour, and there was one other person on the platform. I could always tell an African. Their clothes were too new or if they were old, it was not in the shabby way that was trendy. But it was more the way they held themselves, loose but alert. They actually looked at the passers-by and saw them as people, thus acknow-ledging we are all part of a greater community. And sometimes their faces were flat with anxiety and I knew they were thinking, *Where am I*? Very often, we smiled at each other.

She wore short lace-up boots and a raincoat with a flap on the shoulders. Her hair was straight and she was pretty. She asked me which was the train to Euston Station. I told her and added that it was the one I was taking. She could follow me.

As it pulled up to the platform, I said, 'This is it.'

We stepped through the doors and found seats. I liked the fact that I had spoken with someone and wanted to continue the intimacy. 'Are you from Africa?'

'Ghana.' She smiled.

'I'm from Kenya. On a visit?'

'I'm studying. Law.'

'Great. Are you going to practise back home?'

'Yes.' We smiled at each other again. Then she added, 'This is an important trip for me. I've got to get back up to university because I'm sitting my finals tomorrow.'

The shared confidence made me warm and happy. Here was someone doing something important and I was helping her achieve it. I was going to see that she reached Euston Station in time. The responsibility, for that moment, gave my life meaning. I lifted my eyes above the windows to where a map of the underground stations was fixed to the side of the carriage, and something strange happened. I had been so sure of where we were going, but now the map didn't make sense. We were travelling in the wrong direction. In fact, we weren't even on the right line. I'd never been to Euston Station, didn't even know where it was. Who was I to give advice?

I leapt to my feet and cried, 'We're on the wrong train! We're on the wrong train!'

Her hand was on my coat sleeve, tugging. 'Sit down. It's all right. We've got three stops to go.'

'Sorry. I just thought . . . with your exams . . . Sometimes I get confused.'

'I know,' she said. 'It's difficult when you're away from home.'

CHAPTER 7

Within a month of arriving in London, Peter had written to say that his Aunt Naserian was ill. 'She is growing weak and weak every day. Her age set has all passed away and I don't know her day.' He was haunted by the fear of being abandoned again. It overshadowed all else. 'I don't want you to get moved, but when her time comes, I will be left all alone in the world and will know what is called loneliness.'

Naserian soldiered on and Peter rallied. His aspirations resurfaced.

Do you remember what once you told me when we were driving to your home in Langata? You told me, 'Peter! A good duck teaches its young ones to wade through the mud. A good lioness teaches its cubs to hunt.' It means that a good mother doesn't give children gifts forever but instead she teaches them to find ways of getting presents for themselves when their mother isn't present. These days I have a very big change in me as you predicted. I want to cool down and think before taking an action. I will reduce my football-playing in order to get more time to study. So many times I think that if I can be given a chance to prove to you my love I would actually demonstrate it with actions rather than empty words.

Behind this muscle-flexing lay another plan which soon unfolded on the lined notebook paper. Peter's age-mates were about to become warriors and leave their mothers' huts to sleep apart. He wanted to do this, too. But how can you leave home and your mother when you have neither? It was a time when he should have been protecting the cattle from lions and driving them long miles in search of water. But he was doing none of these things. Instead, like most teenagers, he was wondering what life held for him and indulging in a good dose of self-pity.

'As a grown-up boy other people might think I am after young girls, food, or a rumour-monger if I go to them for accommodation.' His answer was to build his own house. A wooden one with a corrugated-iron roof. It would only cost $450. If not quite in the warrior tradition, it was a fair approximation given the jumbled worlds he lived in and a declaration of manhood for all that. I set about trying to find the money for wood and nails and sheets of corrugated iron. I would send it to Gabriel, who was monitoring Peter's finances.

The letters were no longer damp with tears but long-winded and urgent. A vein of anger and frustration ran through them. The money wasn't enough. Naserian would die soon and leave him on his own. He needed more, much more. Gabriel put his foot down and gave him a talking-to.

Peter wrote to me immediately, his words bristling with indignation. There was a conspiracy being mounted against him.

Mary Anne, daughter of Fitzgerald, Gabriel gave me a lecture on how to be a very good boy, very economical, very respectful and so on. He says that plans of building a house should be put out of my mind until I finish schooling. I know you wouldn't listen to the advice of primitive peoples. If I adhere to dictations they will ruin me. I can say that Gabriel doesn't want to see me progress. Is he a critic or an underground movement for my downfall?

I wrote back to say that Gabriel was right and he should listen to his advice. Peter calmed down and reverted to his old form, love and ambition blazing from the pages. It was now his last year at school. He had been made a prefect and was captain of the Kashanga Football Club. He said he walked like Michael Jackson and was studying so hard he was keeping 'a burning coal' on his head.

He wrote, 'When I visit my uncle's home in the holidays, boys of my age admire me a lot. They would like to walk with me wherever I go and when I sit down to rest, some even go as far as wearing my clothes just to feel the comfortability of them.'

I read the letters and smiled and didn't notice that it was the first

70

time he had mentioned he had an uncle. I was preoccupied with my own problems. The girls and I didn't have a house to live in either.

As time went by, we emerged from our exile with a calm that gave us the flexibility to function as a family, irrespective of geography. Parted from our house in Kenya, we kept our home within us and took it wherever we travelled. We were like house finches – nesting under others' eaves and considering them our own.

Both Tara and Petra had by then acclimatized to England to the point where they seemed almost British, which they were, according to their blue passports. Tara had reacted to her first winter like a hibernating bear. She went to bed as soon as it got dark in the late afternoon and stayed there until daylight reappeared. She struggled to learn how to use mechanized gadgets and earned the nickname 'caveman'. With her sister to lead the way, Petra settled in quickly, adopting the slang, the music, the jet-black clothes. Theirs was a virtuoso performance compared to my snivelling despair.

My parents were critically injured in a car crash, and I flew to Johannesburg in South Africa to nurse them back to health. Tara, who had graduated from university, flew out a month later. We house-sat together and got jobs; I, with a magazine; Tara, as a cashier in a restaurant. Petra, who had left school and was going to work with underprivileged children in Mexico, joined us for Christmas. Back in Africa, the wild joyousness of their childhood reignited. They walked barefoot and there was restless moonlight in their eyes.

It was far better to be wandering the continent than to be depressed in London, but it still wasn't home. Then my luck came through. I landed a two-week assignment in Tanzania for the Audubon Society's magazine. I was to write a story substantiating the theory that the Maasai are excellent conservationists. I'd pitched this angle to the editor in New York a few months earlier. Anything to get back to East Africa. My companions were a New York photographer called Lori Grinker and an interpreter. I spoke good Kiswahili, the lingua franca of East Africa, but had yet to master the intricacies of Maa.

The interpreter was a school graduate whose previous job had been at a tourist lodge at the foot of Mt. Kilimanjaro. He'd spent a week sweeping the bedrooms and then packed it in because the work was menial and boring. He wanted to be a safari guide and, with this in mind, had taken some French lessons. He wasn't exactly fluent, but he felt confident enough to sign his letters *Au revoir, Pierre*.

He was learning to drive too. At the house where he lived in Nairobi he sometimes manhandled an old Land Rover past the deep verandah at the front of the house, the garage overhung by a rusty tin roof, the frangipani trees speckled with trumpets of scented flowers, and aimed for the wrought-iron gate at the bottom of the drive. Although there was no traffic except for the gardener weeding the lawn and the dogs basking in the sun, he'd grip the wheel tightly with both hands, swerving onto the grass and correcting this with a detour through a flowerbed. He said he wanted money for proper driving lessons at a driving school so that he could get a licence.

His name, of course, was Peter Lekerian. He was on the payroll, a necessary expense if we were to find out what was happening in this very remote part of Tanzania. After four years apart, the prospect of spending two weeks together delighted us.

The place I had chosen – at random – to research the story was in the Rift Valley, called Ongata Enchani Pus, the Plain of the Blue Trees. It was a strange moonscape of dust and volcanic mountains at the back end of the Ngorongoro Crater, which is one of the natural wonders of the world. Spawned 4 million years ago by an erupting volcano, Ngorongoro is a precisely formed caldera of magical beauty; a ten-mile-wide cameo ecosystem which contains the Big Five: lions and leopards, elephants, rhino and buffalo; God's footprint, the Maasai say.

The crater's crumpled outer slopes were stacked up in a tumble a few miles away. The dark shadows of myrrh-bearing Commiphora trees marked ridges where buffalo and rhino sheltered. The undergrowth was thick and tangled, as primitive as when man's ancestor Australopithecus walked here 3.6 million years ago. Yet down on Ongata Enchani Pus, there was hardly any vegetation except for the trees and thickets which lined the water courses. The Maasai were the only tribe who cared to live here. They nurtured scarce resources with a frugality no Westerner would care to emulate.

The wind-ruffled Plain of the Blue Trees was an ecological disaster wreaked by thoughtless land policies. In the old days, earlier this century and before, the Maasai shifted with the ebb and flow of the rains. Their survival relied on rotating pastures, seeking new ones while old ones recovered. Now they could no longer move freely and the environmental destruction caused by overgrazing had become permanent.

The theft of ancestral grazing lands began soon after the Second World War, when British colonial administrators targeted the game-filled forests and craters of the Ngorongoro Highlands, the Maasai spiritual homeland, as a tourist site. They drew up a conservation blueprint which claimed people and wildlife would have equal rights, living side by side. But in the 1970s the Tanzanian government evicted the Maasai from the Ngorongoro Crater and its vital dry-season waterholes.

It was the age-old battle between ranchers and farmers. Agricul-turalists from other tribes appeared clutching leasehold title deeds to the most fertile land, pushing the Maasai into the marginal areas. Thanks to the careless dynamics of officialdom, they were being painted into a corner.

This particular part of the Rift Valley was way off the beaten track, even by African standards. It was 100 miles from the market town of Arusha as the crow flies, but it had taken us seven hours to get here in the Land Rover I'd hired. We'd got lost in a hunting block and driven for a good part of the previous night over a rutted and narrow footpath which had never before received four wheels. It was wonderful because it was African. It was home.

We'd slept on the road and spent the day doing the sort of things you do when you have come to a place that is the next best thing to home. We'd stalked a caravan of thirty giraffe across the dusty plain as they made their way to the acacia brush of a riverbed. It was an awesome sight. Giraffe are twenty feet tall, most of which is neck and legs. Then we'd veered off, our attention distracted by a herd of zebra until the ground had trembled under our feet: the giraffe cantering off on noiseless hooves.

As day drew in once more, our meanderings led us to a *boma* that stood on the edge of a grove of acacia trees. Sounds carried clearly in the stillness of dusk. If you stopped to listen, even with your eyes shut, nothing was secret. Two women called to each other across the plain, exchanging the news of the day. From behind came the patter of hooves, as soft as spring rain falling on the earth. A girl's shout was answered by a young boy's whistle. The goats passed, and the acrid mix of dust, urine and dying heat tickled our nostrils. It was an hour of activity for the Maasai. Their livestock had to be herded home before nightfall and penned beyond the reach of lions on the hunt.

'So who's going to put us up for the night?' I addressed the question to our guide and mentor.

'We can go there,' Peter said, pointing to the homestead.

'What, three total strangers? Just roll up and say . . .' I gestured expansively, 'Here we are. Take us in.'

He had no qualms. 'We are travellers. They must.'

The *boma*'s loaf-shaped huts stood in a circular arrangement inside a high thorn fence. They were the same khaki colour as the surroundings. You hardly noticed they were there. But the plain was a moving kaleidoscope of red and blue figures and spirals of copper-coloured dust. The herd-boys were driving the cattle and goats home.

I edged the Land Rover slowly forward and stopped by the gate. Lori clambered out first amidst a rattle of cameras. Everyone froze. It was as if a switch had been thrown on the activity. Then the children started howling and scuttled behind their mother's skirts. They could see that *wazungu* were as red as raw beef, just as they had been told, and smelt bad. They wore strange clothing which prevented the breezes from blowing their body odours away. They were *illoorridaa injikat*, the people who confined their farts.

'They're more frightened of you than of lions. They've never seen white people before,' Peter said.

It's a Maasai belief that some people have eyes which can bore straight through your flesh and see the heart and liver and bones. They can make you fall sick. They can strike little children dead. X-ray machines also have eyes and so do the little X-ray machines like the one that hung around Lori's neck. No wonder they were screaming.

Peter said something in Maa which must have reassured them because the children peeked out at us and stared. We took a few steps inside the *boma*, smiling all the time, not knowing that we should have spat on the ground to dispel any evil we might be bringing with us.

A man approached Peter and they began to converse in an unhurried fashion. The children sidled closer. Lori stretched out a hand and they dashed away, screaming at the top of their lungs.

In due course Peter came back to us. 'This place belongs to a man called Mereso. He's away but we are welcome to stay. You're sleeping with this woman here.'

We stooped low to pass through the doorway and fumbled in the darkness. I breathed in the warm milky scent of baby goats and stumbled over a stool. Lori blinked and coughed as she inhaled a mouthful of smoke. The hut, like every other hut, had no windows or ventilation. It was tiny, just large enough for the two low beds made of branches covered with cowhides. Between them, on the earth floor, was a cooking-fire. The woman giggled a lot as we hauled in our gear: mugs, bowls, sleeping bags, torches, hats, cameras, tea, *posho*, carrots. The paraphernalia seemed cumbersome and excessive in this cramped space.

'Are we intruding?'

She understood my outspread hands and apologetic look and shook her head. Her laughter was accompanied by the wind-chime tinkling of her earrings.

It didn't take long to discover that moon-faced Noonkepa, The Breaking of Water at Birth, collapsed into giggles often. Mereso had six wives and she was one of his favourites. Her overt sex-appeal gave her confidence and made her flirtatious.

That evening we sat round Noonkepa's fire and people came and went in the darkness. They plonked down on the bed or pulled out a tin container from the shadows and sat on that. Or they brought their own stools with them. We felt welcome, but they behaved as if we weren't there. They chattered away in Maa and ignored us.

Peter didn't say much. I could tell he was in awe of these people.

I'd expected him to slot in, but he didn't. Lori and I may have been strangers who farted into our clothes, but he too was an 'alien'. He came from another country and was a city-slicker. A whole world lay between them. Aware of this, Peter wrapped a *kikoi* around his head, turban fashion, and joked that he was a Somali. It was his way of keeping his cultural dignity intact.

A different sort of space separated Peter and I, one filled with experiences we hadn't shared. While he had been scrambling up the foothills of maturity, I'd been travelling through war zones, living with pygmies and tracking gorillas in the rain forest as the *Sunday Times* roving correspondent in Africa.

His wish for a place of his own had at last been realized. But as is so often the way in life, it hadn't materialized quite as he had expected. While his Aunt Naserian was sick he had been spending the holidays at the *boma* of an uncle, who beat him 'like a horse'. When Naserian had at last died, he had gone to live with Kathy's ex-husband Mike Eldon. He had a room of his own in the servants' quarters. Mike, who was gentle, funny and tremendously caring, had instilled a new confidence in him. He had become the father-figure Peter had been seeking all these years. Mike was the managing director of a computer company. With his briefcase, business suit and gleaming shoes, he was the Wise Old Man. Peter, who was twenty-one, looked up to him and wanted to emulate his managerial, executive style.

He developed a habit of lurking by the front door and ambushing Mike when he got home from the office. He bombarded him with questions about his embryonic career. He wanted to go into tourism – showing foreigners around suited his gregarious nature. Yet there was something to be said for joining the army. Military men had stature. But he also had a vocation as a cattle-trader. He was Maasai and cattle were in his blood. Mike was a Rotary Club member and enjoyed moulding enthusiasm into purpose. He fielded Peter's fusillade of questions with tact and care.

Peter had kept me abreast of his endeavours by chronicling them in his letters. The government was allocating the tribally owned land in his home area and he had managed to acquire title to 150 acres down in the Rift Valley behind the Ngong Hills. Land deals were inevitably mired in corruption and Peter had engaged in a protracted battle with local officials and parted with $150 before the papers were finally in his hands. Mike was impressed. He said that Peter was a pro when it came to working the system, and Peter basked in Mike's approval. 'Mike told me you must always go straight to the top. He doesn't tolerate slow moves,' Peter said.

With Mike's help he drew up a plan to utilize his land. He was going to market goats bred from a core herd of 200 nannies. The project would be underwritten by a $7,500 loan at 10 per cent interest with repayment over five years. There was just one drawback. A rather big one. The government land allocation scheme which Peter was part of had been challenged in court by a group of Maasai. The chief litigant was Peter's best friend, Joseph Simel. As long as the legality of ownership was being contested, the banks refused to consider his goat project. So Peter was looking for investors. He had sent me a copy of the ten-page development plan.

I had praised his business acumen but ignored the subtext: a plea for a large amount of money. Likewise, I never bothered to follow up on the cruel uncle, who was the only relative he had ever referred to. I had been too busy trying to cobble my life back into something worth getting up for in the mornings. For the moment, the challenge of making the goat project become a reality had been supplanted by a simpler one: interpreting the nuances of life at Mereso's *boma* for the benefit of Lori and me.

I had stayed often enough in the *bomas* of friends, but even by Maasai standards life moved at a glutinous pace. In fact, it was so slow that my thought processes tended to glue up. It was hard for me to keep our brief from the Audubon magazine – Maasai and conservation – as a fixed point in my mind. The daily routine was measured by the arrival and departure of the sun and, concomitantly, the livestock. Dawn heralded a burst of activity when the herds were milked, then shooed out onto the plains. An hour or two before dusk the scene was rewound as the cows and goats trooped back home and were milked all over again. In-between times we were wrapped in a blanket of heat which made us lethargic. The men lolled in the shade of *enchani pus*, the blue trees, while the women fetched water with the donkeys. They spent a lot of time doing this. It was a six-mile trek to the nearest stream and back.

The evenings were the best time. Mereso was away, at the *boma* of another wife, who lived near Arusha. Even though we stayed in the *boma* for a week, we never did meet him. Encouraged by his prolonged absence, his wife Noonkepa had a lover, a man in a red-and-black-check *rubega* who always arrived and departed at night. As I never saw him properly, for me his voice became his face. It was rich and dark in a gently wicked sort of way, like a coffee liqueur. It lapped about the women and set their hearts beating. When he told stories, which was nearly all the time, the rhythm of his words slowed and quickened so that they danced in our ears. He had the comic's gift of timing which sent everyone into gales of laughter. Even his name was funny. Ololokidomo – he who comes from the *boma* with too much cow dung.

Peter was slow to translate Ololokidomo's stories, perhaps because he hadn't quite got the hang of what his job entailed or more likely because he was embarrassed. When I pressed him, he said Ololokidomo was gossiping about other people's sex lives. He refused to elaborate.

The formalities of Maasai sex allow for a certain amount of wife-swapping within the framework of age sets. Warriors chatting up older women is taboo. However, it is common practice for men who have been circumcised in the same age set to share their wives. Much has been made of this practice, where a socially accepted steam valve for desire has been confused with impropriety. Men and women only take advantage of the custom if there is a genuine mutual fondness. And there is absolutely no stigma on the children of these liaisons. They are embraced as the sons and daughters of the husband.

Ololokidomo was an age-mate of Mereso, which was why, I presumed, he was so bold in his affair with Noonkepa. Several times I woke up in the night and heard soft grunts and urgent shiftings coming from the other bed. I wondered what Peter would have thought of that. Eat neatly, the Maasai say. If you leave crumbs on your mouth, people will ask questions.

Love seemed to be in the air. Peter was smitten, too, by one of Mereso's daughters. She wore a coil of copper wire twisted around one wrist. Her only other adornment was the red top of a toothpaste tube, which hung from her stalklike neck. She had a delicate beauty, but I could tell she was as durable as a kiln-fired earthenware pot.

On the evenings when Noonkepa and Ololokidomo stretched out on a cowhide under the stars, like moonstruck lovers, and everyone congregated around them, she came and stood beside me and rested her hand lightly on my shoulder. Her name was Nanyokie, which means red, and she was eleven. She was just the right age for Peter. In another year or so she would be wooed by warriors. Once that happened, it would not be long before somone negotiated with Mereso to marry her.

The attraction blossomed in Peter's mind, fuelled by surreptitious glances from Nanyokie which could have been curiosity about the 'aliens'. Peter fed on this and became overbearingly polite to the wives. He thanked them lavishly for giving him a mug of tea, to which they replied that it was nothing to do with them as the milk came from their husbands' cows. 'I am addressing you with my chest a bit open because I would like to become your relative,' he replied.

He wasn't conventionally handsome, but his face was constantly alight. He had always laughed often but now he was vibrant with happiness and the smallest event excited him: teasing Nanyokie, helping Noonkepa load the water containers on her donkey or standing in the dawn mist with his hands in his pockets surreptitiously taking stock of Mereso's cows and goats. It was a pastime which had to be conducted with discretion because some Maasai still believed counting a man's herds meant the animals would die. It was probably a tribal protection mechanism against jealousy. A bit of snooping by Peter had ascertained Mereso owned about 200 cattle and 3,000 head of goats and sheep.

Peter announced to Lori and me that he would marry Nanyokie and that I had already become her mother. 'See how inquisitive she is and eager to learn. She will make a good wife, but I must send her to school first.' He said these things casually so that if we thought it was funny, he wouldn't lose face.

I had stayed with Maasai friends often before, but this time it was different. Peter's interpretations of what he saw around him

79

had opened our eyes to the petty dramas of the people we were living amongst: Noonkepa, Ololokidomo, Nanyokie. So we were outsiders and intimates, both at the same time.

It was Nanyokie's job to take the goats into the glade of fever trees behind the *boma*. There was no grazing there, but they foraged the mustard-coloured fever pods which fell onto the ground. It was a peaceful place filled with the liquid cooing of doves and the tinkle of goat bells. One morning Nanyokie's squawks for help came floating on the heat-laden air. Everyone stopped what they were doing immediately. The women raced over the thorns barefoot. The warriors carried their spears at the ready.

When they got to the glade, Nanyokie told me that a large snake had just slid past, and pointed at the bush where it was hiding. She was quite calm about it. I think she was more frightened of being blamed for losing a goat than by the snake itself. She'd seen it curled up in the dust the previous day, she said, but she had taken no notice as she'd thought it was an old cooking pot.

The boys were very excited. They had surrounded the bush and were throwing their spears into it. They picked them up as they ricocheted out and did it all over again. Nanyokie was running around fetching and carrying the spears, too, like a retriever.

Peter said, 'They are no good at spearwork. These guys are very peaceful so that don't have a chance to practise. For us it would take no more than half an hour.' It was clear that he wanted to join in, but I wouldn't let him. It looked quite dangerous and, despite his boast, I had no idea what his spearwork was like.

The throwing and ricocheting business went on for about twenty minutes. There was no sign of the snake but it must have been feeling a bit out of sorts by then because you could smell the blood from its wounds. Then suddenly it slithered out into the open, dark olive splodges on a dark skin flashing along the ground. The boys jumped back, sending a flock of quelea birds into flight. One or two of the women made as if to shin up a tree. There was no need. The snake had suddenly stopped. It was dead.

The skin was seven feet long. I would have liked to have kept it, but the boys insisted on building a bonfire around it. Someone was sent back to the *boma* to bring a pat of smouldering cow dung to light it with and the whole thing went up in a blaze. The cremation of the carcass derived from a belief that if a cow lies down in the place where a snake has died, the cow assumes serpent-like qualities and sheds its skin.

I started to make notes of the whole episode, sitting at the base of a fever tree with my back against its trunk. Nanyokie soon wandered over. She chipped at the bark with her *panga* until the ochre sap oozed and then balled it in her fingers and popped it into her mouth. She liked the gum because it swelled her stomach and stopped the hunger pangs. She hovered above me, chewing, and watching my hand tracing strange squiggles across the paper. She was fascinated by writing. She said something in Maa. I knew she wanted to try out the pen herself.

I was on the point of handing it over, but something was wrong. Nanyokie had leapt away as if stung by bees and was howling with rage. I looked up. A warrior was whipping her legs with a thorn branch. Hard.

'Hey! Stop that! Stop that!' I scrambled to my feet gesticulating.

The warrior ignored me and so did Nanyokie. She was furious, but custom dictated she had to accept the beating. The frustration of it made her rake her face with her fingernails. I looked around for help. Peter had been watching, but he had retreated and his head was turned the other way. Everyone else had melted into the bushes. It was a strange feeling, as if it was us who were invisible not them. I stepped forward with my hands up, palms outwards, and said firmly, 'All right, now that's enough.'

The warrior stopped, glared at Nanyokie and strode off with that bouncy stride typical of his age group. Even by the most optimistic of interpretations, it was obvious my interference had had no bearing at all on the outcome. Nanyokie walked away, too. Even Peter had vanished. I was invisible again.

Later I said to Peter, 'What was all that about?'

'Nanyokie's thoughts and ambitions are with you. She wants to learn more about you. This is bad because you are only passing through. They need her here to look after the goats.'

'Bright girl like that would do well in school . . . Pee-eeter?'

'Yes, M. A.'

'Would you really like to marry Nanyokie?'

He crossed his arms, rocked back on his heels, tilted his head way over to one side in that familiar mannerism of his, and gave me a prolonged wink.

'She's very nice,' he said.

CHAPTER 8

After a week or so, the three of us packed our belongings and moved to a nearby village. Engaruka provided another aspect of how the Maasai adapt to their environment. The village backed onto the Ngorongoro escarpment and was fed by streams that tumbled down from the highlands above. In an unusual departure from their pastoralist traditions, the villagers had channelled the stream into irrigation canals and turned to farming. There were plots of maize and beans everywhere. It was an oasis of vegetation. Mango trees and acacias shaded small mud bungalows. Their leaves filtered the sun, throwing lozenges of light onto the bonnet of the Land Rover as we drove along the dirt road. The calls of the doves from the branches mimicked the liquid splashing of the rivulets that fed the fields. In Maasai country, water is everything. It was paradise.

We had an introduction to Mereso's brother, Pashet Sengeruan, and his wife Mary. Pashet was the government-appointed chairman of Engaruka Chini, the lower half of the village. Their one-room house was dwarfed by the mango tree which stood in the centre of the compound at the back. Beyond stood a grove of banana trees with black, malacca-like trunks. To one side of the compound was a crude mud hut where Mary cooked on a fire laid on the dirt floor. The children slept in a row beside it at night. Next to this were two wooden cubicles. One was the long drop. In the other, which was empty, you could wash in privacy. Lori and I dossed down on the floor of their storeroom. Peter was farmed out elsewhere.

Life was slow-paced, but there were always things to do. We gatecrashed Pashet's development meetings, where the elders squatted on their heels and gave rambling discourses in sawing Maa that revolved around building the village hospital. A fundraiser amongst the local inhabitants had been sufficient to pay for the delivery of the cement blocks. They had been lying in a pile on an empty stand of ground for the last six months. A cheque written out by an assistant minister who had visited the site had bounced. No more funds had been forthcoming and construction had yet to begin.

Pashet, who was lean and young and eager, presided over the meetings on a rickety chair. He liked to unstrap his watch, an item which few in the village owned, and place it in front of him on the rain butt that served as his desk. It was a nice touch but did nothing to curtail the proceedings. They dragged on for hours. We attended church and immortalized a choir practice on Lori's tape recorder. And in a ceremony made formal with speeches and much hand-shaking, we donated $100 towards the hospital fund.

One morning we learned there was to be an *emorata*, the ritual circumcision of a young girl before her marriage. Pashet was doubtful we should attend but left the decision to us. It was, after all, *shauri ya wanawake*, women's business. An erupting volcano wouldn't have kept us away.

Mary was in the compound pummelling a shirt in a plastic bucket of soapy water. It was a chore which she addressed with combative energy. Her arms rose and fell like pistons and water dripped off her wrists. She was giving vent to a fit of pique brought on by the circumcision gift. We had decided on a slim golden ring which Lori had fished out from the depths of her duffel bag. Mary coveted it.

'The girl's only a Maasai. I should have it,' she pouted.

'You're a Maasai, too,' Lori pointed out.

'I'm a Maasai from the town. I've been to school and finished Form Two. *I* won't break it.'

Like all married women, Mary had been circumcised and so could elaborate on its aftermath from the moral high ground of experience. 'It hurts as much as childbirth, but sex is good. Making love is much better when you're circumcised.'

I caught Lori's eye. There was a flaw in this argument. Maasai girls are not supposed to have penetrative sex until they are married so how would Mary know?

We said nothing. We knew that any social gaffe would be dissected and embroidered around cooking fires for years to come. As rare representatives of the outside world, we were at pains not to offend. So we upped the ante of house presents with a shirt and bracelet.

Mary pressed home the advantage by extracting the promise of a handbag to be sent from London. The bargain was sealed. The ring would be presented to the bride-to-be.

At the circumcision *boma*, no one seemed to think it strange that two dirt-encrusted women in slacks were amongst the guests. The women bustled about in their finery of copper and beads, ignoring seventeen-year-old Cecilia about whom all the fuss was being made. She wore black and her head had been shaved. She stood apart, defiant but vulnerable, and a little fearful. You could see it in her eyes. She managed a small smile when we said hello and smiled again when we admired a crude mural of lions, elephants and shields which had been painted with ochre onto the wall of her hut.

The circumciser's face was webbed with wrinkles and her hands gnarled by arthritis. We'd brought her packets of tea and sugar which she quickly tucked into her *shuka*. She was calm and business-like, saying Lori could take photos as long as they weren't of *there*.

In due course, Cecilia was led to the entrance of her hut, where she was sat on a cowhide with her legs spread wide. Another girl squatted behind her, the muscles of her legs tensing where they pressed against Cecilia's hips. Her arms snaked under Cecilia's and enfolded her chest, as if by doing this she could absorb her friend's pain. As the old woman bent over and set to work, the two girls turned their heads in profile and shut their eyes, oblivious to the women who had crowded round, aware only of the soft sound of the razor blade cutting into flesh.

The Maasai equate the clitoris and labia minora to a foreshort-ened penis. To have this extraneous part of the anatomy excised is an essential rite of passage to becoming a woman. It was not my place to protest against entrenched custom and, knowing this, I tried to suspend judgment and thoughts of septicaemia, painful menstruation, difficult childbirth and death.

It didn't help. I could not bring myself to watch those withered hands moving so persistently in the tremulous V of Cecilia's legs. Yet as the minutes dragged by, my imaginings of what was happening became as graphic as the reality. My stomach felt queasy. I moved away to stand alone, staring at the sky and inhaling great lungfuls of air.

Peter came up beside me. 'She's very brave. Did you see how she won't move or cry out? I gave her 200 shillings,' he confided. When it was finally over, the circumciser plastered a handful of ash onto Cecilia's wound and she was dragged into her hut.

Soon after that, some thirty warriors trooped into the *boma*. They were in fine spirits, having successfully killed a marauding lion that had been eating their livestock. The previous evening the lion had attacked a donkey and dragged it away. They had followed the spoor through the night and surprised the lion at dawn as it fed on the carcass, encircling it from behind a wall of overlapping shields. The paws and ears and tail of the lion were stuck on the end of their spears. They held them aloft for everyone to admire and brandished their trophies in my face.

When Maasai warriors hunt lion, they protect themselves by crouching down low behind their shields. They move forward in a line with their shields so close together that it becomes an impenetrable armour. I tried to imagine what it must have been like for the lion to be hunted down by these spear-throwing warriors.

In my mind's eye I saw the lion crouching over the dead donkey and snarling angrily when it was interrupted by the approach of an undulating line of shields. The shield animal drew nearer, heedless of the warning, and he snarled again, lifting his head as he did so to show his fangs. He knew that a demonstration of ferocity always scattered the hyenas and jackals and vultures that came scavenging for a bit of meat. It worked this time too because the shield animal stopped and stood motionless. Yet he was on his guard. The shield animal had brought with it humans. He couldn't see them, but he knew they were near by. Their sickly sweet smell filled his nostrils and made him uneasy. He sank low to the ground and flattened his head and neck. His tail snapped impatiently in the dirt. The shield animal must be taught a lesson.

He bunched his muscles and sprang and, as he did so, he saw a human in front of him and was pleased because it presented an easy target. In that split second of recognition, he shifted his weight to adjust the direction of his charge so that he could land on the human and pin it to the ground. But in mid-air he saw an animal the shape of a snake leaping at him. It was too late to get out of its way. The snake animal bit him hard in the chest and knocked him to the ground. It was painful, but he rose to his feet and ran forward. Where was the human? He could only see the shield animal, which was shivering and undulating. He was enraged because he wanted to crunch the head of the human between his jaws.

Something bit him in the leg and again in the shoulder. It was the snake animal. He could just see it out of the corner of his eye. It wouldn't let go. He sank to his haunches. Why couldn't he get up? He could see the humans now. They were all around him. Their stench was so suffocating, it was impossible to breathe. He must chase them away, but he couldn't see them properly. His strength had gone. He thought he snarled but it was only a whimper. He shut his eyes and lay still.

Cecilia was still, too, as she lay in the darkened hut with her legs drawn up and wide apart. Her breath came in pants. The pain was excruciating even when she didn't move. An empty tin mug stood on the floor. She had drunk *asaroi*, blood from a bull's jugular mixed with milk. It was supposed to help the wound to heal. She could hear the party in full swing outside: the high-pitched ululations of the uncircumcised girls and the snorting chant of the warriors as they leapt and spiralled against the sky in celebration of sexuality. Alone and in agony, Cecilia made a poignant counterpoint to all the festivity.

'How are you feeling?' I asked.

'Fine. The waiting was hard. When it was happening, I pretended I was dead. The warriors have killed a lion for me. It's good luck.'

'Doesn't it hurt?'

She shook her head emphatically. It was a threadbare denial.

'Give me a gift,' she demanded.

Lori and I presented the ring and were about to depart when Peter stooped through the door and sat down on the opposite bed. He had two warriors in tow. He was looking very solemn.

'M. A., there is a problem. This man is Cecilia's fiancé. He is very angry that Lori took photographs without permission.'

'That's not true. It was all cleared with the women,' Lori protested.

'He's angry that you took photographs without *his* permission.

87

And he's very angry that you took photographs of her private parts.'

'I didn't,' objected Lori. 'You couldn't photograph *that*. It's too gory.'

I had a great desire to leave quickly, but it was too late. We had already been sucked into the maw of debate. As there was no way out of this except through protacted discussion, as litigation is settled by the elders, and as the *boma* was situated in the upper part of the village, I suggested we put the matter before the chairman of Engaruka Juu. The fiancé and his friend deliberated on this, then agreed. So we took our leave of Cecilia, and the five of us set off through the thickening dusk to the chairman's *boma*.

As we neared his compound, I said to Peter, 'Tell them we'll be along in a moment. I need a pee.'

The men marched on and I turned to Lori. 'Quick. Get the film out of the camera.'

'I can't do that. It's dishonest.'

'You may be insured for theft, fire and war, but I bet there's an exemption clause for confiscation by Maasai chief. Rewind it and stuff it down your sock. Put an unused film in the camera.'

Lori made a face, but she did as I'd suggested.

The chairman stepped out of his hut into the darkness. He was a big man called Moses Lekor. Even in the darkness you could tell that authority came naturally to him. He called to his wives to bring stools for the guests. Our offence, a grave abuse of hospitality, was a weighty matter and could not be resolved quickly.

Cecilia's fiancé launched into a lengthy monologue in Maa, outlining the case for the prosecution. He paused every few sentences to allow Peter to translate into English. It seemed his accusations centred around invasion of privacy. When the warrior had finished, his friend, the witness for the prosecution, repeated most of what had been said. This all took the best part of an hour.

Next it was Lori's turn. She spoke with dignity, explaining that she had worked amongst many cultures and that she respected and honoured the values of each society she visited. She said it was not her wish to offend as she considered the people of Engaruka her friends and would never want to do anything to cause their disapproval. Peter translated this into Maa for the benefit of the warriors, who were unmoved. They grunted and looked dissatisfied. But the speech went down well with Moses. He was punctuating Lori's sentences with approving nods.

I was impressed by the way he listened to her without interrupting and appeared to be weighing the merits of her argument. He was not seeking to ascertain guilt, which is a condition that pits an individual against his moral universe. His concern was whether or not Cecilia and her fiancé had been shamed in front of their community.

The depositions of Peter and I were aired as the constellations rose in a tarred sky. Peter spoke well. He enjoyed the intricacies of Maasai negotiation. Yet in the absence of the key witness – the circumciser – our testimony was far from watertight.

It was getting chilly and I could barely restrain an urge to fidget by the time Moses turned to Lori and asked her, in Maa, to take the film out of the camera. 'I believe you, but I have to satisfy my clients because I work for them,' he added in English. With feigned reluctance, Lori unloaded the camera and handed the film to Moses. He took it and held it up in front of him. 'The warriors' honour must be satisfied, which is why I have asked you to give me the film,' he said sternly in Swahili. 'Lori, you have satisfied your own honour by surrendering it without protest. The case is now closed.'

Cecilia's fiancé, looking mollified, stood up and strode into the night with his friend beside him. We stood, too, trying to get the feeling back in our numbed feet. Moses, still seated, beckoned us over and shook hands with each of us in turn.

As we walked back to the car, Lori grinned at me and raised a clenched fist.

'The film?'

'Yes.'

The shadows of bushes and trees threw strange shapes into the headlights on the drive back to Pashet's compound. For many minutes, we sat in companionable silence.

Then Lori said, 'Peter, what happened to you when you were a child? Why are you an orphan?'

'My father gave me away.'

'Oh?'

'He didn't like me.' He shrugged. 'Maasai people can do these things, Lori. They sent me away. That is why my aunt took care of me.'

A thought occurred to me. 'You mentioned visiting an uncle's *boma* in one of your letters. You've never mentioned any relations before.'

'Yes, he lives beyond Kisamis. Sometimes I would visit him in the school holidays.'

'Peter, how were you circumcised?'

'By a doctor in a hospital because I couldn't miss school to attend the proper ceremony. I was twelve. It was just before I met you. I had a local anaesthetic, but it hurt a lot afterwards.'

I tried to envision it. A sallow-eyed man in a shabby white coat making Peter lie down on a table in a dirty room at the end of a mud alley. Circumcision is one of the most important moments of a Maasai boy's life. It serves the purpose of testing his mettle. It is the key to becoming a warrior. And a man. Yet the rituals last several months and only the boys who don't go to school have the opportunity to follow them from beginning to end. Those boys, his agemates, would have received nothing to dull the pain of the knife. They would have worn sheepskin cloaks which their mothers had dyed black with a mix of charcoal and fat. They would have used arrows topped with tree gum to shoot birds which they would stuff with grass and hang from their ostrich-feather headdresses. Their mothers would have shaved their heads with milk and removed their coiled copper earrings to drape over their sons' ears. They would have sung: *Surua lai impurronieki. Na mapiknyileti!* My light brown bull roars for I will not bring dishonour! Afterwards, they would have been given a heifer as a token of their courage.

It was impossible to be a true warrior without having done all this. Peter had taken a day off from school. Small wonder he had an identity problem.

'If you marry Nanyokie, will you want her to be circumcised?'

He cocked his head to one side and smiled, flirting to cushion my stupidity. 'Of course. Otherwise, how could she be my wife?'

CHAPTER 9

'You got through.'

'Yes, I got through.'

'No one stopped you?'

'No one. It was easy. They treated me like any old person out for a holiday.'

In the year since Peter and I had been together in Tanzania I had become obsessive about returning to Kenya. Some months earlier I had begun negotiating to this end with immigration officials. I rang almost daily to inquire about progress and kept a suitcase packed in case there was time to catch the evening plane. Finally the holding pattern shifted in the mysterious way that things do in Africa. Nothing was formalized on paper. The decision, made by someone 'high up', had simply come about. It was low key, sudden, decided on a whim, out of compassion perhaps. Hope being the hardy creature it is, I had always known I would return home. I'd caught the plane the day after I was told I was allowed back. Now here I was standing in the airport next to my son.

Peter was still thin, although this was deceptive. He enfolded me in a bear hug, and my feet swung off the ground. Was he this tall in Engaruka? This strong? If you see each other daily, the role reversal of hugger and hugged can pass unnoticed, which is a shame. The first time your son picks you up in his arms is a seminal moment.

His face was different, too. In the photo by my desk he looks as if he has been designed by committee: mouth awash with teeth, fleshy lips, buds for ears, a Roman nose that surely must be on loan. Now the planes of cheek and chin have settled into their just proportions. How is it possible to portray power and gentleness all at once, I wondered. I looked and marvelled.

We stood back and exchanged shy grins. '*Karibu*. You're home.'

I sensed a sharp edge to the hubbub in the airport concourse.

Women clutched their handbags too tightly. The taxi drivers hustled harder for a fare than they used to. They slavered in the faces of passengers and grabbed their luggage trolleys the moment they emerged from Customs. Was all this activity malign or benign? It felt at once familiar and remote. I could no longer read the signals. I was glad that Peter took my hand in his as we filtered through the crowd.

At least the taxis hadn't changed. We chose one with peeling seats. Two of the door handles had fallen off. But the fare into town was higher than before. One of the spin-offs of the mismanaged economy was a derelict currency. Runaway inflation had long ago outstripped the Kenyans' ability to feed and clothe their families.

Marching along the skyline was a ragged frieze of low-cost housing, some of it under construction, some of it lived in and already shabby; beyond that, parched plains, like a room in shadow, muted by a low grey sky. Maasai herders were driving cattle beside the road. I wondered if the rains had failed again.

As for the city centre, it was overcrowded, dirty, crumbling beneath the weight of all the rural people drifting aimlessly, looking for work. Nairobi buoyed and broke their hopes. The taxi scraped in and out of potholes as it nosed its way past beggars on crutches and glue-sniffing street kids. Men loitered by pavement kiosks which sold cigarettes and matches and squares of chewinggum. They appraised the world with sullen stares and looked incredibly young. Sometimes they prised their backs from the wall to saunter after passers-by, with no apparent purpose.

'These boys are pickpockets. You must watch out. Even in shops. They run in and take your bag,' said Peter earnestly.

As I looked out the window, pleasant memories were superimposed on the decay. My first sight of Nairobi had been quarter of a century back when I'd taken months to drive a zigzag course through the bush from South Africa with a friend. The city was much smaller then, bungalows and two-storey office buildings contained by topography: the swell of the Limuru tea estates, the Kikuyu escarpment still freckled with thatched huts and, of course, savannah swarming with herds of zebra and gazelle. In those days it still bore the traces of the wife-swapping, bar-propping, stake-it-all frontier town it had been between the wars. It was this undercurrent of uncertainty that had attracted me. That and the wilderness I had been waiting for ever since my ramblings through the woods of New Jersey.

My travelling companion was a childhood playmate of my brother's. Until that safari I hadn't known him as an adult. We'd slept in the open beside the Land Rover and woken each morning to follow the smell of adventure. Unlike my brother's friend, I'd eschewed a camp bed in favour of the ground. It was my statement about connecting with nature, graphic but excruciatingly uncomfortable. We'd been bickering for weeks over pathetically petty issues. He used too much water for shaving. I forgot to punch holes in the tins of food I heated up in the campfire, with the result that they exploded. By the time we'd reached town, the Land Rover was in danger of being galvanized into a firestorm.

At the root of this sparring was my refusal to sleep with him. I'd made my stand in the first week, knowing I risked being abandoned. It was, after all, his vehicle. I'd wanted to do that trip more than anything in the world. Viewed from the boggy marsh of middle age, I was amazed I'd sought the moral high ground. Youth defines choices in bold black and white. It turns its back on frailty and imperfection.

I looked at Peter slumped on the back seat beside me and sensed again the freshness of the future as seen through the eyes of a twenty-three year-old. He too was a *tabula rasa* waiting for life's experiences to be written on him. My trip up Africa became a rite of passage. I left home and decided, on my second day in Nairobi, to settle in Kenya. That commitment severed the umbilical cord to childhood. In the next year or so, Peter would be doing the same.

He was keen to be considered a man, kept on referring in his letters to how grown-up he was, his newfound 'wisedom' and how he would soon be able to repay Mike's kindness and mine. His correspondence danced with dreams and ambitions.

Life with Mike is really interesting, Mum. He has made me popular and loved, just like you did. I have a lot of friends now in Kenya and they are really proud of me. I think one day I'll write a novel entitled *My Growth and Joy in the European*

Family. Mary Anne daughter of Fitzgerald and Mike ole Eldon will be major characters in it. Give my love to Tara the Tamarind girl and Petra the rocky girl. It's your African boy
    Peter Lekerian.

Life was looking up for Peter. He had a job at the Ostrich Park seven miles outside town in a suburb called Langata. The park had opened only recently. Business was still slack. Gravelled paths led through the trees to rondavels where woven bags, soapstone animals and assorted curios were on sale. A larger, open-sided rondavel displayed eggs and feathers. Behind this the ostriches stood in a pen like tutued ballerinas waiting in the wings.

Peter was a trainee in the shop at reception. He sold guidebooks to overseas tourists and sodas and packets of crisps to mothers herding fractious, overheated children. He joked with the children and chatted to their parents. He took longer than was necessary over each transaction, but the visitors loved his style.

He was still living with Mike in the stable row of servants' quarters. The back part of the garden between the servants' rooms and the main house was always awash with people who were adept at reducing the infinite possibility of the day. Mike's cook, gardener and night-watchman looked after not only their families but a raft of unemployed friends. The women sat square-legged inside the doorways stirring pots over small charcoal braziers. They cooked bobbly white *posho* which gave off a dry smell of nothingness. Bare-bottomed children crawled around their feet. The men collected on the back verandah by the kitchen, where they smartened up their well worn clothes with Mike's iron or sat on broken chairs nursing tin mugs of tea. They swivelled their eyes round to give Peter a courteous *jambo* when he passed. Everyone was on an intimate footing whether they liked it or not because it was impossible to be secret. In the day, life was communal, led outside in the open. At night the soundscape of coughs, creaking beds, arguments and tardy arrivals seeped through the stone walls of the rooms.

Peter was expected to be at the Ostrich Park by eight every morning of the week except Monday, which was his day off. He caught a *matatu*, a combi converted into a taxi, soon after six. The *matatus* passed by the bottom of the road and were packed to the gunnels even at that early hour. He squeezed between bottoms and knees, tunnelled under armpits and rode half-standing, half-suspended between the compressed bodies. In town he changed to another *matatu* which brought him to the Langata Road. The last few miles were on foot, walked through mud or dust, depending on the weather.

I pictured Peter waking to the crowing of the neighbourhood cockerels, stepping into the dark with a towel wrapped round his waist, padding over dew-damp earth on bare feet, sluicing down with cold water and emerging covered in gooseflesh. His room was cosy despite the harsh light thrown from the unshaded bulb dangling by a length of flex from the ceiling. Its signature was a poignant privacy ordered against snooping eyes and hands: tiny padlocks on tin trunks, a suitcase with a lock on it, a heftier lock on the wooden door: Peter's World. His bed was rickety and had a troughed mattress. His clothes hung from nails banged into the wall. He was a virtuoso of the wardrobe and had an ability to step out of the mud and smoke of domestic Africa dressed like a yuppie. I imagined him putting on his slacks, shirt and blazer, lacing up his black shoes, spending a minute or two working his hair flat with an Afro comb and scrutinizing the result in a plastic hand mirror. He might spot a pimple – he still got them – and rub it hard with Vaseline. Then he would carefully double-lock the Yale, walk past a bed of canna lilies and under the washing line, unlock the kitchen door and put the kettle on for tea.

I was privy to his routine because I too was living at Mike's house. Yet, in ways that counted, Peter was a stranger to me. He was always keen to talk about work, but I didn't know much about his social life. Neither did I know how he viewed himself or the world around him. He'd suffered when Petra, Tara and I left Kenya. It must have undermined his faith in relationships. He probably thought there was no point in opening up to anyone because they'd leave him soon anyway. Peter and I had begun to be reacquainted in Tanzania. In Kenya, which was his place, I hoped we would become comfortable with each other. While we were parted, Peter's letters had revealed muddling glimpses of his life which left me confused. It wasn't that he hid things; he just refrained from revealing them.

First of all, there was Rosina, who'd never once graced his correspondence. Neither had her name come up when he was talking of marrying Nanyokie. But there she was, his old high-school sweetheart. They had been seeing each other on a regular basis for several years. She was the daughter of Kikuyu parents who had scrimped and saved to put their children through school. They didn't own a phone or car and went to church on Sundays. The new bourgeoisie. Rosina was taller than Peter and had the tremulous beauty of a forest creature. She taught at the Shining Falls Church Kindergarten. Every Saturday she caught a *matatu* to Mike's house to sweep Peter's room and do his laundry while he was at work.

I let Rosina pass. No point in making a fuss about it. But there had been references to other people which had made me wonder what was going on. Eighteen months after his aunt had been lowered into the earth, Peter had mentioned a sister who had looked after his aunt on her death bed and put on her ornaments as was the custom. 'This practice bonds us with the living dead, who we believe dwell with us even after their physical departure,' he wrote. He wanted me to underwrite the purchase of a cow with a heifer, a goat and a sheep which were needed to cleanse the sister after mourning. In case I hadn't grasped the importance of the request, he added, 'Several issues and practices are mandatory in our society, and if you diverge or ignore the practices, you will be regarded as a slave.' Before the letter concluded with 'Your lovely son Peter', there was one final goad to my conscience. He was the girl's only brother and thus bore the entire responsibility of preventing her from being cast into ignominy. They were random facts which made little sense to me. But one thing I knew for sure. My bank balance wasn't up to purchasing livestock. I wrote Peter and told him so. After that, the mysterious sister vanished from the correspondence.

Three months later he wrote to say his elder brother had got married and he had helped with the wedding preparations. That was it. Nothing more. I knew that the Maasai used family terminology differently from us. Brothers and sisters didn't necessarily share the same parents. As I understood it, people from the same clan and age set referred to each other as brother and sister. So I let that pass, too.

Then one day Peter wrote the following, 'I am becoming a young man who needs property of his own and earn his daily bread by working. Right now I am ashamed of receiving money from you and Mike when I can work for myself.' I nodded in approval as I read. Then came the bombshell. 'In my uncle's home my mam has young children who need to be cared for and I am their only expectation.' He was supposed to be an orphan. Who were these shadowy people who populated his letters?

Now that we were reunited, The Family was at the top of my agenda. We were on Mike's front porch. Peter was sitting on the wicker settee. I'd perched on the concrete sill with feet planted in the flowerbed between some ragged geraniums. They were coated in the dust thrown up by the cars. At the far end of the lawn the gardener was cutting the grass. It was as good a time as any to pop the question.

'Is your real mother still alive?'

'Oh yes, M. A. Her name is Nnee.' He pronounced it *Nay.*

Even though I had been expecting it, the answer introduced something unfamiliar. The feeling puzzled me. Was it confusion or curiosity? Anger? Or perhaps a sense of detachment. I looked at Peter sitting there so unperturbed and saw him with double vision. He was the same boy I had always known, but he had a secret history which I knew nothing about.

'*Tumbo moja*?' I asked, which in effect meant, had he come out of her stomach.

'Yeah.'

'Why didn't she bring you up?'

'When I was born, I was not born in my father's home because there was an arranged marriage between my mother and my aunt.'

'Your mother and your *aunt*?'

'Yes, Mama Safi, my father's sister. My father married my mum and exchanged Mama Safi to my mum's brother. So it was two men exchanging sisters for wives.'

'Okay,' I said slowly. I didn't want to rush it. 'So who's your father?'

There followed a convoluted story in the best African tradition. It took about an hour to tell, but in essence it was this. Peter's father and his father's sister were the children of a *whydoe* (widow, as I realized later). The family was poor and couldn't afford a dowry so a barter marriage was arranged whereby Peter's father and another man gave each other their sisters as wives. It was in this way that Nnee became the second wife of Peter's father (I forgot to ask how he could afford two wives) and soon gave birth to a son. (This must have been Lankisa, the elder brother who had just got married.) Peter's aunt (his father's sister, Mama Safi, not Naserian, the aunt who brought him up) didn't like her husband and ran away. When this happened, Nnee's brother went to Peter's father's *boma* to fetch Nnee back home. As far as he was concerned, the swap deal had fallen through. It was while she was back at her childhood *boma* that Nnee gave birth to Peter.

Then I asked the name of Peter's father.

'Mebikie. Mebikie ole Kepaeka. But I'm not sure he's my father.' Peter exhaled his breath in a pouf to denote a laugh, but it merely served as a preface to something which was obviously difficult to articulate. 'I think my mum got pregnant at my uncle's home. I think I was born there and that's how my father found out he was not my father. When I was young I was always being told by other boys, 'That is your father. That is your father.' My mum had a boyfriend. I was really ashamed and angry and at times I would go off and cry. I just didn't want to look at him.'

'So what did your father do?'

'He wanted to kill me.'

'It wasn't *your* fault.'

'If a family doesn't want a child they can put a curse on it or kill it.'

'How would he have killed you?' I couldn't believe I was having this conversation.

'Probably with a stick. Like this.' He put his index and middle fingers together and made a whipping motion. 'Or he would have thrown me into the fire.'

'If he'd tried to kill you, would anyone have stopped him?'

'No.'

There was a silence which neither of us tried to fill. The rhythmic swish of the gardener's machete floated on the still air. Then I said, 'You would have just passed away.'

'Yup.'

Another silence.

'I see. Hmmmm. So what did your mother do?'

'She really cried and sent messages that her husband wanted to kill her child. My aunt heard about it. She had never had an opportunity to have a child . . .'

'Your father's sister?'

'No, my aunt who's my mum. She's a distant sister. My aunt's father and my father's father . . . Her grandfather and my father's father shared a father. I think she must have got to the stage of menopause so she knew she would never have a child and she said to herself, "I have to adopt a boy to look after me in my old age." It's very difficult to adopt a child in our tradition so when she heard the news, she came down from Naivasha. She lived there with my father.'

'Your father?'

'Her husband. He was a herdsman at Ndabibi.'

'And you thought he was your father.'

'Yes. So my aunt took me to Naivasha. I think she breastfed me, but I could always drink milk from Lord Delamere's cows.'

'So what happened to your father? I mean, your uncle. Your aunt's husband.'

'He ran away. But first my father . . . my aunt's boyfriend's father . . . was killed in a war in Maasailand and blood cattle were paid as compensation. So my father didn't have to work anymore and we left Naivasha and moved to Kisamis. He started to drink and sold fifty cows. Then my uncle moved. My father. He moved to . . .'

'Your uncle or your father?'

Peter paused momentarily. 'My father. Because I have not yet started calling my father my father. I have always been calling him my uncle. Because by then I was still in the house of my mother . . .'

'Your aunt?'

'Yes, my aunt who was my mother.'

'Did you know that Nnee was really your mother?'

99

'At times I would ask my mum who my mother was. Because when my father ran away, my aunt took me to live in my uncle's *boma*.'

'The *boma* where Mebikie and Nnee lived.'

'Yeah. My brothers knew they were my brothers. And when we went after the young goats, they would say, "Nnee is your mother. Nnee is your mother."' He had lowered his voice to a whisper.

'Did you believe them?'

'When I went home, I would report them to my aunt and she'd tell me not to listen to those crazy children. She said she was my mother and told me not to go to Nnee's house. But in the evening Nnee would come to my house and ask for food for her children. And my mother would give her some and a cup of tea and they would talk. A relationship developed between my mother and my aunt. My aunt became my mother's mother.'

'Your aunt became your mother's mother.'

'Yeah. She was like my mother's adviser because she was very old by then. My mother would always come to my aunt's house and tease me and play with me.' His voice became gentle and softened. 'I think she was taking care of me.'

'You love Nnee very much, don't you?'

'Yes I do.'

'It must be good to be back with your family.'

He grinned. 'When I go to see them, I sit with Nnee at night and we talk very sweetly about many things.'

'Well, I'm glad we got all that straightened out.'

There is only so much you can try to absorb in one go so we never got round to talking about how – or when – Peter had met up with his family again. I was just glad that he'd done it. I didn't feel that I had lost him. Instead, our family had grown bigger. He had two mothers instead of one and more people to love him. I was happy for him.

Mike still subsidized Peter because he couldn't make ends meet on his tiny salary. Now that I was around, I helped out too. The handouts – reasonable but not overly generous – were shadowed with resentment. Peter's family lived at Ol Tepesi, down in the Rift Valley beyond Kisamis. By this time he was visiting them on a regular basis. I guessed my money was being used to buy their food, and I didn't like it.

To my mind, I had provided for their son when they had refused to do so. Now, with the elusive logic of the Maasai which no *mzungu* will ever come to understand, they expected me to look after them as well. We call it sponging. They call it the tradition of the extended family. I felt like a one-woman social-security department. I reproached myself for my meanness but couldn't help feeling that way.

Unlike me, Peter was fiercely conventional. Maasai protocol doesn't allow for capitalism. Whoever has the privilege of a job is beholden for the school fees, the hospital bills, the new shoes. To ignore this ethos is to be a man without respect. That was Peter's dilemma. He said, 'My dad is a beer drinker and my elder brother rarely looks after my mum's needs. I vow to take care of my family in every way. I love my brothers and sisters and I would not want them to suffer and look like me when I was young.'

He couldn't look after himself on what he earned, let alone anyone else. So he told white lies and extracted dispensations from my wallet. To honour one mother, he had to deceive the other.

There was an added dimension to his predicament. After such a long absence, he was something of a stranger in the *boma*. He saw largesse as the leverage to insinuate his way into this close-knit group. It was an acceptable ploy, according to Maasai etiquette. Peter never alluded to it, and I found it difficult to express my thoughts.

One day when we were in the kitchen I tackled the subject. I asked him about the money I'd given him for the *matatu* fare to Ol Tepesi.

'How much does it cost?'

'Two hundred and ten.'

'How much does it really cost?'

No reply.

'It's seventy there and back . . . Isn't it?'

He said he didn't know.

'You go there all the time. Of course you know.'

Peter hung his head. Delamere, the terrier, jumped up and licked his hand. He gave the dog a perfunctory pat, then stared at the kettle.

'Look, it's not the money I object to. It's the fact that you tell lies to get it. If you want money to buy food for your family, then tell me that's what it's for.'

Silence.

'That's it, isn't it? You wanted to take a present back to the family. That's okay,' I lied, 'but just tell me the truth.'

He looked out the window at the washing line. More silence. Then he turned to me, still with that faraway stare.

'I lied to you, M. A. I am bad. It was a very bad thing to do. You have made me see that I will never tell lies again.' He recited it as if it was a creed, an article of faith which he would adhere to even though he hadn't pinned down the real meaning of it.

'You're not bad . . . of course not.' I shook my head. 'It's just that . . . if I can't be sure you're telling the truth . . . well, there's no trust between us.'

I shrugged and screwed up my mouth. Peter was crestfallen. He put his arms around me and laid his head on my shoulder.

'Thank you, M. A., for telling me I lie. Even if you become furious like a loose bull, you are my mum still. Let the money issue go and I can struggle, but our love should be intact. I think that you doubt me, but that can only happen if you don't love me. I will never let you regret why you made me your son.'

I felt terrible, like an inquisitor. But I knew I was right.

Peter's family. I didn't know how many brothers and sisters he had, what their names were, who was married. In fact, despite our talk, I knew precious little about them. And he didn't offer to tell me.

'Peter,' I said, 'Do you know what I'd really like? I'd like to meet your mother.'

'That would be good. I'll ask for some leave.'

CHAPTER 10

That first visit to Kenya was only for a month so time was precious. Peter knew this and moved quickly to arrange a few days away from work. A week after suggesting I meet his family, I hired a four-wheel-drive car, and the two of us set off on safari to the Kepaeka *boma*. My feelings became increasingly ambivalent as we cornered the Ngong Hills by Kipenget's house and descended into the Rift Valley. Curiosity was tempered by doubt. I wanted to meet Peter's mother and father but feared that Nnee and Mebikie would look on me as the *mzungu* intruder who had snatched their son away from them. I worried that I too might be resentful. My Western instincts made it difficult to accept that parents could cast out their blood-and-flesh baby. I wondered too exactly when and how Peter had come to discover that his orphaned boyhood was a myth. Had he tried to explain the web of Maasai relationships before and I'd missed it? My twinges of guilt at not paying sufficient attention to him were overlaid with relief. By seizing the past, Peter had gained a present and a future. The sense of belonging to his family would give him cultural identity. As it turned out, my fears were groundless. From the moment I arrived at Peter's family *boma* I felt even more at home than I had in Nairobi, even though it was a low-key sort of welcome.

Peter's parents evinced no astonishment at our surprise appearance. Mebikie, who was sitting some yards away in the shade of a thorn tree, made no move to come and greet us. A sidelong glance and an extra flick of the fly whisk were the only signs he was aware that his son had arrived in a *mzungu* car driven by a *mzungu* woman. Nnee, for her part, gave me a handshake and a shy smile before disappearing into her hut to brew tea for the visitor. Shortly after that, Peter wandered off to inspect the goats, leaving me with children swirling around my legs and a pair of skeletal dogs sniffing at my ankles.

In the days that followed, the *boma*'s unchanging daily ritual imparted a sense of comfortable reliability. Each morning I watched the sun sketch the ragged ridges of Olorgesailie mountain and spill yolk yellow onto the stubbled plains below. In that first dawn hour after the night had sluiced away the heat and dust, the day was still too fresh for the chainsaw buzz of flies. From inside the huts came the low murmur of voices. Nnee had already released the baby goats from the pen beside her bed. Outside in the dung-splattered stockade the kids competed for their mothers' udders with Mebikie's first wife and Peter's sister-in-law. The women's straight backs and legs were bent into a perfect right angle. The milk plinked into their tin cups.

As the sun sailed higher, the young boys took the goats out to graze and the men drifted into the shadow of a T-shaped tree. They squatted on stones and on their heels and discussed the weather, livestock. Sometimes they were animated in their opinions, fishing for attention with a raised stick or pointed finger. They emphasized points by chanting the same word over and over again. The listeners provided a chorus of elongated vowels: *eeeeh*, *aaah*, *uuuuhuh*. What was the mantra carried through the stillness? Was it a cow or sickness? Perhaps it was someone's name: a man who had been bewitched; a woman who had committed adultery. I couldn't speak their language so I couldn't tell.

Mebikie, Peter's father, talked more than the others. He was lean, had the legs of a marabou stork. His impassive face, shaded by a snappy leather cap, was defined by points: a sharply tapered chin, slit eyes, a thin smile. This was the man who had disinherited Peter, who had wanted to kill him. The man who later beat Peter 'like a horse', who spent his money on beer rather than his family. This was the man to whom I must show respect. For Peter's sake.

I watched and knew that what I saw differed not a jot from yesterday nor would it six months from then. I felt protected and secure. I was a voyeur bestowing on this pastoral scene my own convenient interpretation because I had no way of knowing what they were thinking. These people had a different sense of honour and shame, right and wrong, which I couldn't fathom. It would take days, months, years to understand what they were thinking.

Peter was more than just an interpreter of the rattling Maa cadences. He was the guardian of cultural nuances and clan secrets, rivalries and ambitions. But he was not renowned for relaying an impartial, straightforward rendition of events. I had to draw on intuition and second-guess what I saw happening around me. I had no confidence in my ability to finger the rhythm of the *boma*. Its languorous heartbeat was to elude me in that brief stay. Perhaps it always would.

Nnee stoked the ashes from last night's fire to redness and filled a battered and blackened tin pot with water and tea leaves. Her pale brown skin was plump about the upper arms and thighs. A faint web of lines framed her eyes. She was recovering from malaria and still not feeling well. I knew this because I'd paid for her stay in hospital.

A halting sort of Swahili was within her grasp, but when she wanted to tell me something, she channelled it through Peter by talking in Maa. When she spoke, Nnee looked at neither of us, staring straight ahead as if practising for an after-dinner speech. 'Nnee says come and sit here beside her . . . Nnee has made *chai* for you. Come and drink it.' I turned to listen to Peter and her eyes followed me. When I turned my head back, I caught her looking. Her expression was as blank as a potato. She called me Mama. Sometimes she called me Mama Peter.

She must have been wondering how we would get on. I was. I'd brought up her son – fed him, clothed him, put him through school. I'd listened somewhat impatiently to his problems, met most of his demands for shoes, sweaters, lamps, books, beds, cupboards, although not the heaviest outlay of all – a house of his own. Was she jealous that I'd done these things instead of her? Perhaps she worried that Peter had a greater affection for me, my begrudging generosity creating a schism in his love. I wondered if she would be influenced by the insidious asymmetry of largesse and poverty. For us it may be harder to receive than to give. Not, however, for the Maasai. They can take with remarkable equanimity. Outsiders are often left with the impression the Maasai consider gifts as belonging to them by birthright.

Beneath the smiles I was guarded, only too aware I was looked upon as a source of comfort to ease the daily burden of life in the bush. My concern was that I would accidentally reveal my resentment over what I'd given or, more likely, what I'd be asked to give while I was here. It was niggardly behaviour, this taking stock of the ledger of received and paid, kindness and gratitude. It was inappropriate in the context of our generous surroundings.

The Kepaeka family holding, slightly larger than Peter's recently acquired property, was perched on a hundred-foot scarp on the eastern wall of the Rift Valley. Down below, the land was gullied, the watercourses rimmed by straggles of thorn trees. The fluffy trees, the rivulets of livestock tailed by corkscrews of dust were small and toylike. About the same size as the kites working the thermals against a cornflower sky. I could hear the wind in their pinions as they swooped above my head.

The Rift runs down Africa from the Red Sea to Mozambique. Of those thousands of miles I estimated nearly 200 were in my vision. It stretched north to Ndabibi where Peter had played hide and seek as a toddler and south to Tanzania and Engaruka where Nanyokie was doubtless still herding goats. I could just discern the indigo smudge of Gelai mountain across the border in Tanzania. Beyond that Ol Doinyo Lengai, the Mountain of God. From time to time it belched lava into its cone and dark grey smoke plumed up into the sky. I liked to think the Maasai had sanctified Lengai because it moved to a primal force they could not quantify.

The genesis of this magnificent topographical scar came 17 million years ago when the earth's crust buckled and volcanoes popped up through the cracks. They spewed molten lava and vomited ashes over vast areas such as the Serengeti Plain (where trees still cannot grow). Then the earth moved again and wrinkled the Rift walls into a series of tip-tilted escarpments. It was hard to come to terms with this titanic creative process.

We had arrived in the early evening when the goats had already been shut in for the night. Peter had excused himself quickly, saying, 'Do you mind if I visit the office?' and disappeared into their pen. I could just see his head and his brothers' heads above the branches. Peter had about thirty goats of his own which he had bought after his stint as a translator on the Audubon payroll and on the proceeds from other jobs. He could identify each one by the shape of an eye or an ear, the colour of its belly. He knew at a glance if it was sick or healthy or pregnant. Peter was focused on goats.

The herd wasn't just money on the hoof. It was the equivalent of a shopping mall. From the goats came milk, meat, dung for plastering the huts, hides to put on the beds, and fat – which is a delicacy. With the nearest water source several miles away, the goats provided a water substitute too. Nnee used their urine to clean out the milk gourds. She dribbled it in and shook the gourd like a cocktail shaker. It was sound practice. Urine is free of bacteria and therefore sterile. She used it for tanning leather, too. Just as I did. When I was doing long walking safaris, I stood in a puddle of pee to toughen the soles of my feet. You don't need a goat to do this.

It was 'the month of the healthy oxen' and the rock pools of rainwater had dried up. The week before we arrived, the boys had taken the animals to drink at the waterhole for the first time since the short rains. On this particular visit Peter intended to hold a meeting with Mebikie and his brothers to decide which pastures to use. The recovery of the vegetation was a concern for them. When the dry weather set in, the goats would be sent to graze on the communal land of Boulder Mountain, which rose a mile or two to the north. *Oloorruka*. The way he pronounced it, with angular vowels and rolling consonants, made it sound like rocks tumbling down the ancient volcano's slopes.

I asked how many goats there were. Peter looked uncomfortable, drew a number in the dust with his foot and quickly scuffed it out. When I inquired how many brothers and sisters he had, he was vague and skirted round the answer. I got the impression it was impolite to have asked in the first place. I didn't push it. Peter hadn't introduced me to anyone except his parents. It was as if the Kepaekas were not individuals but a collective organism. So the family tree took shape through chance remarks and endless questions.

I soon formed a tentative connection with Peter's sister-in-law, the recently married wife of his elder brother Lankisa. I was quietly passing the time of day on the little bench outside Nnee's hut when she joined me. We sat with our backs slouched against the mud wall. Her Swahili was scratchy and limited so we didn't talk much.

After a bit she pressed her thumb against her nostril, snorted hard through the other one, flicked the contents of her nasal passage onto the ground and walked off. It had never bothered me before, but for some reason I was having trouble coming to terms with the hygiene aspect. Maybe it was because I had been living in London. Regardless, I would have liked to have known more about The Noseblower.

'What's her name?' I asked Peter.

'I don't know her normal official name because I am not supposed to call her by her girlish name.'

'So what do you call her?'

'The same name I call my brother. By the present I gave them for their wedding. But the names are different. Lankisa is Entawuo, a young female heifer. My sister-in-law is Paashe, which is what you call a woman you give a heifer to. They call each other "my heifer".'

'And as I wasn't at the wedding, what do I call her?'

'Nalotu-esha. It means married during the rainy season. That's her real name.'

Another time we saw a girl in her teens standing by the road. The stacked firewood at her back was secured by a strap that hung from the top of her head. Her fists tightened on the leather and she turned away to avoid the dust as we drove by in the car.

'Traditionally, that girl is my daughter,' noted Peter. 'She is from my Ilukumae clan but in a different age group. It would be very rude for me to call her by her name.'

The Maasai apply different guidelines to relationships. For instance, a girl cannot marry a man of her father's age group. That would be incest. The taboo regarding Peter and the girl wasn't immediately apparent, but I didn't inquire further. We had been deep in discussion about The Incident.

'You were wrong to do that, M. A.,' he was saying.

And I was saying, 'I know you've got your culture. I'm doing my best to conform to it. But I have values, too. In the *boma* we'll go by your culture, and when you're in my car, we'll go by mine. That's fair, isn't it?'

He said nothing, obviously considered this a dubious proposition. This is what had happened.

On our first day I did what any good guest would do. I offered up the services of my rented four-wheel-drive Suzuki to collect water. The women disappeared into their huts and came out with about a dozen plastic containers which they loaded into the back. Then Peter said two of his brothers would come with us to help fill the *debes*. They were seventeen or so, warriors and very aware of themselves. I agreed because I could see that the water trip was going to entail a lot of hard work.

Down at the borehole at the Ol Tepesi trading centre, Peter toiled away in the hot sun while his brothers lolled about talking to their friends. When we got back to the *boma* the brothers got out and stood watching while Peter heaved the full containers out of the car onto the ground. There were little bubbles of sweat on his face and his eyes and teeth seemed to have grown bigger. I suggested the boys take over for a while, but he would have none of it.

By this time the women had gathered round and were shouldering the *debes* onto their backs to carry them into the *boma*. Mebikie's first wife, a skinny woman in late middle age, was summoning up all her strength to lift her *debe*. It was the height of a small child and must have weighed about thirty pounds. The brothers watched, their *rungu* sticks tucked under their arms, legs crossed at the ankle. They were a picture of repose.

'Help her,' I said to one of them in Swahili.

He looked at me, gave a little snort and sort of smiled to show he had noted the attempt at humour.

'Help her,' I repeated.

I think he grunted but the smile had gone.

I took a step forward. 'I mean it,' I said in English. I was talking with my body.

He didn't move.

Everyone was looking. They hadn't gathered round so much as stopped whatever they were doing and just sort of floated nearer. Peter was half in, half out of the back of the Suzuki. His face was frozen, his eyes even bigger. 'M. A., warriors don't carry water, it's women's work,' he said in English.

I knew he was right but ignored his muttered warning. 'She's old and it's heavy. She can't carry it by herself. Help her.'

'I'm sick.'

'You came in my car because you said you'd help . . . so do it.'

He shrugged, bent down and picked up a container the size of a handbag. He started walking towards the *boma*, which meant he was walking towards me.

'Not that one. That one.'

I took a few steps backwards and stood guarding the entrance with my arms folded. We eyed each other. You could have heard a fly faint.

He dropped the handbag container and went back to pick up the small-child container.

'Ri-iight. Thank you.' I stepped aside to let him pass.

It was shortly after that that Nalotu-esha had come and sat with me on the bench. 'He's lazy, that boy,' she'd confided. We'd grinned at each other. I'd sensed sisterhood.

One day Peter took me to meet Joseph Simel, his best friend. Joseph lived a mile away at his family's place. It was the adjoining property at the foot of the scarp. We walked there at night down a winding footpath littered with lava rocks.

The Simels had a compound of straight-walled houses with roofs and windows and doors. We sat with Joseph and his friends, drinking soda served by Joseph's wife Anastasia. She wore haloes of bead necklaces and a blue *shuka* trimmed with white. She was exquisitely beautiful.

There was much relaxed talk of politics and Joseph's land case. He was challenging the adjudication of the land in Loodariak, the Place of the Red Rivers, which was roughly equivalent to a county. He had proof that some of the land had been wrongly allocated to politicians' relatives and rich businessmen from Nairobi – 364 in all – who had no proper claim to it. As a result, over 1,200 Maasai, he was one of them, had been dispossessed and made squatters on their ancestral land. He was deep in litigation with the government, which was a brave thing to do as he was being harassed by the local officials.

Joseph's victory would be bittersweet for Peter. If Joseph succeeded in overturning the Loodariak land adjudication, Peter would lose his 160 acres. Peter was both pragmatic and generous about it.

'I don't get involved with Joseph's case because I want to keep him as a friend.'

Peter had taken me to look at his land on the flats beyond Olorgesailie. He was full of ideas on how it could be utilized. It would carry goats, of course, and perhaps cattle. It could be a tourist site, he said, for campers. Maybe he could hire it out as a film location. He'd heard that film companies paid a lot of money. It stood at the foot of another scarp and was peppered with drought-resistant trees. There was no ground cover, just pale, pale earth which sparkled in the sun. And, of course, no water. Peter said he could walk the goats back to the pump at Ol Tepesi, a trek which would take the best part of a day. It would be better, he said, to sink a borehole and create a dam. The barrenness didn't bother him. Maasai are used to harsh conditions.

There was another topic of conversation that night at Joseph's. Peter's trip to England. The idea had been generated soon after I had arrived in Kenya. I had spent so much time thinking about it that, by then, in my mind, it had already fleshed out into reality. Peter thought it was a great idea, too. I had been looking for a flat to buy in London, and it had been decided that as soon as I found one and we had settled in, he would join us for a year or so. I wanted him to be under the Fitzgerald wing for a while. He needed to know that he still had this other *mzungu* family, that we loved him as much as we always had. In fact, we loved him more than ever. Besides, exposure to a different culture and another value system would broaden his horizons. I hoped that he would be able to learn about the technology of livestock husbandry and put it to good use when he returned to Kenya.

Peter had written often in his letters that he wanted to come to England. He was excited at the prospect of new horizons, looking forward to it, and masterful at disguising his apprehension. That evening Joseph acted as point man for finding out what England would be like.

'Can you live in a polygamous state in Britain?' he asked.

'No, it's illegal.'

Joseph's eyes popped.

'What about having an affair?' said Peter.

'That's not illegal. It's just bad behaviour. Particularly if you're indiscreet about it,' I said.

'Peter will be all right. White men are good and honest. The British people will look after him,' Joseph put in.

'Not necessarily. The English are no different from the Maasai. There are nice ones and bad ones. People in London don't always have good intentions towards strangers,' I said, then added, not wishing to frighten him off, 'but most people are very friendly. It's just that it's not a good idea to automatically trust every stranger you meet.'

On the way back to Peter's *boma* we stopped to have a companionable pee in the dark a few yards from each other. As I drizzled onto the hard earth, I thought, *I love my son. I'm glad we're going to have more time together.*

There were, of course, formalities to be cleared with Peter's parents. He was an adult who made his own decisions, but he needed their blessing.

Mebikie held court under the T-shaped tree. He was hunkered on a rock and his red *rubega* spread around him like a pool of liquid. Mebikie spoke in Maa. I replied in English. Peter acted as translator.

Mebikie took out a wad of chewing-tobacco and inserted a sliver between his front teeth and lower lip. Then he said, 'Thank you for looking after Peter. I'm pleased you came and glad to see you're middle-aged. You deserve respect. We share a son so you are like a sister or a wife . . .'

When he'd finished, I praised Peter in reply and gave assurances he would be well looked after in England and on the trip there. Mebikie cut me short in the middle of all this and started all over again. 'I'm glad you're middle-aged and have your own children . . .' He ended by referring to Nnee, 'She is my wife. I am the boss.'

The interview with Nnee was held over a mug of tea in her hut. She sat on one bed, I on the other bed on the far side of the fire. One of the lazy brothers came and sat next to me. Lankisa joined Peter, who was sitting by the doorway on a stool.

'When a mother loses her eldest son, it's like a home with a pillar removed. Another pillar must replace it,' Nnee began.

I knew where this was leading. I pointed to Lankisa and said, 'He can be the new pillar.'

'No,' said Peter gravely. 'He's married and must look after his wife.'

'Of course.' I turned to the boy on my left. As far as I knew, he was the second eldest of the unmarried brothers and followed Peter in age. 'Then you will have to be the pillar.'

Nnee and Peter looked serious, but Lankisa and the lazy boy fell about laughing. 'He's too young.'

I said, 'I agree with Nnee. She has a point. Mothers must be looked after. I work hard from morning to night to earn money to support the family. No one sees that I'm all right. Who is going to look after us?'

Peter looked confused. He urged Nnee to speak in Swahili so he would no longer have to translate.

She said, 'My head can hear you, but my mouth can't return the words.'

Silence fell. I picked up the conversation again. 'Shall I tell you how Peter will live when he is in England?'

Another silence. Then Lankisa took up the challenge. 'Tell us about the milking machines.'

I did so: how the machines ran off electricity and were attached to the cows' udders and sucked the milk into large metal *debes*.

Another silence. Then Nnee looked at me directly and spoke of what was in her heart. 'Will my son live with your family?'

'Yes. He will. I will look after him as you do because he is my son too.'

'In your house?'

'Yes. My home is his home.'

Relief stirred her perceptibly. She smiled and said, 'That is good.'

I looked across at Peter. 'I think we've just been given the green light.'

As it turned out, a year was to pass before I was ready for Peter. I found the flat I wanted, hard on Hampstead Heath, but it was old and delapidated and needed extensive renovations. I did them slowly, as one does when you are living on the breadline. By this time I had hung up my African boots and was trying to make a go of it as a freelance journalist writing about things that happened in Britain. Work was tedious but family life was fun. The flat was large and sunny, with enough bedrooms to accommodate several children. I shared it with Petra, her boyfriend John, and Yvonne, our lodger. One bedroom stood empty – Peter's. Finally, after nearly ten years, we were going to be a family with a home of our own.

It never occurred to me that Peter's visit would be anything but perfect. Then one Sunday as I lay on the living-room sofa, the newspaper I was reading clawed me back to reality. Leafing through it, I came across a picture of Tom Cruise and Nicole Kidman holding a baby. He had a cherubic face framed by loose black curls. His skin was the colour of a Mars bar. He was called Connor and they had adopted him. I started reading. I already knew that there were two African-Americans in Mia Farrow's tribe. The article said they were called Isaiah and Keili-Shea. It said that Michelle Pfeiffer had adopted a mixed-race baby called Claudia Rose. It was a new trend: the United Colours of Beverly Hills.

I read on and learned a number of things. In the States, parenting across the colour line was suddenly very PC. The Multiethnic Placement Bill had been enacted the previous year to free the way for what was termed 'transcultural adoption'. The legislation prohibited welfare agencies from delaying or denying the adoption of children on the basis of race, colour or the national origin of the adoptive parents.

This was a policy volte-face. A de facto ban on the practice had been in place in the United States for nearly twenty-five years because the National Association of Black Social Workers had condemned it as 'cultural genocide'. Apparently they weren't happy about the recent liberalization. A spokesperson for the organization was quoted as saying, 'Children who are adopted by a family of a different race grieve over the loss of their culture. Kids have a human need to know the connection to their heritage. Transracial adoption should be a last resort.'

Transracial adoption. Catchwords are pretentious. What they meant was a white mother and a black child. I pondered over Peter's imminent arrival. Would he yearn for the *boma* when he came to England? Or perhaps the woman from the National Association of Black Social Workers was referring to something more profound. Peter's spiritual umbilical cord was connected to Maasai rites of passage – *olamal engipaata*, *emorata*, *eunoto* and *oringesherr*. Each one conferred status on a Maasai man. Even if he couldn't celebrate ritual circumcision, graduation from warriorhood and the transition to becoming an elder, these ceremonies should be honoured to reaffirm his sense of identity. Tradition is the matrix of every society.

The British authorities agreed with this and, according to the article, had yet to be persuaded of the merits of tampering with social birthrights. Exposure to white middle-class values, it was felt, would tear up the child's cultural heritage by the roots. So white parents were not allowed to adopt black children.

I detected a subtext here. It was race not culture which bothered the authorities. From what I'd seen of English xenophobia it was alive and well. The Channel was as great a divide as the oceans which lay between Britain and her former colonies. Yet no one argued the pros and cons of a baby of Portuguese or Greek origin being adopted by an English couple.

I'd never given any of this much thought before. Africans accept whatever help they're offered. There are literally millions and millions of orphans and street kids. The state coffers certainly aren't deep enough to look after all those children. There are over a million orphans in Uganda whose parents have either been killed in one of the civil wars or have died of AIDS. They are fostered by uncles, aunts, grandparents. When their foster parents die of AIDS, too, they trek across the countryside in search of more distant relatives. Some couples have twenty orphans living with them. Many children end up looking after themselves with no adult around. In Kenya, parents and children of different colours are commonplace enough to have their own catchword – zebra families. No one thinks it is wrong.

If Peter had been with me, he would have taken the article to his room to read carefully. Afterwards, he would have said, 'That is very interesting.' We had never discussed racism.

I started taking note of what was happening around me. Race issues cropped up on the television news, in the papers, in the way people talked to Indian shop owners and West Indian porters. I drove through the endless streets of Asian suburbia in south London, tried to stop a fight between two white teenagers and a young Asian man who was closing his shop late one night. Racism. It would have been naive to ignore this seemingly unchanging reference point of British thinking.

One evening I went to meet a friend at a club on Piccadilly. It was one of those safehouses the establishment use when they come up to London from the counties or on their way home from the City. The threadbare carpets gave off a masculine smell of cigarettes and damp tweed. I passed the Men's Room and caught a whiff of Jeyes Cleaning Fluid. In clubs such as these, steep membership fees and stern economy are not mutually exclusive.

My friend was late. I settled into an armchair and ordered a glass of wine. Late shoppers and early drinkers sat in groups beneath the high ceiling. Their conversations were muted, observing the convention of their class that it is vulgar to talk discernibly in public. Occasionally voices lunged at my ear: '. . . play golf . . . *already* blackballed . . . a darky, wot?' A burst of laughter rose above the chink of ice against glass. The man who had said this puffed on his Davidoff and released a trail of smoke into the air. He looked very pleased with himself.

A week later I was at the Queen's Club to watch a tennis match. Here there was a different compendium of smells and sounds. The atmosphere was less muted, verging on the boisterous, a result of the rich devoting a few hours to athletic activity. The aroma of sweat and breath exhaled in sharp bursts hung above a pungent substratum of astroturf and racket grips.

Afterwards we ate lunch in the dining room upstairs at a table set with silver and thick pink napkins folded into triangles. The man to my left, fiftyish, wore a badly tied cravat that revealed patches of white skin next to his silk shirt. Our host introduced us. 'Bertie's a splendid chap. Farm in Oxfordshire. Cattle. Hardly ever comes to town. Such fun.'

I didn't know any farmers and was still wondering how to go about finding work for Peter. Bertie might have some ideas. Indeed, he might need someone to help him through the calving season. He had returned from the buffet with a thick wedge of chocolate cake which he was regarding with the greedy satisfaction of a schoolboy. I decided to give it a try.

'Do you have children?'

'Mmmmmm. Two girls. Grown-up now.'

'So are mine. Two girls and a boy. All looking for work.'

'Your girls don't work, do they? Lucinda wanted to work as a waitress once. Said she wanted the money to buy herself a bike. Such a sweet idea. Told her I'd pay her to stay at home.' Bertie was shovelling the cake in with gusto. He had one of those untroubled faces from the pages of *The Field*. I could see him in plus fours and cap with his dog at his feet and a gun broken at the breech over the crook of his arm. Here was a man who loved his animals, his shooting and his family. In that order.

'My son is adopted. He's a Maasai from Kenya. He's coming to live with us soon to get some experience with English cattle.' I paused, as if an idea had suddenly struck. 'You wouldn't, by any chance, know of any farmers looking for an extra pair of hands?'

Bertie was taken aback. 'You mean work for them? Where would he live?'

'With the family?' I ventured. 'England will be pretty strange for him. He'll need to feel at home. Have some company in the evening.'

Bertie gave me a pitying look. 'Don't think that would go down very well. Very rural where I live. Locals've never seen a black man. Wouldn't have anything in common.'

'He's very easy to get on with. I just want him to get some experience of proper farming,' I said lamely.

Bertie scraped the last smudge of icing from the plate with his fork and popped it into his mouth. 'Can't understand why. The Maasai don't work. All they do is stand on one leg and then the other. Trying to improve the natives is bound to end in tears.' He reached for the wine bottle and recharged his glass. 'Best leave him in the bush where he's happy.'

The conversation had made me distinctly uneasy. I can be oblivious to the constraints of reality, but Bertie's reaction sounded the alarm bells. Was I being impossibly naïve in uprooting Peter from his familiar world?

Tara had taken a year off between school and university, flown by herself to Pakistan and found a job in Peshawar on the Afghanistan border. She returned a young woman, none the worse for wear despite some harrowing experiences with gunrunners and drug smugglers. Petra was doing Latin American studies at Liverpool University. The coming year she planned to enrol at the university in the Colombian town of Cali. I had no qualms about that. Change makes us grow.

England would be even more foreign to Peter than Latin America to Petra or Asia to Tara. Yet I imagined the Hampstead artists and tower-block grunge, prosaic rural England and Prozac-driven yuppiedom – the pastiche of Britain's best and worst – awakening his gentle nomad's soul. I envisioned Peter pushing out the boundaries. This would be the grounding for a future as a politician; or, at least, an iconoclast. The sum of these formative experiences would be a tool to make the world (he could start with Kenya) a better place to live in.

And yet. Peter was different from Tara and Petra. As a child he had never known the love of his biological parents. As a teenager he had missed out on the discipline handed out by the tribal elders. While his brothers had been contained within a traditional, tight-knit society, Peter had wandered free-range through boarding school, the shacks of Kisamis and the random attentions of the Fitzgerald household. It had been a culturally schizophrenic existence.

No child should be a prisoner of his background. One of the greatest gifts a parent can bestow is to encourage exploration, and teach the value of the search. It transcends prejudice and frees you of the fear of the unknown. Yet every child should have the security of belonging to his tribe or community.

What I excluded from all this agonizing was obvious. A child needs to sense right down in the marrow of his bones that he is loved unconditionally: even if he gets bad grades at school, fails to make the football team, forgets to wash the ring of dirt from the bathtub or overdoes it with the booze and throws up all over the Persian carpet. Or, in Peter's case, regardless of whether he gets the hang of living in England, or finds work on a farm; and despite being a child with a lion-hunting warrior as an alter ego.

Peter would know his value as a human being by the value I gave him through my love. The most profound things are always the simplest.

There had been hurdles to negotiate with the bureaucracy of two continents. Obtaining a passport in Kenya is not a simple task. Peter had to furnish an ID card. To get that he had to persuade the torpid clerks at the Kajiado records office to trawl for his birth certificate amongst the mountains of folders stacked against the walls. This exercise took three months and entailed several bus journeys and the furnishing of the wherewithal to 'feed' those who looked for his papers. In England the freedom to travel is taken for granted. In Kenya it is considered a privilege. Peter was justifiably proud of his blue passport.

I sent the money for a ticket and a date was set for his departure. We spoke to each other on the phone, tightening up on last-minute arrangments. 'M. A., what about the issue of blankets? Do I bring one with me? It's a question of being cold.' I told him there were blankets waiting for him. He said that was good. He would bring sheets and a towel. I told him we had those too, but he packed a towel anyway.

Peter had never flown in a plane before. Indeed, he had never been out of Kenya except for the trip we had taken together to stay with the Maasai in Tanzania. Two Maasai elders had once asked me if they used a shrinking machine at Nairobi airport to fit all those people into the tiny planes they saw in the sky above their *boma*. Peter knew that airports didn't have shrinking machines. All the same, air travel would be a novel experience for him. 'I am a warrior, but I was completely worried to death,' he later wrote to Mike. 'I have always thought a plane was like a *matatu* that picks up and drops passengers in different destinations. I never thought that it is a killer box should anything go wrong. While the plane is airborne the passengers are always praying to get to the next destination safely.' Peter put in a pilgrim's share of praying, particularly during take-off and landing, but when I asked what he thought of the flight, he said, 'It was very good. There were no problems.'

However, there was what Peter would no doubt have called The Question of Immigration. The British authorities were cracking down on tourists from former colonies. Too many arrived at Heathrow on the pretext of visiting relatives or friends when they were really in search of work and a more pleasant place to live. More to the point, there had been stories in the press about liaisons between middle-aged women on holiday and gigolo beach boys. A Croydon hairdresser had married a Samburu warrior she'd met on holiday in Kenya. She was fighting to get the right of British residency for her young husband. I worried over how the immigration officials would view Peter's visit. A forty-something woman inviting a young man to live with her was bound to stiffen their antennae.

I phoned the Foreign Office for advice. Nothing concrete was offered, but it was suggested I write a letter to Peter stating that he would be supported by me financially. The woman on the other end of the phone said six months was the maximum period of time he could stay. I put that problem to the back of my mind and sent off the letter.

Dawn was still a long way off when I woke up on the day of his arrival. There was a cavernous black sky spread above the church steeple. The hour hand on its clock pointed to five. For once I didn't linger in bed an extra few minutes. I turned the light on, threw on a pair of jeans and went downstairs to make some coffee without bothering to brush my hair or look in the mirror. The night had emptied the streets of traffic. An early-morning van rumbled past, its gear change reverberating in the quietness as it approached the corner. I stared at it through the window.

When I had first come to London six years ago, it was this intrusion of the outside world which I had found most unsettling. I lay in bed and heard the rapid tap of high heels on the pavement, followed by bubbles of late-night laughter. Disembodied feet, phantom voices, the anonymous on their way to the unknown. Back home it would have been a hyena sending banshee whoops into the all-pervading silence of an African night. Or the rattle of the tree hyrax sounding like a door on a creaking hinge. These unfamiliar urban noises outside his window – Peter would call them alien noises – would make him nervous.

The city was still slumbering as I drove to Heathrow. Not so inside the terminal. The concourse was packed with sleepy people meeting flights. Asians, Africans, Americans, Australians streamed through the arrival gates. I had arrived in good time so as not to leave Peter stranded. I propped myself up against a pillar and waited. After an hour or so my feet began to ache so I found a seat, craned my neck round the forest of heads, got bored with that and returned to the pillar. Two hours passed. Two and a half. Peter's Gulf Air flight had been on the ground for well over an hour. I was beginning to feel distinctly anxious.

It was at that point that an announcement came over the tannoy. Would Hussein Ismael and Mary Anne Fitzgerald please report to the information desk. I made my way there as quickly as I could. I wasn't given to panicking, particularly over air departures and arrivals, but I was imagining Peter, frightened and bewildered, incarcerated with Hussein Ismael's relation in an airless cubicle.

A uniformed official walked me through to the arrivals hall. I was ushered into an office, invited by a man in a suit and white shirt sitting behind a desk to have a seat. He began grilling me about my relationship to Peter: who I was, what I did for a living, why Peter was coming to England, what he intended to do here. The questions were delivered with an ultra-patient expression to show this was not a cross-examination, merely an informal chat. I half expected to be asked which toothpaste Peter used, but I wasn't.

Perhaps that was only for people who professed to be married to each other.

The answers must have satisfied because after that I was led to the desks where the passports were stamped. Peter was there sitting against the wall. To my surprise, he looked completely unflustered, quite in command of the situation. He rose to his feet and we hugged. He was wearing a blue blazer, slacks, shirt and tie. Joseph's old anorak was folded over his arm. He showed yards and yards of teeth when he smiled. He looked wonderful. Peter had been given the third degree as well. How did he know me? Why was he here? Who were my employers? I was working as a freelance journalist so he could have tripped up on that one. But he got it right enough. 'I told them you wrote stories for *The Times* of London,' he beamed, then added, 'This issue of the letter seems to be important. It's hard to keep secrets in England.'

Midwinter doesn't show London at its finest. Battalions of steely clouds marched above the traffic as we edged off the M4. A wind had blown in and brought with it sputtering rain. People walked the pavement with bent heads, clutching their hats and hanging onto their umbrellas. A man stared at us and Peter said, 'He will come and punch us and tell me to get out of the car.' He presumed London was even more dangerous than Nairobi.

Behind King's Cross we passed two prostitutes in miniskirts, hugging themselves to keep out the cold. A sudden gust sent an empty Coke tin tumbling down the street and some plastic bags and bits of paper flapped up into the air. Peter took no notice of the girls or the fantasy red-brick towers of St Pancras and instead commented on how clean the streets were and the absence of *matatus*. I was waiting for wonder or recognition to flare in his eyes, but he said very little at all. I couldn't gauge his reactions from his face. So I chattered away and kept on pointing out landmarks and supermarkets and bus stops. I wasn't a very good guide because, as was becoming rapidly apparent, I knew very little about London or how it worked.

We detoured through Regent's Park. As the city's envoy, I felt an obligation to present Peter's new home in its best light. When we reached the sweep of Nash terraces with their imposing facades the colour of clotted cream, I slowed the car. Ionic columns and statues and cupolas were not common features of Kenyan architecture. In fact, when Nash was in the throes of gentrifying London, architecture had yet to enter the Kenyan consciousness. But if I was expecting a gasp of admiration, I was to be disappointed. Peter was focusing on the strangeness of the familiar instead. He gazed at the naked tree branches. 'Is this a burnt forest next to the fields? The trees are very dead.'

I recalled how I had been enthralled by Olorgesailie's dark volcanic slopes when I had visited Peter's *boma*. It was not at all certain that he was going to be similarly fascinated by what the Maasai would have called my 'home area'.

CHAPTER 12

'Morning.'

'Morning.'

'Hi.'

I flicked the switch on the kettle and surveyed the midden of pots and pans spilling out of the sink. 'Look at this mess. I thought you guys said you were going to clean up before you went to bed.'

Petra gave me a cross look. She was sitting at the kitchen table in a *kikoi* and T-shirt, deftly rolling her first cigarette of the day, running her tongue along the paper and tamping it down with her thumb. Despite the uncombed thickets of blonde hair, she looked beautiful in a tousled sort of way. Her contribution, as usual, was to the point. 'Leave it, M. A. Shut up and sit down.'

My *obiter dictum* that a clean kitchen made a clean start to the day has never been popular. I switched off the kettle, made a mug of instant coffee and, ignoring Petra's instruction, grabbed the broom. I jabbed at John's bare feet with the bristles. 'Move them, please.'

He looked up from the book he was reading and put his half-eaten toast and marmalade back onto the plate. 'Chill out, M. A. I'll do it later.'

'Yeah? Later which day? And by the way, your music's too loud. I don't need jungle shaking the bedroom floor at two a.m.'

'For God's sake. Relax. You're so uptight.' Petra, like Tara, had inherited my early-morning crotchetiness.

'You're not too charming yourself in the mornings,' I retorted, patrolling the work surfaces with a damp cloth. 'I'm the one who'll have to pay for new carpets when seven kilos of dirt have been tramped into every inch. Wait till you get a place of your own. Then you'll change your tune.'

'M. A., I'm always cleaning the damned house. You're paranoid, that's all.'

'All right, you two. Cool it. Petra and I will clean everything when we've finished breakfast. Won't we, sweetie?'

Gentle John, ever the pacifist. He was dressed in some loose-fitting greyish things that looked as if they'd come out of an Oxfam bin and probably had. His fashion sense was expressed tonsorially. This week it was a skinhead crop and black caterpillars of beard crawling along his jawline. Che Guevara meets student grunge.

'Oh yeah, Johnny boy? You'd better be right.' I gave him a wry grin. He raised his hands above his head, stretched and grinned back at me. I caught a glimpse of olive skin rippling over his ribcage. John was spectacularly tall and thin. We teased him that he was a graduate of a Serbian detention camp. I was immensely fond of him, in fact loved him almost as fiercely as I loved Petra. Our bickering was harmless. It went without saying that the three of us would defend each other to the death to anyone who wasn't family.

There was a light thudding on the stairs. 'Is that Peter?' I said, knowing the footsteps were too rushed to be his. 'I've been waiting for the bathroom to brush my teeth.'

'Go easy on him, M. A.,' Petra said.

'Yeah, you're right. But what does he *do* in there?'

'Hi. I'm late. Bye.' Tim's bald, earringed head popped round the door. He gave us a beatific smile before continuing down two more flights to the street. Tim was the boyfriend of Yvonne the lodger and spent most nights with us.

'Bye.' Yvonne threw the word through the door as she raced down after him. She worked as a television news editor and, like the rest of us, had trouble coming to grips with the start of the day. She left no margin for error in her commuting schedule, but the early-morning dash was as unruly as she ever got. For the rest of the time, she moved about the house with the detached, self-contained manner of a cat.

Petra and her live-in boyfriend John were more like puppies, tumbling from room to room and leaving behind them the paper-chase of artefacts peculiar to twenty-one-year-olds. Cigarette papers, dirty ashtrays, socks and Latin American novels covered the tables. A sprinkling of dark ochre tobacco flakes dusted the furniture.

The two of them adhered to the law of anarchic displacement. Nothing was ever where you might reasonably expect to find it. The cooking salt, for instance, led a gypsy existence in every room except the kitchen. It had been usurped as a salve for the wounds they inflicted on their eyebrows, noses and navels in the pursuit of body-piercing chic.

By now I too was sitting at the table. Petra and John had returned to their books. I had my cold coffee and the *Herald Tribune*. We retreated into our private worlds and read. It was the customary routine. A flurry of activity and accusation from the Kitchen Police, some backchat from the Usual Suspects, followed by companionable silence. This fifteen-minute interlude before starting work was sacrosanct. It was as if we had hung Do Not Disturb signs on our backs.

There was the sound of the bathroom door being opened on the floor above; footsteps crossing the passage; the creaking of floorboards in the pink bedroom with the French roll bed where Peter slept. I turned to the foreign pages, reading but not taking it in. Despite myself, my neck muscles tensed. He would be coming down in about ten minutes. Then I would have to emerge from my reverie of newsprint and coffee and reach out to him, be sociable and kind, concerned and caring.

He appeared in the doorway, muffled up in a windcheater and a white Somali shawl and smelling of soap and hot water. 'Hello, M. A. How are you? Did you sleep well? Hello, Petra. How are you? Hello, John. Did you sleep well? I have been having a bath and then I got dressed. Now I am going to have breakfast.'

Peter's words were lilting and singsong, a genetic memory embalmed by generations of setpiece dialogue that dealt with journeys in progress and the state of the clan. Stranger greeting stranger on a dusty track, son greeting father's first wife at the entrance to the *boma*, it all unfolded at a stately pace. But here in London, freed from the cultural context of cattle and rainfall and expeditions made on foot, the courtesies seemed painfully slow. Like porridge being poured into your ear.

'Hey, man,' said John.

'Y'all right, then?' said Petra.

'Did you sleep okay? No noises this time? You weren't too cold, I hope?' I spoke brightly, glancing at Petra for any sign of disapproval.

At some point during that first difficult week that Peter was in London and off his home turf our conversations had become starched with formality. I was painfully aware of sounding like a Universal Aunt, a not very patient one at that. I had shown Peter how to light the gas on the hob; turn on the oven, the kettle, the television; how to operate the locks on the front door; myriad little things which we took for granted. He was an eager student but, like anyone launched on a new learning curve, didn't always get it right. The previous evening he had taken the grill tray out of the oven without using a glove and nearly dropped it. Nothing had broken, but I had snapped at him anyway.

The memory brought a flicker of remorse and I said even more cheerfully, 'What do you want for breakfast? There's toast and tea. Eggs if you want it and bacon in the fridge. Sorry. Forget the bacon. There may still be some sausages. Have a look.'

I had been scouting the neighbourhood shops for beef sausages, but they were hard to come by. Peter didn't eat pork, just as he didn't eat cabbage or peanuts or bananas. The pork was probably born of the fact that there weren't any pigs in Maasaini. I had been meaning to ask him about it but hadn't got round to it yet. But cabbage and peanuts and bananas were staples of the Kenyan diet and on sale in abundance in the markets. It was about as inconvenient as one of us claiming to be allergic to potatoes and wheat. Peter said they bloated his stomach and gave him wind.

Neither did he eat cakes or ice cream or anything sweet. Or fish. Or a lot of the vegetables we put into our stir fries. In fact, finding food that Peter could and would eat had been challenging. He had settled into a routine of spinach (a relation to that other Kenyan staple *sukuma wiki*), mincemeat and rice. Breakfast was tea, bread and sausage – when I could find it. The bottom line was that Peter had landed himself in a household of low-maintenance human beings who were satisfactorily fuelled on lettuce sandwiches. As far as the rest of us were concerned, food wasn't top of our list of pleasurable experiences. Being used to adversity, he never complained, but he was in danger of becoming north London's first malnourished Maasai.

Peter had brewed up some milky tea in a large tin mug and was stirring in three spoonfuls of sugar with a lazy rotary motion. He stood at the kitchen counter with his back to us and stared dreamily at the wall. There was a metallic grating sound as the spoon scraped back and forth along the bottom of the mug. The noise sent steel skewers down my neck again. 'Pee-ter. You're going to wear the mug out doing that.'

'Sorry, M. A.' He looked chastened.

Petra glared at me. 'Well, he *is*,' I mouthed at her.

I stood up and announced, 'I'm going upstairs to work.' Then, for the benefit of Petra and John, added, 'And to brush my teeth.'

'I'll join you,' said John.

'Who are you kidding? You don't even own a toothbrush and you're certainly not using mine.'

Why couldn't I talk like that with Peter? The shorthand of innuendo and jokes which had flowed so easily in Africa had evaporated.

Life in London wasn't as carefree as in Kenya. There was a house to run and a job to hold down. I was pressed with work, shackled to meeting deadlines. Petra and John had the good sense to stay out of the way. They only appeared in my study on the top floor in an emergency. In other words, when they wanted to borrow the car. For the rest of it, they left me alone and announced their arrival or departure by shouting up the stairwell.

While we rushed, Peter lingered and talked. His inbuilt sense of community meant that he liked to share what he had done, what he was doing at that very moment and what he planned to do next. He charted the course of his day, by the minute and the hour, while standing next to my desk, just as he had when he was a boy at school. I listened, smiled, nodded, not really taking it all in.

He must have missed the treacly pace of life in the *boma*. There was no discussion in the shade cast by the branches of the thorn tree where Mebikie sat out the heat of the day; no goats to count in the evening as they milled about in their thorn enclosure; at night, no gentle ebb and flow of conversation in the dark depths of Nnee's hut.

Deprived of any familiar points of reference, he floundered in his new surroundings. Petra and John, the insouciant rebels, took pleasure in giving the finger to the establishment. I could afford to give them a piece of my mind when they stepped out of line. Peter knew no such security about his role in this strange new world that was so grey and sunless. His survival manual had no chapter on how to be an Englishman. As a parent, it was my responsibility to handle his vulnerability with compassion.

The cruellest aspect was the weather. It was 'cold, horrible, murderous'. He had never known such chill, he said, even on the misty peaks of the Ngong Hills. At first he refused the sweaters I provided, saying that the wool made his skin itch. However, principle soon crumbled in the face of necessity. He encased himself in layers of sweaters and abandoned Joseph's thin coat in favour of a cosy anorak I had once used for skiing. He was thrilled with the thermal longjohns Tara bought for him, the gloves and scarf and fur hat obtained from Camden Market. He wore them all. Inside the house. He sat on the living-room couch, looking like a forlorn Michelin Man. My heart twisted at the sight of it.

Peter tried bravely to acclimatize without complaint. When he kissed me hello, which was at every opportunity, he did it with ritual: a kiss on each cheek after which he laid his head on my shoulder. With that contact I sensed his ache. I did my imperfect best to make him feel at home, exuding pleasantries with the finesse of a chat-show host. Our exchanges masked the uncertainty we felt.

A useful act of love would have been to 'chill out', as John and Petra suggested. I should have relaxed, been less intense. But his presence amongst us was still too new. Part of me was in there struggling to compensate for what he had left behind. Part of me watched from afar, through glass, the subtle kaleidoscopic shifts of family dynamics now that he was amongst us. I was eager to do the right thing, but I couldn't quite put my finger on what that might be.

Before his arrival, I'd had visions of taking Peter to Parliament to watch democracy at work, a football match for light entertainment, some photography exhibitions as windows onto other parts of the world. These grandiose plans had been sidelined by magazine assignments. I had to earn a living. Petra and John had their own north London agenda, played out to the throbbing beat of techno while they lay sprawled on the floor in a haze of cigarette smoke. Peter called it tanko, but it didn't seem to interest him. So he mooched around the house. Mine wasn't a new problem. I was at a loss at how to be mother and breadwinner simultaneously.

Peter soon hit on a solution to his boredom. He embarked upon a pastime which came easily to him. He walked. Not as English people do, going out for a stroll to stretch the legs and get a breath of fresh air. He made pilgrimages of epic, Maasai proportions which took him out of the house for the best part of the day.

Soon his routine consisted of a leisurely bath and breakfast followed by an assiduous sweeping of the kitchen floor. Then he ascended the stairs to take his leave before setting off on another odyssey. I made sure he was equipped with some money and a slip of paper on which I'd written our telephone number and street address.

The first time this happened, I stepped out onto the roof garden, pulled a chair over to the parapet and stood on it so that I could see down into the street. Peter soon swung into view. I watched as a young woman with a baby in a pushchair emerged from the council estate at the end of road and came towards Peter. He said something to her but she walked by as if he was invisible. At the traffic lights he stopped and looked carefully in both directions before crossing the street. Then his dark bulky shape disappeared behind the row of houses on the far side. That day Peter found his way back without trouble. He had only been gone for about an hour. The next day he was away for much longer and rang just when I was beginning to fret.

'Where are you?'

'I'm in the phone box outside. I'm locked out.'

Sitting in my eyrie at the top of the house with my earplugs in I hadn't heard the doorbell ring. His initiative was reassuring and I felt a surge of pride.

We lived less than a mile from Hampstead Heath and this was where he set about his orienteering. He crossed the grassy slope which led to the ponds and stopped to look at the Egyptian geese. Peter liked them because they migrated to Africa and reminded him of home even though in Kenya geese bivouacked along the rivers and were not to be found on the plains. A man threw a stick into the water and his dog swam out to retrieve it. The dog paddled back encircled in rings of ripples. It dropped the stick at the man's feet and took a few stiff-legged steps towards Peter before shaking its coat. Water splattered onto his trousers and Peter laughed out loud.

He was intrigued by the peculiar devotion of the English to their 'dog pets'. It puzzled him that they lavished so much attention on animals which had no apparent purpose. The Maasai worshipped their goats and cattle because they were everything: money on the hoof, the primary food source, the matrix of tribal myth. Love made sense when the welfare of man and beast was inextricably intertwined.

Once the ponds were at his back, Peter tramped up Parliament Hill and entered the windswept woods. The trees seemed like castles compared to the squat Commiphora and the toothpick branches of the acacias which dotted the plains. The ground was muddy and the mulch of rotting leaves squelched softly underfoot. When he tired of these strange sensations, he retraced his route. He always returned exhilarated and complaining about the cold. 'My feet are like stones. If I hadn't known here, I would have collapsed along the way.'

Peter injected a hitherto unknown note of conviviality into the Heath, talking to anyone he could persuade to stop and listen. 'I am a visitor to England,' he would say, standing closer than it was customary for a stranger to stand and taking it upon himself to fill them in on his impressions of city life. He dispatched with enthusiasm details of our family and his daily routine until, from what I could gather, they made an excuse about being in a hurry and wandered off. He told me he chatted to women exercising their dogs, couples out with their children. There had been a man who had commented on his dark skin and asked if he walked that way often. What did these people look like? I asked. But Peter was vague, observing 'Europeans seem to be very similar'.

Then one day Peter didn't come home. At first I wasn't worried, but as the afternoon greyness thickened and turned to night, I couldn't banish my mounting concern. By five o'clock I was frantic. Why had I been so cavalier about his expeditions? He couldn't resist talking to strangers. For all I knew, he'd been mugged or even murdered.

While all this was churning around in my head, the phone rang. 'M. A., I'm really lost,' came a subdued voice.

I said I would come and fetch him in the car if he could tell me where he was. This took some time to ascertain. He was next to a travel agent and there was a big supermarket on the corner. In Nairobi this briefing might have sufficed but not in London. After several minutes of interrogation, I suggested he asked a passer-by to tell him the name of the street. An American voice came on the line. 'This is Finchley Road tube station, ma'am.' Peter had walked several miles.

I drove down there as quickly as I could, white-knuckling the steering wheel and muttering at the traffic. It was rush hour and the pavements were filled with commuters. This was before the days of the Camden Market fur hat and I thought that with his white Somali shawl wrapped round his head he would stand out in the crowd. But I couldn't see him anywhere. Anxiety flared again as I frantically scanned the sea of dark coats. Then he tapped me on the shoulder. I turned and we clutched at each other as if we were drowning.

Peter was full of his adventure. He had decided to strike out from the Heath in a new direction. He had walked down streets of white houses, passed a police station, descended a hill and found himself in the midst of an infinite parade of shops. There were phalanxes of buildings amassed on every horizon and he realized that London was bigger than fifty Nairobis. The passers-by ignored him and he thought he would never find his way home. Soon he was in despair. The cold had numbed his muscles and killed his strength, he said.

Soon a more urgent dilemma presented itself. His bladder was bursting. Peter eyed a telephone booth but discarded that option. He might be arrested. He considered letting it dribble down his leg. That would make him colder. What was he to do?

There was nothing for it but to act like a warrior who killed lions. Summoning up the last of his courage, he walked into a garage.

'I need to make a short call.'

A man in overalls was standing on the forecourt. He regarded Peter with suspicion. 'Sorry, mate. We don't have a phone.' Then recognition lit his eyes, followed by curiosity and amusement. 'Where you from, then?'

'I'm a visitor from Kenya . . .'

Peter's well-rehearsed preamble was cut short. 'Kenya? Wot's that, then?' The man had stepped up to him and was running both his hands down the front of his jacket, patting it as he went. 'No gun. Guess you're harmless. It's over there.' He nodded in the direction of a dark blue door in the side of the building and walked off, shaking his head.

Peter concluded the story with a triumphant flourish. 'The English are very kind,' he said.

CHAPTER 13

I worried about Peter on his outings. Although life was cheap in Kenya, people killed for no darker a motive than money. Peter was innocent of the perverts and weirdos thrown up by decaying London. He was far too trusting for his own safety.

One day when we happened to drive past a public lavatory, I pointed to the dank steps leading down beneath the pavement. 'That's where you can go for short calls.'

Petra chipped in, '*and . . .*', giving me a meaningful look.

'And you have to be careful. Places like that are a hang-out for gays. They're looking for good-looking guys like you to pick up. They won't hurt you. But don't talk to anyone just in case. You'll be fine.' I didn't want to alarm him and I didn't want him to come to any harm either.

'They'll try to grab your plonker,' said John helpfully.

Peter seemed unperturbed and said he wouldn't talk to anyone in the 'caves'.

I knew he was conversant with the concept of homosexuality because of a story that had come tumbling out one day. It had been just the two of us in the kitchen. I had broken off work to come down and have lunch with him.

He stood tucked into the right angle where the two counters met, with his feet thrust out slightly to take his weight. The sausages and mashed potatoes he had prepared were at his elbow. While he spoke he kept on picking up one of the sausages and holding it in front of him between thumb and index finger like a science-class specimen. Then, without taking a bite, he would return it to the plate.

Peter began to tell me about an Englishman he had met in Kenya. 'He was forty, maybe fifty, and very huge. Maybe one hundred kilos. Eighty. Something like that.' A friend had asked him to do a favour and show this man how the Maasai lived. Peter had taken him to watch the circumcision of a teenage boy.

I had been to several such ceremonies and in my mind's eye imagined the boy sitting on an ox hide outside his mother's hut, his legs splayed stiffly. The circumciser squats down on his heels beside him and pulls the foreskin forward with thumb and forefinger. He makes a rapid half-circle incision with a razor blade and pulls the penis through the hole. The operation is performed cleanly, without blood. The foreskin will, in due course, shrivel and hang at the base of the penis. It is known as The Tie. *De rigueur* for Maasai men. Hopefully, but not necessarily, the razor blade is a new one, in these days of AIDS. The circumciser's head is cocked to one side in concentration. With infinite care he skims the razor over the blue-black flesh.

The initiate gazes steadily ahead. Circumcision is the no-man's-land which separates boy and warrior. It must be endured without complaint. One cry or whimper and he will be ostracized by the warrior fraternity. He will not receive his gifts of cattle or run with the warriors after lions. The boy knows this and says nothing as the elders watch. He is mute, rigid with pain.

The circumciser has completed his circuit around the boy's cock and sloughs off the skin. It is the rebirth of the snake as it sheds its scales, the ancient imperative of the renewal of life. But it is hard to tell if the elders who stand about are aware of this. Their culture has hit the pause button. It is impossible to rewind to the pre-Independence era when they were unencumbered by the corruption and greed that spills forth from urban Africa. And the future is too uncertain to fast-forward to universal education, trousers and cars, individual plots of land secured by title deed. So instead they murmur approval that a job has been well done and shuffle off in search of the crates of beer which their host has secreted somewhere in the compound.

Soon, Peter said, the guests became very rowdy. The more inebriated of the partygoers began to disappear into huts to sleep off their drunken stupor. Until now I had thought Peter liked the man he was chaperoning, but as he became more animated in the telling of the story, I realized that he didn't hold him in high regard.

'He wanted to sleep with me but I told him it was wrong because I can only sleep with my agemates. Then I got worried this guy would go off and sleep with the *wazee*. If he started messing with the *wazee* they would beat me up. And what if in their drunkenness their *shukas* came up and showed their nakedness? I would not want him watching them. They would say I have brought a man to look at their nakedness.' As he said these last words Peter thrust his head forward and gestured with his jutting chin as if to bring my attention to some object at the far end of the kitchen. He gave me a googly-eyed stare. A whoofing sound vibrated in his throat. It was the carnival-dragon look the elders adopted to express disapproval.

He decided to take the man to Nnee's *boma*. If he was at home, he would have more control over the course events might take. Just as important, he would not be disgraced in public by the man's unpredictable behaviour. They would spend the night in Nnee's hut as he always did when he visited his family. Peter's countenance softened at the mention of his mother. He picked up the sausage which, in the telling of the story, had been returned to the plate.

Nnee's hut consisted almost entirely of wall-to-wall bed. There was just room for a stool or two, but most people who came to see her chose to sit on one of the low divans which flanked the hearth. This was where the Englishman lowered his huge bulk after Peter had introduced him to Nnee. The beds were like bowers, framed by an arch of sticks and hugging the contours of the walls. They offered dark and unknown recesses where much could happen without fear of discovery.

Nnee stoked the cooking-fire that smouldered at her feet and put a pot on the stones. The heavy ovals of beaded leather at her ears swung idly as she nodded her head to Peter's explanation of his appearance so late at night with a stranger, and they shifted and fell forward as she bent to stir sugar into the *sufuria*.

They sat there bandying news of the *boma* and the circumcision ceremony back and forth. The man was beyond the pale of the easy companionship of mother and son, but from time to time Peter repeated portions of the conversation in English for his benefit. When Nnee handed him a mug of tea he smiled and thanked her.

Eventually Peter yawned and said it was time to go to sleep. The suggestion pleased the man and he lay down with his head pushed up against the wall and his feet hanging over the edge, wreathed in the smoke that rose from the fire. The mattress was constructed of interwoven branches. Animal hides were spread on top.

Peter bit into a sausage. As he chewed, I recalled the night I had shared a bed with five tall men, a sleeping arrangement which had ruled out the indulgence of tossing and turning. We had lain in the solidarity of tomblike stillness, moulded to each other, curve for curve, like a mass burial of ochre-swaddled corpses. I love Maasai beds. They are great for bad backs although an ordeal for delicate respiratory systems. The smoke from the fire tends to hang there like city smog.

That night Peter was on the alert. At the circumcision ceremony his guest had shown no interest in the women. He recalled the three girls who had been drinking sodas. The cloth draped from their shoulders had fallen away as they raised the bottles to their bee-stung lips, revealing secret clefts between armpit and breast. Yet the man's gaze had not delighted at this erotic sight.

Peter summoned his little brother, a skinny boy of six – 'to put between us on the bed like a curtain' – and continued to talk to his mother across the red and grey embers of the fire. It was a smart move, but the little boy wriggled like a worm on a hook. This and Peter's low-toned conversation annoyed the man. He was restless and complained he was being kept awake. Peter told his brother to move to the far side of the bed where his squirming would not disturb the man. He said goodnight to Nnee and the quiet mixed with the smoke from the dying fire.

'You didn't have any problems?' I inquired.

'He put his hand on my leg like this,' Peter said and laid aside his sausage to stroke his long fingers up and down his thigh.

I leaned forward in my chair, unconsciously mimicking the movement. Kenyans are unabashed in describing bodily functions but circumspect when it comes to discussing sex. I was shocked. I felt my hackles rising. The sleazeball. I visualized a chance meeting. At first polite, he would crumble beneath my stare, reduced to quivering penitence. A few succinct words and this fat, middle-aged man with suspect sexual ambitions would grovel with shame. But no suitably scathing condemnation came to mind so instead I said evenly, 'What did you do?'

'My body was shaking. It didn't feel normal.'

'So what happened?'

'Nothing.'

'Nothing?'

'I didn't react.'

'And?'

'I lay there very still, not moving at all, until he fell asleep.'

You never can tell about people, even your own children. You think nothing has debauched their innocence until casually they reel off the type of encounter you have been trying to shield them from. The juxtaposition of experience fascinated me. We were opening doors for each other onto new worlds. Each time one of us questioned what we saw, as with the 'dog pets', the interpretation reinforced or realigned our values.

There were meals, for instance. It was the family routine for everyone to go about their own business during the day and come together as a unit in the evenings. We made an informal show of supper: sharing the cooking, tripping over each other, smoking and chatting. John was a master of mashed potatoes. I supervised the stir fries and chicken dishes. Petra's cooking expertise didn't reliably extend beyond salads, but she always set the table. Once it was all prepared, we spent a good hour or so enjoying the meal and each other's company.

Peter, on the other hand, had been raised to think of eating as a solitary affair, a chore to be dispensed with before settling into the more pleasurable pastime of conversation. His favourite feeding site was the corner between the sink and the dishwasher. Standing there, he could survey the entire domain of domestic chaos. But in the evenings our milling about usurped his strategic viewpoint.

He sang loudly – quivering descants and plaited harmonies from the plains, as he stirred mince in a saucepan – to defy his confusion at oscillating between happiness and despair. When the meat and rice were ready, he took it to the table. If we were still cooking, he ate with his back to the room, ladling it in at a steady pace. He hunched over his food, addressing it with singular concentration, like a teenager who gulps everything down so that he can join the other kids on the block for a game of football.

In fact, he would have loved nothing better than to sling his boots over his shoulder and run downstairs to do that. Football was an obsession with Peter and had been ever since the days when he played number nine for the Kashanga Football Club and scored all the goals. He religiously watched every match on television, giving a running commentary whenever I came into the room.

One day we pulled off the motorway to have lunch at a Little Chef. At the next table were three men in red shirts. Their plates were loaded with pizzas and pasta and cakes. They were massive. Late-night TV and Carlsberg boys. I couldn't figure the glint of recognition in Peter's eyes.

'Why are you staring at them?'

'Those are Manchester United supporters. There are a lot of them here. Look. They are a bit proud today because on Saturday they might win the FA Cup.'

Peter regarded my blank face and expanded. 'Last Wednesday they beat Crystal Palace, two-nil. Now they're going to meet Liverpool. It's the most dangerous game in the world to attend. They throw rocks and stones at each other. And the supporters of the defeated team even hang themselves or shoot themselves.'

He was attuned to the team rivalries and philosophically accepted the violence they engendered amongst the football hooligans. Peter had seen it all happen before in Kenya. He supported AFC Leopards. His great friend Kashoi was an ardent Gor Mahia fan. The Leopards and Gor Mahia were to-the-death contenders for the Kenyan Super League. He and Kashoi couldn't go to matches together as they would end up fighting.

I had heard that African football teams had in-house witch-doctors who massaged the players' superstition. They travelled with them from match to match.

'Do they really do that?' I asked.

'Yes, for the most part they do.'

'But does it work?'

Peter was a devout churchgoer yet there was no scepticism in what he next said. 'You worship different deities and if you believe in them, then it works for you. You take their energy and make it your energy. I believe in prayers . . . Do you?'

'I'm not sure,' I replied and felt uncomfortable.

Peter was as undeviatingly loyal to his chosen sport as he was to his church. He gave cricket short shrift – referring to the bats as 'those sticks' – and showed no interest in the World Cup rugby matches which were in progress. If we felt like being couch potatoes in front of the TV on Saturday afternoons, we were obliged to watch Manchester throw off Chelsea in mud and rain.

Peter participated in each match he watched with such intensity that he might as well have been sitting on the front bench. But afterwards when we switched on a documentary or the news or – Petra's speciality – a soap, his interest waned. Then he stared at the TV screen as one does at distant mountains. His gaze was dreamy and unfocused.

One evening we watched a documentary on the American evacuation from Saigon. It was gripping and strangely moving. Vietnam. The watershed war that made the West question its values. I asked Peter if he had heard of Vietnam. 'What is that?' he said.

Another night we tuned in to a period drama. Peter was on the couch, looking like Nanook of the North. John slouched in the armchair while Petra sat on the floor in front of him, her shoulders wedged between his knees.

A woman in expensive silks rustled on-camera followed by a younger, prettier woman who was pleading tearfully with her. It soon became evident that the younger woman was having an affair with the older woman's husband.

Peter was having trouble following the dialogue. 'Why is the woman crying? Is she a worker?' Employers being beastly to their employees rang a familiar note.

'No. The woman in white is somebody's wife and the other one is his mistress,' said John.

'What's that?'

'She's his girlfriend,' I elaborated.

'Does that mean she's just a friend?'

Petra chipped in with 'A proper girlfriend,' as the wife gestured at the door with an outstretched arm.

'Why is she sending her away? Can't they live together in the same house?'

'Wives don't share their husbands here. Polygamy is illegal.'

Peter nodded and continued to stare at the screen, happy not to analyse English mores too much at this early stage.

That day the four of us had been discussing an article in the paper about a forty-year-old French teacher who had fallen in love with one of her pupils. She had taken the boy to live with her. He had spent all her money, then left. Petra, John and I had laughed at her foolishness. But Peter had come to their defence. The boy was not to be blamed because he had behaved as any young man would, he said. He felt sorry for the woman because now she was broke. He was like that, brimming with innocent compassion.

One day Peter and I took the train to Cambridge. The wheels rattled and clicked beneath us as we sat facing each other. It was his first ride with British Rail. In Africa, train trips are a diverting soap opera. Smugglers hide their contraband – yards of plastic shoes stuffed along the ventilation pipes, branches of bananas stowed in the lavatory – and play cat and mouse with the border police. Women with flashing eyes parade the corridors, their swaying bottoms running a gauntlet of boisterous, beer-swigging men. Passengers hang recklessly from the doors to blow away their hangovers. Others hitch free rides sitting cross-legged on the roof, outriders to the conflict and romance that swirl beneath them. And at the stations lissome girls argue the price of the pineapples and cane rat they hawk from bright enamel plates perched on their heads. The recollected sounds and smells of those journeys were underscored by the present buttoned-up offerings; the potato-chip smell of the seats and the fusty overlay of wool and stale sweat.

I scanned Peter's face and wondered what was going on in his mind. He was staring at the rows of terraced houses relentlessly flashing by. Suddenly he half rose from his seat and pointed out the window at a distant rise of green rimmed by naked trees. 'Isn't that where we live?' It was Hampstead Heath – the magnetic north of Peter's London compass. Pastoralists read the landscape as they journey. It comes of travelling on foot in places where there are neither road signs nor roads. Peter had proved to have an uncanny talent for recognizing vegetation but was impervious to mortar and brick. This explained why he always returned safely from rambles on the Heath but got lost when tramping the streets. In those early days his quirky sense of direction never failed to surprise. I was going to Cambridge to interview a prosthetist and had dragged Peter along to show him one of England's most historic towns. As we left the station, we stopped to wait for the traffic lights to turn green. Peter looked around him with interest. 'Is this north-east London?'

I was writing an article on Richard Leakey, the Kenyan conservationist and palaeontologist. His legs had been amputated below the knee after a plane crash and the article dealt with Leakey's battle to learn to walk again. Peter showed scant interest in the prosthetist's litany of stumps, limbs and wheelchairs, the snail's-pace tour round the workshop's kilns and casts, or the interminable retrospective of amputee evolution beside a display case of wooden legs. Boredom plastered over with polite interest was a fact of life for journalists. 'Oh really? How fascinating. Are you the only ones to do this?' I murmured as we trailed round the centre. A glance at Peter's vacant eyes told me he was astral-travelling through some private world.

Peter's reward for his forbearance was to be an educational stroll amongst the venerable spires and courtyards of the Cambridge colleges. At last we took our leave and set off on foot down the main road. The city centre was a few miles away so it seemed a good opportunity to embark on some career counselling. The Path to Take in Life was a major item on the agenda of Peter's visit. By the time he returned home, his future would be clearly charted. It was an ambitious objective, but I foresaw no problems.

We strode past two-storey stone houses set back from the pavement behind privet hedges. It was an overcast day and the wind was sharp enough to make us both shiver despite the brisk pace.

'Have you given more thought to what you want to do when you go back?'

'Oh yes, M. A. I want to do the goat project. And I want to do tour-guiding.'

Mike Eldon had pulled strings through his business contacts to shoehorn Peter into the tourism sector. It suited his gregarious personality to be amongst people. Before the Ostrich Park he had worked as a trainee for Austrian Airlines. Before that there had been the brief stint in the lodge at the foot of Mt. Kilimanjaro. Tourism was an important foreign-exchange earner, but it was vulnerable to Kenya's high crime rate. Too many visitors had been mugged in Nairobi and held up by armed bandits as they drove between the game parks.

I reasoned that Peter's career shouldn't be vulnerable to the breakdown of law and order. If he went into livestock-ranching, he would be his own boss. No one would lay him off during a recession. Whatever happened to the country, Kenyans would always be in the market for meat.

If he stayed in England for a year and garnered some technical expertise by working for farmers, one day in Kenya he would be able to expand out of the dry, goat-sustaining terrain of the Rift Valley. He could acquire land in the fertile highlands with the profits from the 'buying-and-selling-goat business' and populate it with sleek, moist-eyed cattle. He would build himself a house and patrol the pastures in a cloth cap, Barbour and green wellies like a country gentleman. He would do what was needed to take advantage of the EC, GATT and the new world order, and export chunky carcasses of beef to the Middle East, possibly Europe.

When it came to the mechanics of how this would be achieved, my vision misted over, but I was optimistic. It was merely a question of learning at the knee of the English farmers. Somewhere in Britain there was a lode of information on international agribusiness and breeding cattle in the tropics. Between us, Peter and I would mine it.

I had it all mapped out. In a few years other, less successful ranchers would be flocking to him for advice on marketing and veterinary practices. He would be an influence in the community, holding court in the living room of his spacious stone house. As we walked with our hands thrust into our coat pockets, his sunny future was etched sharp in my imagination. Peter would prosper. He would become a Big Man.

'People who have just one goal in life find it easier to reach that goal than people who have two goals. Don't you think?'

'Oh yes.'

'Perhaps you should first of all figure out what your goal is.'

'Uh huh.'

'What do you *really* want to do?'

'The goats.'

'Good. If you go with the goats you can live on your land, fatten up the kids and sell them. Then you can buy more goats with the profit, breed from them and gradually build up the herd.'

'I can't live at home.'

'Why?'

'I'll be living in Nairobi.'

'Oh?'

'Because I'll be working as a tourist guide.'

'But I thought you said . . .'

'Then I can buy goats out of my salary.'

'Mmmmm. Can't count on it. So far your salary hasn't been enough even to buy food, has it?'

'My brothers can look after the goats,' he went on. The discourse was beginning to ramble.

'Okay . . . your brothers will be down there with the goats and you'll be up in Nairobi. But you'll be working as a tourist guide to get money to buy goats because your *goal* is to be a wonderfully successful goat-farmer. Right?' Silence from Peter. I went on, 'What if you're not earning enough to save?'

He reflected. 'No problem.'

'Why?'

'I like working in tourism.'

'Yes, but what's your ultimate objective?'

'To have a goat farm.'

'Your objective is the goat farm but you'll be working in tourism and not saving anything?'

'That's okay, M. A.' He gave me a reassuring smile. 'I'll be happy.' Round one to Maasai logic.

After that we wandered the cobbled streets. It was a question of the blind leading the blind. I knew nothing about Cambridge. We found our way to the River Cam and stood on a bridge watching a swan glide beneath us. Two students, a young man and his girlfriend, both dressed in jeans and duffel coats, were leaning against the parapet, one against the other. By a prismatic trick of the fey late-afternoon light their reflection in the glassy water seemed truer than the surface reality of their lovers' embrace on the bridge.

Peter took my hand in his and confided in a low voice, 'You are like a newly delivered mother. I am so helpless that I must follow you wherever you go. It takes a lot of time and patience.' He leaned towards me. 'Thank you for looking after me,' he said and kissed me on the cheek. There were times when I felt that the added burden of Peter's minute-by-minute welfare was too much on top of the demands made by my work. But when he showed this gentle side, it melted my heart and I vowed to be a better mother for him.

CHAPTER 14

Peter looks up to Tara as the elder sister although no more than a year or so separates them in age. She is the sage. Her pronouncements are set in stone. He loves her dearly. She's The Word.

Within a week or two of his arrival Tara issued an invitation to spend a weekend with her. This seemed like an excellent idea. He needed to be amongst people his own age. It would be invigorating and reassuring to be in her company for a few days. The only problem was the train ride. I was apprehensive but upbeat, almost entirely sure he would make the trip without incident. So was Peter.

Tara lived in Brighton. She had first come to know it in the days when she read social psychology at Sussex University and then stayed on. She loved the laidback seaside feel of the place and the way the seagulls mewled above the town's steep narrow streets. She liked it because her friends were there, former students like herself who shopped at organic food stores, listened to Zap Mamma and endlessly discussed relationships and politics. Tara ran a rape crisis centre and was studying to become a counsellor. She paid for the course out of her skimpy salary. When she felt strongly about something – refugees, the mess the Tories were making of things – her green eyes would flash then soften. They were at once luminous and capable of great stillness, the moonlight playing across a swell of dark water. Very seductive.

Peter enjoyed talking politics with Tara. It led to vigorous debate. She was left-wing. He was an arch-conservative. Begrudgingly, the Kenyan government had changed the constitution to incorporate opposition parties prior to the last elections. But like all Maasai, Peter had voted for the ruling party, the Kenya African National Union. To him KANU represented schools, piped water, the security of the known.

Encouraged by Tara, he read the English papers. His eyes were being opened to other possibilities. 'What I can see is that we are still a young and poor nation and we are lagging behind. Our problem is tribalism not nationalism. Our problem is greed not hard work. I have a vision for Kenyans when we are all brothers and never spill blood from one another. I don't think I would ever go to politics. Not at least for the next twenty years.'

He was thinking about his goats and about being a tourist guide instead. Peter could not understand why most of the people he met of his age were uncertain about what to do with their lives. 'The most confused students come from England. They still do not know what they need to do in life. I would call this late maturity and lack of self-realization. They need to go to university first and then they can select their careers later.'

Petra earned money in the holidays doing odd jobs as a receptionist, as an assistant to photographers and journalists. John worked in his uncle's travel agency. Peter could very well have been referring to them.

Peter and I took the underground to Victoria Station. The benign bustle took on a threatening aspect as I put myself in Peter's shoes and imagined how difficult it must be to make sense of the departure board as it clacked up a seemingly random appendix of urban geography. Peter had confessed that trains made him anxious. 'Everything is so quick.' He still spoke with a pronounced African accent. If he got lost, would anyone take the time to understand what he was trying to say?

A weatherbeaten porter glanced at us as we walked up the platform. He fell into step beside Peter. 'Wheah you goin', man?' The inquiry was embalmed in lilting West Indian vowels.

Peter looked cool, in charge of things, and cocked his head on one side. 'Bray-*ton*,' he said, betraying his Kenyan origins.

The brotherhood faded from the porter's face and he moved away, unhurried and disinterested.

It was early afternoon and most of the carriages stood empty. I walked on, saw a young couple sitting by themselves in a second-class carriage halfway along and heaved open the door. 'Here.' We climbed aboard. Peter was muffled up in coat, gloves and scarf and carrying his blue polyester duffel bag. He had pulled down the flaps of his fur hat but left them sticking out at an angle so he could hear properly. This simple sartorial detail, more than the colour of his skin, made him stand apart from everyone else. Those flyaway flaps gave him another personality. He was a Battle of Britain fighter pilot who had just jumped down from the cockpit of his Spitfire. This impression was underlined by the shellshock in his eyes.

We stood very close to each other in the carriage corridor. 'Okay. The train stops at several stations. I don't know what they're called but just ignore them. Don't get out until it stops completely and doesn't move on again. Brighton is the end of the line. Tara will be on the platform to meet you. She knows the time.'

'Okay, M. A.'

I turned to the couple who were chatting, engrossed in each other. 'Excuse me. My son hasn't travelled on his own in England before. Do you think you could possibly be so kind as to tell him when the train gets to Brighton?'

They nodded, smiled politely and said nothing.

Peter threw his arms around me, kissed me on both cheeks and tenderly laid his head on my shoulder. We hugged. Three times. 'You've got my number. And Tara's. If anything goes wrong, just ring. Get someone to help you.' The train jerked under our feet. 'It's leaving. I have to go.'

'Bye.'

'Bye! Have fun!'

I stepped back onto the platform. Peter had sat down opposite the couple and was staring at me through the window, a rapt expression on his face as if he had forgotten something and must go quickly to fetch it. He waved. The engine sighed and groaned as I waved back. An image from World War Two flickered across my mind's eye. Sweetheart bids farewell to troops departing for the front. Goodbye! Goodbye! With a lurch the train rolled forward. Peter turned away and leaned towards the couple. 'Hello, my name is Peter Lekerian. I'm a visitor from . . .' They were oblivious.

Brighton was an eye-opener for Peter. His peer group didn't take life as seriously as I did. He made himself useful by washing up all the dirty dishes, a Sisyphean task, but no one expected him to do it. He could slouch around on the sofa or spend as long as he liked in the bath, making hippo splashes and emerging looking as if he had been sluiced down by a firehose. It didn't matter if he dropped something. There was already so much clutter no one noticed if he added to it.

More to the point, they knew how to enjoy themselves. On his first night Tara and a group of friends took him to a ceilidh at a church hall in Lewes. Peter should have felt at home. He had seen a cross-dresser teeter past Camden Lock in high heels and tight, gold lamé skirt and been confounded. But here were men who wore their skirts like men. Just like the Maasai. Yet he was amazed. The Scots stood in a line in their tartans and pirouetted the girls round as if they were spears. You should *dance* at a dance. He preferred raves.

He had been to one with Petra and John, who were acolytes of north London's club scene. They dressed down in trainers and loose clothes and got down to the dentist-drill beat of trance and techno. Petra was determined that I should join one of their all-night jaunts and had even promised to stick by me so I wouldn't feel out of place. The spirit was willing, but my stamina invariably fell by the wayside. There had been a time when I waited up for Petra to come home from parties. These days I stayed up waiting for her to go out.

I had attempted to paint portraits of the girls in my letters to Peter before he came to England. In one of them I described Petra in Liverpool. She wore boots and a Rasta hat and looked like a *matatu* tout, I said.

Peter had picked up on this with enthusiasm. He wrote back that Petra was a *manyanga*, a beautiful girl. In Nairobi slang a *manyanga* meant a flash *matatu* that blared a monotonous African beat through a speaker in the cab and had a name painted on the side. Sharck of the Ocean. The God Help Us Leopard.

A *manyanga* if mentioned raises the eyebrows of the people and leads them to look around for a beautiful young girl bumping around or for a *matatu* with a good shape. Does Petra like Music? Does she dance a lot? I hope yes and we should size one another! I dance like a robot and I am too funky. I like bands like the heavy and quick London beats and Dolly Patron [sic]. Does Petra dance until she starts sweating?

Petra wondered about Peter, too. When he went clubbing, would he shuffle his feet as Africans did to the repetitive Zairean music that sounded like a scrubbing-brush being run over a washboard? Or would he get down to the rave scene with all the tower-block *vérité* of the insolent-looking young men who hung out on the streets around our house? The challenge had been issued. His ability to blend in with the lifestyle of contemporary British youth would be assessed not with clothes or drugs but on the dance floor.

Petra and John counselled on his attire. They settled on slacks and a batiked jacket he had been given by a visitor from Los Angeles. Peter never wore jeans. A beaded Maasai medallion dangled from the back of his hair like a rat's tail. There were several brightly coloured Maasai bracelets at his wrists. Nothing too *outré*. Petra grabbed him by the hand and led the way through the spiky, body-pierced crowd fanned around the door. 'Hey, Petra! I don't do mind-altering substances.' He wondered if this lapse would meet with her approval. 'That's okay. Just know that a lot of people around here do,' she said over her shoulder.

He danced on his own all night, tirelessly, the strobes freeze-framing his medallion in flight, head thrown back, snatched from his surroundings. The Maasai move to their own type of ecstasy. 'He's fly. All fluid. Not jerky like some of the geezers,' John said approvingly.

Peter was not impressed with his first rave – The Fridge at Brixton. 'It was an alien's place. There was a lot of cigarette smoke and a lot of water-drinking. People danced as if they were drunk but there was no beer. And they vomited.' He didn't seem to mind that.

Tara took him to see *Star Trek: Generations* on a wide screen. 'It was terrible. There were airplanes without wings and cars without wheels. They were mad.'

'It's about intergalactic diplomacy,' Tara explained.

'I don't do intergalactic diplomacy,' came Peter's firm reply.

He was intrigued by the people he saw in Brighton. They had metal in their lips, their noses, even their eyebrows. Like Petra and John, they were bent on self-mutilation. He wrinkled his nose in disgust when Tara told him that some men pierced their foreskins. Eeeerrgh. Barbaric. But he admired the tiny silver rings that rimmed her friends' ears like tassels. 'He told us in great detail about having his ears pierced at fourteen with a metal poker that had been heated in the fire and cow's piss being poured on it,' she said over the phone. 'I think I'll stick to sterilized needles, thank you very much.'

On Sunday Peter rang to say he was having such a good time he thought he would stay on in Brighton for a few more days. Was that all right? I agreed, with enthusiasm. He sounded the happiest he had been in England. The other truth was that I felt relief at having the house to myself for a bit longer. It gave me a much needed opportunity to catch up on my work. I suggested he ring again with his time of arrival so that I could meet him at the station. He turned the offer down, saying he knew how to use the underground. He told me not to worry. He sounded so confident that I left it at that.

Peter had been away for six days. His ticket was valid for five. He had also run through all the money I had given him, which was not nearly enough I concluded with hindsight. It never occurred to me to check on any of these things when he told me on the phone that he would be all right.

Peter had spent his money on food, movie tickets and a trip to the jewellers to join the ranks of the Britpop crowd. In addition to the holes introduced by a red-hot poker, he now boasted two gold studs at the top of his ears. Perhaps it was my imagination, but I thought the weight of them bent his ears down fractionally in an echo of the fighter-pilot flaps of his fur hat. I secretly thought they looked a little strange. But he was proud of these new adornments. He twiddled them round between thumb and forefinger while he talked. He wanted to make sure the skin healed properly. In the absence of available cow's pee, the kitchen salt resumed its perambulations from room to room. That was reassuring. House-hold tradition lived on.

He was fiddling with the studs when he told me the story of his train ride from Brighton to Victoria Station.

Things were fine until the ticket inspector made his way down the aisle and stopped by his seat. The inspector leaned over, wafting stale cigarette smoke into his face. 'Ticket, please.' Peter gave it to him.

The inspector glanced at it. 'This has expired. You'll have to buy another one.'

Peter cocked his head to one side and frowned. 'A new one? I have one already.'

'This won't do. As you're no doubt aware, this ticket is only valid for five days. It's expired. That will be ten pounds, please.'

'Sir, I only have three pounds left.'

'Three pounds, eh? It's ten pounds now or you're off the train at Croydon.' He tilted back on his heels and regarded Peter down the bridge of his nose. 'Might call the police,' he added.

Peter flushed. A bottomless abyss would open at his feet once they got to Croydon, wherever that was, and he would be tossed into it. 'Sir, I am a foreigner in your country. I am just a poor boy who doesn't know London. What am I to do if you throw me off the train? I will have to look for a Samaritan.'

The inspector modified his tone to something a shade more avuncular. He said, speaking slowly, 'Your ticket isn't any good anymore. So you have to buy a new one. Are you sure you don't have the money?'

Peter pursed his lips and shook his head to say no. 'I'll run home to get some and bring it back to you. I live near Hampstead Heath.' He stared up at the inspector and didn't take his eyes off him. It was not surrender. It was a look that children use when they are very small.

The inspector pondered the dilemma momentarily. 'Tell you what, son. I haven't seen you yet. You're going to get on at Croydon, a'right? That's Croydon to Victoria. You have the money for that.'

'Yessir.' Peter tried not to look relieved and dug into his pocket for the change.

The train pulled into the station and Peter stood to leave. His way was blocked by a young woman in a bomber jacket and jeans who was struggling to heft two bulky suitcases onto the platform. She was blonde and pretty. About Petra's age. In fact, she reminded him of Petra. Another *manyanga*.

'Shall I carry that for you?' he asked. He reached for the handle and their hands brushed as he did so.

The girl stiffened and shrank back. 'I'm fine, thank you.'

Peter didn't notice the warning note in her voice. In Kenya women carried suitcases balanced on the head while the men walked in front. He knew this wasn't the English way. The girl obviously needed help. Perhaps she was shy. He moved past her onto the platform and gave a toy-soldier bow from the waist. 'Let me help you with your suitcase. It is too heavy.' He looked her straight in the eye.

For a moment the girl was confused as she weighed her in-built prejudice of strangers, especially dark ones, against his open face. 'All right,' she conceded.

Peter lifted the larger of the two suitcases – he could show her he was strong – and they set off through the throng of commuters.

'My name is Peter Lekerian. I'm from Kenya . . .'

'Kenya! I used to live in Dar es Salaam. I was at school there until I was seven. Then we moved to England . . .'

'I'm living in England, too, now. With my foster mum. I haven't been here long . . .'

Soon they were chatting easily about their love of Africa and how they missed it. They didn't notice the inspector as he came past. He gave them a wry look. 'Don't let him travel again without checking his ticket,' he said.

'Nothing to do with me. I've never seen him before.' The girl laughed.

'You mean he's just carrying your bag? You've got a right one there.' He walked off shaking his head in wonder.

'You know, M. A.,' said Peter, 'I will see that man again and he will say to me, "Hey, have you looked at your ticket validity today?" Actually, the English are not racist. You make them open their hearts and then you can enter.'

Peter did go back to Brighton on the train – several times. But he never met the inspector again.

CHAPTER 15

We live in a nest of council houses. Some are highrise blocks that blot out the horizon. Others are sprawling and low. All these concrete boxes piled one on top of the other speak not of architecture but the backroom of a shoe store. But there is a certain nostalgia attached to the dank courtyards and broken windows. They evoke the less salubrious quarters of Nairobi.

I had been surprised by my house – the Camden Council call it a maisonette – when I'd first set foot in it not quite a year ago. The same reaction is attendant upon anyone who chances to drop in. 'I didn't realize it was so big,' friends say as they puff their way up flight after flight of stairs. And when they reach the top floor (my floor), knees buckled from the exertion of mounting sixty-six steps, and see the church spires soaring above the parapet of the roof garden, they exclaim, 'This is *wonderful*!' Once they have reclaimed some oxygen, they always remark on the stairs. Just taking a break from my desk to go and make a mug of coffee in the kitchen is a major expedition. I have the flanks of a racehorse.

The flat is in one of the neighbourhood's few remaining rows of Victorian houses. It consists of three floors running across two houses, a honeycomb of landings and corridors populated by African mementoes and potted plants. You have to climb two storeys just to reach the living room and kitchen. Above that are Peter's room at the top of the stairs, Yvonne's room next to his, Petra and John at the far end of the corridor and the bathroom.

The top floor is my domain. The stairs give straight onto my study, which in turn leads into my bedroom. It is just two rooms and would be ordinary enough if it wasn't for the sky. It streams in the windows on one side and positively floods through the wall of glass that stretches the entire length of both rooms on the other side. The sensation of infinite space is important to me. More so than the panoramic view which meanders over the rooftops to embrace a corner of Hampstead Heath, St Paul's Cathedral, Canary Wharf and even a spur of countryside beyond. I have no curtains. That way I conjoin with the elements. Often clammy rain lashes all around me. In the summer I sweat in a sauna. I don't mind the exposure. Even when the winter gales rattle the rooms so hard in their casements I imagine I am clinging to the crow's nest of a frigate and the faint thud of techno from Petra's stereo is the wind bellowing the rigging.

My study is an inspirational eyrie where I sit at the word processor and live in my head. It is here that I summon up descriptions of amputee athletes, women bodybuilders and other extraordinary human beings. While I write for the magazines and newspapers a frieze of pale savannah and pebble-coloured mountains marches above the brash city skyline. Up there next to the sky is where I dream of Africa.

The wall by the stairs is lined with shelves filled with box files, documents, taped interviews, photographs, Maasai beadwork, a smattering of bullet cases and spent land mines picked up in the trenches. Beyond the wall of glass is the roof terrace, larger than a squash court and as empty. I couldn't be bothered trying to keep plants alive in the winter.

Pushed up against the glass is a reed armchair from Western Kenya over which an Eritrean *kushuk* has been thrown. The chair is customarily piled with books. Petra had shoved them to one side so that she could perch on the edge.

'Petra,' I said, working an earplug loose but leaving it lodged halfway in my ear to indicate the conversation would be short. They were effective. I had missed her preamble. 'Coming to borrow the car?'

'I want to talk to you,' she said sternly. I knew I was in for it. A temper of great vitality (not my genes, of course) had been one of her guiding emotions as a child. Somewhere in her teens she had more or less tamed it, allowing it to take over only in specific circumstances: early in the mornings or when she couldn't get a gadget to work; and if she considered my behaviour to be incorrect. That day her temper was swimming close to the surface like a cruising shark.

'It's Peter,' she went on. 'What are you doing about him?'

'Doing?'

'Yes. What are you going to do about him?' She enunciated the question slowly, perhaps an unconscious echo of the many reprimands I had dealt out to her over the years. 'You've brought him over here and now he spends the day sitting in the living room bored. It's not fair.'

She had a point. But I have never been comfortable with criticism.

'I *am* doing something about him.'

'What?'

'I've been trying to find him work. It's not that easy, for goodness' sake. He's not exactly qualified for much.'

'So? You knew that.'

'Look, I'm very aware of all this, I promise you. But I can't expect anyone to take him on just yet. He's too new to England. He doesn't have a clue about how the system operates. We've got to give him a few weeks to settle in. It wouldn't be fair to him to throw him in at the deep end just like that.'

'Hmmmph. He's miserable and you've got to do something about it. Oh, and I *do* want the car.' She yanked my bag across the floor, rooted around inside and fished out the keys. As she was leaving she stopped at the head of the stairs. 'Get on the case, M. A.,' she said and gave me a beady look.

My children have an uncanny knack for making me feel guilty.

The previous year Tara had announced she would not be moving into the new house with us. She was going to find a flat of her own in Brighton. She was twenty-three and led an independent life. I had been mildly reprimanded by several friends for my timing. Having been homeless for five years, why acquire a house and albatross mortgage just when the girls were flying the coop? 'They can't leave home if they haven't got one,' I replied.

There was, of course, a subtext to be dealt with. I have since learned that many children dislike their parents at this point. It is easier to dismantle the existing structure of a relationship if it's afflicted with a sort of emotional rising damp. Tara was definitely going the traditional route. She had been stewing over many offences, real and imaginary, which I had committed during her life. Discussion and apology had so far done nothing to assuage her inner-child hurt.

I was emotionally lacerated by guilt while Tara cheered from the benches. In desperation I phoned Parentline. 'She's twenty-three? Earning a reasonable living? From what you've said, you've done a good job bringing her up. She's an adult now. Get on with your own life and stop feeling guilty.'

Not feel bad if she came up for the weekend and I played tennis with my brother while she slept late on Sunday morning? I had spent so much time working when she was a child (five days a week and business trips – just like fathers) that I was convinced it was wrong to spend leisure time out of the house when Tara was there. I carried around the detritus of our early years like a bag lady. The woman from Parentline had suggested I dump it on the nearest garbage heap. What a liberating notion. I gave it a try and it felt good.

I had been trying to lead a guilt-free existence for nearly a year. But now temptation presented itself in the form of Peter's brooding presence. The added weight of Petra's tirade pushed me over the edge. I was very worried that I had done the wrong thing by Peter to bring him to England, but I shared my doubts with no one.

In fact, there had been activity on several fronts regarding Peter's job prospects. Tara had taken Peter to the library in Brighton to show him how to research higher-education opportunities in agriculture. Later on, I'd taken him to our local library and fished out suitable prospectuses, explaining what they were and how they could be located if he needed them again in the future. The courses were either one or three years and expensive. If he was serious about learning how to ranch livestock, we would raise the money somehow. But it wasn't worth the effort for a tourist guide moonlighting as a goat farmer. I gave him the brochures and led him through them, pointing out the phone numbers for inquiries. Then I left him to it. I wanted to see where he would take it.

Meanwhile, I had been busy. I knew nothing about the world of livestock and farmers, but I was a journalist. I'd had practice in becoming an *aficionado* of subjects about which I'd known nothing the day before. I picked up the phone and started ringing around the country: the Beef Breeding Society, the National Cattle Breeders, the New Zealand Dairy Board representative. No stone was left unturned. The cattle community turned out to be remarkably co-operative. I'd had long chats with *Farmers Weekly* and Send A Cow to Africa. They had given me names to network and were keeping their ears open, they said. Somewhere out there was a farmer who needed an extra pair of hands (Kenyan ones) through the calving season.

Finally, Peter and I had put together his CV and composed two covering letters. One was targeted at tour companies specializing in Africa and one at farmers and cattle societies. I had spent the previous morning ringing up all the likely tour companies and had not only pinpointed a specific person to send each letter to but had also had a little chat on the phone with them, all syrupy charm.

Despite this groundwork, it took us all day to get the CVs and letters out. Peter had drawn up one of the white chairs from the roof terrace and placed it at a right angle to where I was positioned in front of the word processor. He sat leaning forward with his arms resting on his knees, unsure as to his role in this procedure.

I took things slowly because I was hoping that down the line he would be confident enough to do job applications on his own. 'Now then, let's have a think about how best to do the CV . . . Shall we lay it out like this . . . easier to read . . . yeah?' I typed a few lines onto the screen and sat back to show them to Peter. He leaned forward and stared at them, nodded his agreement. I wasn't sure how much he was taking in but ploughed on anyway.

I started off well enough, but as the day wore on, I tired of drafting and printing and explaining. I took a sheaf of envelopes from a drawer and handed them to Peter. 'You can do these. Get the addresses off the letters. Sign the letters, then you can stuff the envelopes.'

Peter took them from me and put them on the desk. He picked up a pen and placed one of the envelopes on his knees. He looked at it, hesitated, looked at me. 'Should I do large letters or small letters?'

'You mean you don't know how to address an envelope?' I snapped. 'Who cares? Just *do* it.'

His eyes dimmed and sank back into their sockets.

'Sorry. Sorry. I didn't mean it. Choose whichever you feel comfortable with. It doesn't matter as long as the postman can read it.'

I hate bullies.

Guilt.

It was around this time that a friend called Bill Forse invited Peter to take a look at his well capitalized smallholding near Arundel. On it he grew wheat and ran a 150-strong dairy herd. Bill was a bachelor in his forties who had a passion for Africa. He was writing a book aimed at pastoralists. It was called *Where There Is No Vet*.

Spring was trying to establish a foothold the day we drove down there. The sun pierced the clouds for minutes, sometimes only seconds. When it did, it highlighted a silo or tractor or barn. Most of the time, however, we were forced to brave squalls of rain-laden wind. We stared at Bill's black-and-white Jerseys standing in the mud. The cows stared back at us.

'Those little ladies are pretty pleased to be out here. They've been kept inside for the last four months because the winters are so cold.' Peter nodded and stamped his feet to get the circulation going. Flecks of mud flew up and splattered my jeans. Bill wore gumboots. Peter and I, the townies, had acquired a thick excrescence of mud around our shoes.

'There isn't as much disease here as there is in Kenya,' Bill continued, warming to his pet subject. 'But it's very contagious in winter when the cows are living at close quarters. We have to keep them healthy because they have to earn. Around here one acre of land costs about three thousand pounds and a cow is worth about one thousand on top of that. The return on investment on bought land is only two, three per cent at most. Most farmers – I'd say three-quarters of them – rent their land. Like I do.'

Peter had never been a front-runner in his maths class at school. Nevertheless, he must have been getting the gist of Bill's discourse. There was no room for shirkers over in the dairy. This high-tech, capital-intensive approach geared to the bottom line was very different to the Maasai way of doing things.

'How much milk do you get from a cow?' Peter asked.

'Sixty-five thousand litres a year. Twenty litres a day on average. Forty litres peak production.'

'Uuhuuuh. Our cows at home produce a litre in the morning and a litre in the evening. But they produce more in the rainy season because there is a lot of grass to eat.'

'I always supplement their grazing even in the summer. Profit margins are so narrow that you have to.'

'Aahaaah. Our cows are very resistant to drought and disease.'

Bill was talking to Peter in a very gentle way. He launched into the manifold intricacies of the Common Agricultural Policy milk quota – 'The EC licence works out at about seventy pence a litre . . .' – as we headed back to the pebble-dashed nineteenth-century barn he was converting into an office.

Peter kept on nodding and uttering soothing syllables of assent. This was Bill's forum. It was impossible to tell what, if anything, was at work in Peter's mind.

Bill pulled open the door of the office and ushered us into its pristine, cement-glazed depths. ' . . . and so the Church of England is the largest – or is it the second largest? – landowner. They have seven thousand acres of excellent soil right here on the Chichester coastal plain. Tea? I've run out of milk. The delivery man won't be coming round 'til tomorrow.'

'M. A., does he buy his milk from a shop?' Peter inquired discreetly into my ear.

'Guess so.' I made a face.

'But where is the milk from his cows? Why can't he take some for his tea?'

I grimaced again and shrugged to show that I too was stymied. The Maasai milked their animals into a gourd or a tin mug, took it inside the hut and drank it. It was that simple. It seemed senseless to sell the milk to the Milk Marketing Board and then buy it back from them.

If the Maasai were criticized for being minimalist, by the same token we would have done well to cool off on the consumer fervour. Ethiopian refugees wept tears of amazement the first time they saw three zillion items of packaged food lined up on Sainsbury's shelves. Heaven or hell? The Europeans would have it the Ethiopians were looking on the Promised Land. I still found it an effort to push a trolley along supermarket aisles with any calm. All that potentially creative energy turned inwards to the gratification of a nation's intestines made me want to cry.

We were invited to lunch at Bill's flat in Arundel and planned to follow him there in the car. We strolled over to my Peugeot, which was parked beside a small mountain of second-hand tyres. Bill opened my door, shut it again, stuck his face up against the half-open window – 'Do you know why we have them? To put on the black plastic that protects the hay so it won't fly up in the wind' – and stepped back as I flicked the key in the ignition. The engine gave a little cough, then purred as the starter motor turned over. Bill disappeared round the side of the barn to fetch his own car. Peter threw back his head and pointed his chin at the lowering sky. He was laughing.

'What's up with you?'

'I'm thinking of when I rang the agricultural colleges. Now I understand why. This is very different from home. It's like heaven.'

He had said nothing about his expectations or, to be more accurate, his doubts. At that moment I realized he had assumed English farmers penned their livestock outdoors and trailed after their animals all day, stick in hand, watching over them as Maasai herdsboys did. He must have wondered why I was making such a song and dance of sending him off to learn what he already knew. In presuming he understood what I had omitted to explain, I had failed him. Peter hadn't complained. Before he had even left Nairobi he must have resigned himself to being besieged by the inexplicable.

Peter's mood changed soon enough. Something was obviously bothering him as we drove the overcast country lanes to Arundel. He became quiet and observed me intently like a jackal waiting for the hyenas to leave so that it can rush in and devour the remains of the kill.

'M. A.?'

'Mmmm.'

'Do you mind if I ask you a question?'

'Go ahead.'

'I know that you're always working and never still for me, but I must be keen to show that I'm serious. How am I going to get money for the goat project?'

The question had an innocuous façade but we both knew what lay behind it. I had been waiting for it and here it was. Peter had thrown the issue of finance, as he always called it, right into my lap. He wanted me to give him the money to buy a herd of goats.

At one level, I didn't have any problem with this because it was so unequivocal. Peter had yet to furnish any clues to indicate he was serious about the goat project. Apart from ringing the numbers of the agricultural colleges which I had placed before him, what had he done to persuade an investor he was a good risk? A habitual spendthrift, he still had no idea how to handle money. Also he was a self-confessed absentee landlord. He didn't even want to live with his goats.

There was another factor which rendered these ruminations academic. I was broke. It had cost me money I didn't have to bring Peter over. Now he wanted me to go further into debt to buy goats. If I'd had the money, I would rather have bought a car for Petra or contributed to a down-payment on a flat for Tara.

In our family you worked for your goals. You proved yourself. Peter wanted everything handed to him on a plate. Europeans were always excoriating Africans for their dependency mentality. They said they expected to live on handouts. Was this an example of it? Peter was in danger of becoming spoilt.

But amongst the Maasai the richer members of the family are expected to assist the aspirations of the less successful ones. It is a system of obligation rather than reward. An inverse Maasai code of behaviour where the offer that can't be refused issues from the supplicant.

Who was responsible for elevating Peter's expectations if not me? I had to see him good. Guilt, however, was tempered by pragmatism.

'How do you think you're going to get it?' I kept my eyes on the road.

Peter, too, looked straight ahead. 'I don't know.'

'What would Mike say if he was here?'

'I don't know.'

'Well, I would have thought you'd have to put a plan down on paper. You've got that. Then you'd have to persuade the investor you'd implement the plan properly. He – or she – might be convinced you could do that once you have had some experience in the accounting and technology of farming. That's one of the reasons you're here. To acquire that. The investor doesn't want to see his – or her – money go down the drain. Does he? Or she?'

Silence.

'Do they?'

'No.'

'So how do you think you should go about raising money?'

'I don't know.'

'Hmmmm.' I turned my mouth down and lifted my eyebrows, a gesture of resignation usually reserved for shop assistants who tell you they have just run out of the item you are looking for.

CHAPTER 16

It was well over a month before Peter landed his first job. In the interim I gave him pocket money and after a while found tasks for him to do around the house. I paid him five pounds an hour, the going rate for cleaning ladies. He washed the windows, swept and hosed down the roof terrace. Spring was on its way and in my mind's eye I could already see the garden abloom with tubs of fuchsias, busy lizzies and pelargoniums. He performed these chores according to Parkinson's Law. It took a day to do the vacuum-cleaning, two days to get the grime off the windows. For a day and a half he scrubbed and sluiced the cement squares on the terrace, making inroads into the grey-green slime that had accumulated through the winter. I watched through the study window as he persevered at it and felt nostalgic for the unhurried pace of life back home.

He was happier these days. The clown in him was coming out. After supper one night he suddenly stopped sweeping the kitchen and launched into an impromptu skit. It was the Maasai being interviewed by a Kikuyu housewife for a job as her nightwatchman. First he was the fawning supplicant and then the harridan employer. He crouched down to make himself smaller. The broom, which was his spear, looked pathetic and ineffectual. 'Please take me on. I am brave and strong and I never fall asleep,' he whined in a high falsetto. Then he drew himself up, puffed out his chest and frowned. His whole presence had changed. The broom, which was a broom again, became large and threatening. 'You are lazy and stupid. I know you Maasai. I will only pay you a hundred shillings and don't steal my *posho*,' he said with a booming voice and stabbed the broom's bristles at the air.

It didn't matter that Peter was talking in Swahili. The satire was universal. Even John understood what was going on. We were laughing and clapping. And I was smiling because Peter was smiling.

Spurred on by our reaction, he seized the broom handle and held it in front of his mouth. Then he rearranged his face into something more solemn and glared at us. 'Ummmm-hmmmm.' It was a deep growl.

'Kenyatta!' I shouted. 'It's Jomo Kenyatta giving a speech.'

'*Hamjambo wananchi! Sikiliza maneno yangu . . .*'

'Peter, you're mad!' Petra giggled.

'Yes! I am mad! I am mad!' he cried, delighted.

I watched him pirouetting around the kitchen. The planes of his face were more defined, had a new symmetry to them. The protective love I had felt when he was thirteen surged inside me. The boy was on the cusp of manhood.

Peter was at pains to demonstrate this. As if we needed reminding. We were in the kitchen for the evening. John had excavated two beers from the back of the fridge and shared them out amongst us – John, Petra and I. Peter refused to touch alcohol. John was pouring them into the square tumblers I had bought at a sale. He shook the last few drops from the cans and put them into the plastic bag next to the rubbish bin.

Peter fished one of the cans out of the plastic bag, examined it, then tore the tab off and put a finger through its hole. He twirled it absent-mindedly. 'Metal that is thrown away should be made into jewelry,' he observed.

This is what happened in Kenya. The four silvery snakes above my elbows had once been part of an aluminium cooking pot. The Maasai prefer small arrows and circular discs made from tin. They hang at the throat and from the ears, making seductive tinkling sounds and sparkling in the sunlight. Keys and buttons are incorporated into the beadwork, so are spent torch bulbs and the ridged red tops of Colgate toothpaste tubes. *Wazee* insert Kodak film canisters into the stretched loops of their ear lobes. There is no junk in Africa.

'Not a bad idea,' John agreed. 'If you're going to recycle, go all the way.'

Peter nodded, sage and serious, and said, 'That is the warrior's way.'

Everything was the warrior's way: walking fast, eating alone, getting up early, staying in bed. Peter had missed out on this rite of manhood because he had been at school and because his aunt had plucked him from his *boma*. When you are far removed from familiar surroundings and therefore not constrained by the imperatives of custom, something you shoved to the back of your mind can elbow its way to the fore and become a major preoccupation. Peter was obsessed with warriors. And the more he thought about it, the more he became a warrior in London.

I noticed that when I invited people over to meet him he acquired a certain stature. He mixed in well, sitting hunched over with his hands clasped on his knees as close as he could to the other person, looking them straight in the eye, engaging in intimate tête-à-têtes. They were fascinated by his stories of lion hunts. Imperceptibly these accounts took on a personal aspect and the 'they' in the stories became 'we'. He had never entertained the family with tales of these exploits. My friends were film directors, writers, art historians. Peter wrapped himself in the more dramatic aspects of his culture so that he too would be seen as a person of dignity and consequence. The guests made their way over to where I was putting bowls of salad and rice onto the table. 'He speaks such good English', and 'He's very intelligent', they said kindly. There was no condescension in their voice. But the parenthetic 'for a Maasai' was ever present.

I'd answer, 'He seems to be settling in quite well.'

Only one friend took a different line. He had grown up in a family of eight in a Welsh mining village. As a child, he had never been given pocket money and had earned everything he spent. 'If he were my son, I wouldn't let him lie in bed till midday. You're too soft on him,' he scolded. 'You're his mother, goddamnit, so behave like one and lick him into shape.'

Peter and I both wanted him to be an equal amongst equals. We just had different visions of the path to follow. There was no danger of his losing his cultural identity. He was Maasai right down to his giraffe-skin sandals. I longed for him to step beyond that and be a citizen of the world. Yet his sense of self was so fragile. He lacked the innate security of knowing he was loved simply because he existed. He was driven by the desire to excel, to please, never to put a foot wrong.

We went about our daily business, met at meals, talked of his ambitions, visited friends, behaved on the surface like a family. And all the while we walked on eggshells. I looked at him and wondered if his thirst for love would ever be slaked.

Peter's first gainful employment was a stint with a travel agency. The company was preparing for a tourism exhibition and needed someone to sort brochures, stack boxes, generally help out. The evening before his first day at work we discussed what he should wear – white shirt, grey slacks, navy-blue blazer and paisley tie. Then we got out the A–Z and perused the underground map. I showed him where to change from the Northern to Circle lines. I still felt uneasy about the underground. I fantasized about Africans returning home and talking of 'a great metal snake that shoots under the earth'. Peter had no such qualms. He worked it with the nonchalance of a mole.

Success depended not only on finding the office but arriving on time. In marked contrast to the British concern for punctuality, Peter operated like a wildly swinging pendulum. He was either senselessly early or ludicrously late. His time management needed stabilizing. He had been told to report at 9:30. I wanted to make sure that everything was in place because I had to be out of the house early the following day for an out-of-town interview. I planned to leave at 7:45.

At seven o'clock the next morning I stumbled down the top flight of stairs in a T-shirt and *kikoi*. I was on the way to the bathroom. When I got there the door was shut. I could hear the hiss of running water. I banged on the door. 'Peter! Is that you?'

'Yes, M. A.!' he sang back.

'Well, hurry up. I've got to leave in forty-five minutes.'

I continued down the stairs, made myself a mug of coffee, took it back up to the bedroom. Due to some inexplicable quirk in the plumbing, it took a good ten minutes to draw a bath. He could have one and I'd go without. I put on a suit and some jewelry, stashed my notebook and tape-recorder in my bag and took it with me to the kitchen. On the way down I paused on the landing. 'How you doing, Peter?' I called.

Silence.

I stood by the living room window, nursing the second mug of coffee, the one you notice you're drinking. Across the road a priest was walking down the cloister path, his robe swishing about his feet, on his way to fetch the paper. There was a primary school attached to the church, but it was too early for the parade of children walking hand in hand with a mother or father or hopping and skipping erratically along the pavement like tennis balls that have been shaken loose from their canister.

I looked up at the clock on the church spire. 7:30. This was ridiculous. The effect of the power dressing would be somewhat mitigated if I wafted last night's garlic into the air with every question I asked. I needed to brush my teeth and put on some make-up. When I reached the bathroom door I banged on it.

'Peter?' The taps were still open and he couldn't hear above the noise of the running water. Was he having a bath or going for a swim?

'Peter!' The handle yielded as I rattled it and I pushed it open. He was standing there in his boxer shorts, holding a toothbrush aloft like a salute. His mouth was covered in a white froth of toothpaste. It was a way of teeth-cleaning singular to Peter. It had always intrigued me. But not this morning.

'Sorry, M. A. I won't be long.'

I threw the door open wider, keeping a grip on the handle (but little else) and stood aside. 'Out! Now! I'm late.'

He sidled past me into the corridor.

Nothing was said of the incident, but Peter took it upon himself to ensure our timetables didn't clash after that. At 7:30 the following morning I went downstairs to fetch the *Herald Tribune* that had been thrust through the door slot sometime before dawn. He buttonholed me as I passed the kitchen door. He looked very pleased with himself. 'M. A., I have changed my schedule. I am going to have breakfast first and then I'll have a bath afterwards.'

We left the house together – Peter on his way to work; I to the paper shop. The day was brisk but carrying with it the promise of spring. I had almost put on bicycling shorts.

Peter paused by the front door, the horse scenting the air as it steps out of the stable. 'It's quite warm today,' he remarked. Spoken

Tara, at the age of three, trying her hand at being a Maasai herder.
(*Mary Anne Fitzgerald*)

M. A. as a foreign corre-
spondent with dancing
partner, a Tanzanian
soldier and his AK47, in
Kampala after the fall of
Idi Amin. (*William
Campbell*)

Peter and Godfrey sitting on the packing cases of M. A.'s possessions shortly after she had to leave Kenya overnight. The Alitalia bag is the same one Peter was clutching when he was stricken with malaria and stumbled away from his job at the safari lodge. (*Meriape Sankaire*)

Peter (left), an earnest seventeen-year-old, in Form Three at Oloolaiser High School.

Mama New York and Noonkepa at Enchani Pus pose in Lori and M. A.'s hats and sunglasses. (*Mary Anne Fitzgerald*)

Peter in Noonkepa's hut at the *boma*. During the visit, he took to wearing a turban in an effort to assert his individuality. (*Mary Anne Fitzgerald*)

The two mothers, M. A. and Kipenget. (*Helen van Houten*)

Mebikie (holding staffs) at the circumcision of three of his sons. Mbele (on right), now sixteen, stands with shaved head in the black circumcision cloth. (*Guillaume Bonn*)

Maasai warriors draining blood to be served as recuperative mugs of *asaroi* for Peter's brothers to drink after their circumcision. (*Guillaume Bonn*)

Peter with goats – animals central to his plans for the future. Tumpeni is on the right. (*Guillaume Bonn*)

(Left to right) Nalotu-esha (Peter's sister-in-law), Nnee (Peter's mother), Betty (a friend), Susanna (Peter's half-sister by Mebikie's first wife) and Tumpeni (Peter's younger brother). (*Tara Fitzgerald*)

Peter risks his fingers while feeding *sukuma wiki* to his friends the ostriches.

(Left to right) Tariq (owner of the Ostrich Park and Peter's boss), Peter, Tara, a friend and Mike Eldon at Mike's house.

John, Petra and Peter in London. (*Mary Anne Fitzgerald*)

Tara and Peter in London. (*Mary Anne Fitzgerald*)

Peter with an English bull – sadly not Fiston. (*Mary Anne Fitzgerald*)

Paul, M. A. and Mereso on the morning Peter and M. A. left the *boma* for their long walk through Maasai country.

like a true Englishman. The change overtaking him was as subtle as a faint blush but definitely there.

He phoned from a callbox in the underground that evening. 'What shall I bring home? Would you like some wine? Some beer?' I suggested a bar of chocolate and when he got home he dropped it on the table along with the *Evening Standard*, saying, 'I thought you'd like to have a look at the news.'

I imagined him strap-hanging between Sloane Square and Chalk Farm, a newspaper slotted under the other arm. Or perhaps he unfolded it and creased it in half and held it up next to his face to read, a stance that was the acme of a commuter's indifference to the sweaty crush of the carriage.

Peter had been warmly welcomed into the travel agency. Miss Reddy always greeted him with a *jambo*, drawling the word 'like an Asian'. His colleagues were his own age and they fooled around together a lot while they were working. He blossomed. Ironically, it was the veneer of Englishness he had acquired while working there which restored his self-confidence. In fact, he was so enamoured with the travel agency that his ambition was beginning to assume yet another shape. He should definitely work in an office when he returned to Nairobi. It suited him. And the goats? Maybe not.

Two people had indicated they might be interested in taking Peter on. As farmers, they were polar opposites. Alan Mowlem was a tenant farmer in Somerset who kept goats. He and his wife lived on the smell of an oil rag and relied on visiting students to help them with their livestock. The other, Douglas Mash, was landed gentry. He ran a stud farm for Limousin cattle outside Chesham in Buckinghamshire. It was Douglas Mash who summoned Peter for his first job interview. We were expected there at 1:30 p.m.

I explained to Peter that I didn't know the countryside to the north of London and wanted to allow an extra half an hour for emergencies. In other words, for getting lost. 'We'll leave here at noon. Sharp,' I said, tapping my wrist. I don't own a watch.

A quarter of an hour before ETD Petra and I were sitting in the kitchen. Peter was upstairs. He had been busy all morning getting ready. I stepped out onto the landing and called up the stairwell, 'Nearly ready? Time to leave soon!'

No answer.

I went upstairs. His bedroom door was open. The bathroom door was closed. I knocked on it. 'Peter, we're about to leave.'

'Okay,' he called.

I frowned and pursed my lips. The Victoria Falls whoosh of water was ominous. 'Peeeeter. What are you doing in there?'

'I'm coming.'

'Peter, are you having a bath?'

There was a long pause. 'Yes. I'll be down in a minute.'

'Hurry up. I'll be waiting downstairs.' I said it slowly and deliberately.

When I get truly worked up, I move with the calm precision of a robot. My emotion concentrates in my nose, a part of the anatomy over which I have no control.

I went back down to the kitchen and sat, motionless, at the table. The minutes ticked on. I got up, put on my coat and slung my bag over my shoulder. I walked out onto the landing and stood by the telephone.

'Your nostrils are flaring,' said Petra.

Some time later she added, 'It's quarter past twelve. You're going to be really late.'

Of those of us in the house, Petra was Peter's staunchest supporter. Earlier that week she and John had waited over an hour for him in the car park at the Heath. Finally they had aborted their walk and traipsed home in the dark without him. Peter had returned soon afterwards having spent a good part of the afternoon anxiously looking about for a familiar face on the far side of Parliament Hill. He was contrite about having got confused about the rendezvous point. He expected one of Petra's bollockings. Instead she said evenly, 'I was cross when I was waiting, but I'm not cross now. Don't worry about it.'

You learn from your children. Tell the truth with a smile and no one gets upset. Putting it into practice is another matter.

A vertical crease had appeared just above the bridge of Petra's nose. That funny little frown was the giveaway that she was considering going on the boil too.

At that moment Peter came down the stairs, smelling like a beautiful-baby contest and smiling as if he didn't have a care in the world. We headed for the car. Neither of us said a word.

I got hopelessly lost between Chesham and the farm. We had spent a good twenty minutes nosing up country lanes and driving back down them again. My patience was like pond ice in a thaw. It had become dangerously thin.

I announced that we were going to be late, half an hour late in fact. Peter concurred and said this was because I didn't seem to know the way. I retorted that I had allowed time for getting lost. We were going to be late, I pointed out, because we had left the house half an hour behind schedule. We had left behind schedule, I went on, because he had been taking a bath.

'You had all morning. Why did you do it?'

He didn't answer.

It was survival behaviour. In the bush you rely on an adrenaline rush to trigger a reaction: fight or flight. For the warriors, mostly, it seemed to be fight. In bodyguard training courses you are taught three options when presented with danger. In order of preference, they are: avoid, evade, confront. Peter would have done well on the course. He had the right mental attitude. He hovered between avoid and evade.

I turned into a driveway, reversed and headed back the way we had come. 'I'm not cross with you. I merely want to understand the thinking behind taking a bath when you did. Punctuality is important in England. Don't you want this job?'

I kept looking from the road to him, but he just stared straight ahead. His face had darkened, become as impregnable as a castle keep. He had an annoying habit of pulling up the drawbridge when confrontation presented itself. I knew this and could have retreated, but I didn't. I said, 'Will you please answer me when I talk to you?' And then, 'Well, there's no point in having a monologue. You're worse than a brick wall.' His face was stony. I could discern nothing from it.

In this way we continued to stoke up each other's distress all the way to Douglas Mash's raked gravel driveway. I parked the car and we walked over to the office in silence. Mr Mash was out, coming back soon, the secretary said. Would we care to wait? Mr Mash was obviously not an exemplar of the famous British punctuality I had been lauding. Peter didn't comment on this. Neither did I.

We retired to the lawn that separated the office from the farmyard to await his arrival on the razor-sharp grass. Sitting there in the crisp sun, chatting about trivia, we could have been taken for what I wanted us to be: a responsible young man and his caring guardian. But we were both seething infernos of frustration.

The interview seemed to go well. We followed Mr Mash round the complex of barns, tractors and cattle pens and nodded as he talked. We admired the bulls staring at us with marble eyes. We fumbled for an appropriate remark as we paused to watch one of these large furry beasts having its hooves trimmed with what looked like an instrument of torture. We greeted the farm workers in blue overalls and they touched their caps with gnarled, tree-root hands. When they talked it sounded as if a ferret was scrabbling at their tonsils.

Mr Mash seemed kind enough and I felt confident he would treat Peter well although it was obvious from his *droit de seigneur* manner that Peter could not expect to be welcomed into the bosom of the Mash family. He said he needed some extra help for about a month and Peter could start as soon as he wanted to. I got the impression this was by way of a trial period which would be extended if everything went well. Peter explained he was commited to Mr Mowlem's goat farm in Somerset for the next few weeks but looked forward to coming to Chesham after that. We shook hands on it and left. I wondered how Peter would get on with the farmhands.

Most of that trip home remains blurred. I remember the anxious moments trying to find the motorway, the cars and petrol tankers and refrigeration trucks plaiting in and out of the fast and slow lanes. I have fixed in my mind Peter's unforgiving profile hovering on the periphery of my vision: the sullen jut of the chin, the hooded eyelids. And strangely I can still recall exactly where we were on the M1 when he chose to break his sulky silence.

He drew himself up and inclined his shoulders in my direction.

At that instant his thoughts snapped into focus just as surely as if someone had fiddled with the lens.

'A woman does not talk to a warrior like that.'

I like to think I can be remarkably patient about many things, but I have no time for arrogance.

'Warrior? You're not a warrior. You're my son. If Tara or Petra had done what you did this morning, they would have expected to get a piece of my mind. And quite right too. How the hell do you . . . ?' Suddenly something inside me did a U-turn. My tone became plaintive. 'I just don't know what to do with you. We have two choices here. Either you're a warrior and I treat you like someone very special. Very *different* from the rest of us. Or you're my son and I treat you like Tara and Petra. Like one of the family. Which is it to be? Maasai warrior? Or the Fitzgerald family?'

I had to stop talking at that point. I was crying.

There was a small noise. Peter had taken out a handkerchief and was dabbing at his eye. He looked like a Jane Austen heroine. He handed me the handkerchief. 'I'm sorry, M. A. I love you.'

'Me too,' I said and cried some more.

We had just tumbled through some sort of emotional vortex which was freighted with love, self-awareness, cultural identity and a lot more besides. In our different ways, we were as stubborn as each other. I was pretty sure that at times like this I annoyed Peter as much as he annoyed me. Yet beneath our frustration coursed an indefinable love. I didn't fully understand it, but it had prevented our clashes from becoming deadly. So far. What I did know was that we had emerged, scathed but intact. I put a hand on his shoulder. It was all I could do in that traffic.

CHAPTER 17

Peter had longed for me to summon him to England in the years that followed our precipitous departure. He was too young to accept that life's vicissitudes are impartial and could find no reasonable explanation for why he had lost yet another mum. He was bereft. But here in London he had a mother, two sisters and a brother figure in John. He was awash with family. So he didn't think he should voice aloud what he was feeling. He was homesick for Kenya.

I understood that.

I too occasionally felt a bit alone and in need of a hug. I tried not to think about it because if I did, I would have had to concede that life was getting on top of me. I worked from the moment I got up in the morning to the time I put my head back on the pillow eighteen hours later. Carving a niche for myself in domestic journalism as opposed to foreign reporting was a slog. Still, freelancing had its consolations. There was no risk of being fired.

One of the Sunday magazine editors had made a remark to me which bore a defining clarity. 'From Monday to Friday all people are concerned about is survival and not falling through cracks. So on the weekends they want to read about the rich and famous who have escaped the treadmill they're on. Or about people whose lives are so goddamned awful it makes their own position suddenly look quite attractive. Either way, it gives them hope.'

The rich and famous were guarded by public relations consultants who had the mores of a bear trap. So I sought out the less fortunate. I made unctuous overtures to the lawyer of a woman who had been convicted for murdering her husband, to the guardian of small children who had watched daddy hack mummy to death with an axe. My job was to persuade them to share their horrific tragedies with the entire nation. It was to be expected that they didn't always fall in with such a prurient proposal. I hated imposing on their private anguish. Often enough I was bombarded over the phone by an angry diatribe on my integrity or, worse, had to fend off hysterical sobbing. You needed armour plating over your heart not to be touched by it.

From the time Tara was six and Petra was three, I had raised the children as a single parent. My thirties had been hard going but I still had the resilience of youth. By the time I reached my early forties and had no home and little money, I had accepted what was a tough situation on the assumption that it would improve. Now, as I rose towards the fifties, I was beginning to wonder if there was a cosmic joke at play. With the children grown-up and nearly off my hands, responsibility should have diminished. Life was supposed to get easier. Instead there was some sort of inverse exponential at work which took no account of the stress of the material in relation to the weight-bearing load. I never did understand physics.

These goblin thoughts tended to take the stage in the intervening hours between midnight and that predawn instant when the sky shifts and becomes something other than blackness. They pranced across the soundscape of distant trucks, the gurgling juices of the plumbing, the primitive tick of the clock, with delinquent disregard for the reality of what had happened during the day.

In the time I had spent with the Maasai and Samburu I had acquired an ability to encapsulate the moment and take what it offered. The past is irredeemable and the future is fraught with uncertainty. The present should be honoured. This is how animals live. In one dimension.

Thus it was easy to succumb to the pleasure of listening to the clarinet hoot of the owl that lived in the Belsize woods. I got up, barefoot and naked, walked through the open sliding-glass door and squatted by a tub of South American grasses. The winter winds had dried the papery fronds. They rustled in the breeze, softly strumming my cheek. I looked up at the sky and imagined it stretching seamlessly across Europe, over the Mediterranean and the Sahara and on down to Kenya. While I gazed up at the murky darkness I peed into an empty flower pot. My outdoor latrine. Old habits die hard.

I made my way back to the bedroom and, still naked, lay down on the bed. As I did so, a pain the size and shape of a knitting needle jabbed through my chest. Rubbing it wouldn't make it go away. It was the sort of pain that makes you wish you didn't sleep alone in case you needed someone to remind you to wake up in the morning. I stared at the ceiling and wondered if I was going to die.

The seepage of the rose-tinted dream we subscribe to in our twenties was predictable, I suppose. All the same, it unsettled me. Recently I had been climbing the stairs rather than bounding up them. In the mornings there was a baby python coiled about my head. I had never suffered from migraines before. I wasn't ancient, but then again, I wasn't getting younger. In the old days, when a Maasai became an insupportable burden to the family group, he would be carried outside the *boma* in the evening and laid down in the dirt. By the next morning the hyenas would have eaten him. The Dutch aren't the first to practise euthanasia. Hyenas are quick and thorough.

Owing to a legless girl who had no feel for deadlines, I knew that I was in for a difficult day. The story had been approved by the editor. But we had come to an impasse over the photo. The editor wanted a picture of her ready to rave, her false legs tucked into a pair of platform shoes. The girl was not happy about this. She said her stumps hurt. There had been numerous phone calls: broadsides about my insensitivity from the mother, lachrymose protest from the girl. I listened, said I understood (which I did, for goodness' sake), wheedled and got nowhere. Today we were down to the line. No photo, no story. I wasn't looking forward to the phone calls that had to be made.

When I came down to breakfast, I found Peter was sitting on the couch. He was wearing Joseph's anorak despite the sunshine. He looked intent, compact as granite. I knew there was something on his mind even before he said, 'M. A., can I talk to you?'

It was perhaps a measure of my apprehension that the python stirred and shifted, its coils contracting around my eye sockets and making my head pulse. I put down the teapot and sank into the couch.

'Sure. What is it?'

'First I would like to thank you for everything you have done for me. I know how busy you are but you still find the time to care for me and to feed me and to talk to me about my life. You have been showing me how things are done the English way and I have learned a lot.'

'Thank you. That's very nice of you to say that.'

'M. A., I know that you are very poor. I know that you work very hard. But I am wondering.'

'You're wondering?'

'I know that you will give me money to buy my goats . . .'

The goat project was becoming an obsession. I steamrollered right over it. 'Peter, I haven't *got* money to give you. I *will* help you with the goats. I want you to have a head start in life. I just don't know how or when I can do it. Meantime you must pull your weight and show that you're capable of running a goat farm. You've got to take that on board.'

'. . . I was wondering what I can do for you. I'm not educated but I have understanding.'

Insomnia disorients you. I uttered some platitude about wanting him to develop his potential, adding, 'That's reward enough.'

'No one asks what you want,' Peter continued. 'Sometimes you are sad and shed tears and you need not just a handkerchief. You need someone to put an arm around you.'

'Oh, Peter.'

'You are my mum and I am your son. I will always look after you. When I go back to Kenya, you will come too, and I will make a home for you. Even if it is just a Maasai mud house or one of tin sheets. I will put a mattress under the bed so that you can drop in without notice and will have a place to sleep.'

'Oh, Peter,' I said again.

We profess to be civilized in the West, making much of ambition and output. Yet these are flimsy values in the face of the family matrix. My son was seizing the power, albeit tentatively, and nudging the centre of gravity in the direction of the next generation. Wasn't that what I was longing for? I had to admit it was.

That hug I had been whinging about was interrupted by the telephone's exuberant ring. Peter stood up and went out onto the landing to answer it.

The conversation was brief. He was back in less than a minute. 'It was a lady,' he announced. 'She said she won't do it.'

My head began to throb again.

'Damnit.'

'What?'

'I don't want to be a journalist. I want to go and live in a tin house with your goats. Will you look after me? I can't rely on Tara or Petra. They'll throw me to the hyenas when I get old and sick.' I said it affectionately, to make it light-hearted, but I was probing.

He gave me a tentative smile. 'When I am rich, I will.'

A few days after that, Peter started work at the Mowlems' goat farm in Somerset, but my financial salvation was not imminent. His salary was £25 a week.

It was a grand exodus. Petra and John returned to Liverpool and university the same day. We heaved their rucksacks, Kikuyu baskets and boxes into the car and I drove them to Euston Station. In the underground car park, after we had unloaded all the clobber, they told me firmly they would carry it themselves. I was to stay in the car. I cry when I say goodbye to my children.

We hugged before they hefted their rucksacks onto their backs. 'Goodbye. Ring when you get there,' I said briskly.

I watched them heading for the stairs. Their stride was slow beneath the weight of the baggage and their boots clumped. They looked so good. John the grungey Che Guevara and Petra the *manyanga*. She turned and lifted her arm in a salute. 'Love you!'

'We both love you, M. A.!'

I squeezed out a smile, gave a small wave and reached for the Kleenex.

By contrast, Peter had only a small duffel bag when I dropped him at the underground some hours later. I had booked him on a bus leaving from the Hammersmith coach station. Mr Mowlem would be at Taunton to meet him. I pulled up opposite the underground entrance as the traffic light turned green. Peter got out quickly, started to walk off and came back again. He put his head through the window and kissed me twice.

'Travel well and good luck,' I told him. He was about to say something in reply, but a car honked impatiently behind us and he ran across the road. He'll be fine, I thought to myself. Then I suddenly remembered something.

'Peter!' I shouted. 'I don't have your phone number!'

'I'll ring from the station!' he called back across the traffic.

I was engrossed in work when the call came. He was on a pay phone, he said, and he had missed the bus. It was unclear whether he had arrived too late, should have prepaid the ticket, confirmed, reconfirmed or whether he had been pushed off because the bus was overbooked. He said he had rung the Mowlems' house twice but got the answering machine both times. Peter only speaks to living people. 'You ring them, M. A. The number is oh, wan, too . . .' There was a click followed by a purring noise.

Peter didn't ring again. And the Mowlems' number was ex-directory.

That night I went out to dinner. I left a message for Peter on the answering machine. No one called.

The next morning I woke to splashes of sunlight on the duvet. It was a wonderful day. Then I remembered and my stomach turned. Where on earth was he?

I began to ring around Somerset asking total strangers if they knew Alan Mowlem. If not (which was always the reply), could they please give me the name and number of a friend or neighbour so I could ring and ask the same question. And while I was doing this, I thought of Nnee sitting in her dark hut and announcing she was entrusting Peter to me. In my mind's eye I saw mother and son talking together in low, intimate tones across the guttering fire as they always did before going to sleep. Nnee had placed her faith in me – in a way, she'd had no option – and now I had lost her son. The thought compounded my anxiety. I had to find Peter.

The detective work paid off at lunchtime. Alan Mowlem's wife Leslie answered the phone and passed it to Peter. He said he hadn't rung last night because they had got in late from Taunton and he had been busy all morning feeding the goats.

He was jaunty and full of chat. 'I had a wonderful, wonderful evening. I had so many questions. Mr Mowlem answered them all although he was tired. He is just like Mike and I am a part of the house. Now I see that one of the best things I needed was to come down here and do practical work and seek knowledge. I'm having fun.'

CHAPTER 18

Peter's enthusiasm continued for over a week. He told me on the phone that he started work at six in the morning and stopped at six at night. He had learned to drive a small tractor called a Bobcat and helped dehorn the kids with 'fire'.

'It's very hard. You have to be really fit and strong to do this type of work. Generally I'm very strong and getting used to it. The issue is to have the mental power to understand what you are doing. The way the goats are here, this is really what I need to do.'

'I bet they're very pleased with you,' I said.

'Oh yes, they really love me.'

Unlike the Fitzgeralds, the Mowlem family ate as soon as they knocked off work. It was good solid fare. Peter was intrigued. 'Yesterday I had chips and chicken and then a cake and a cup of tea for finishing. I couldn't understand when I came to your house why we had salad and apple pie and why we needed all these different foods. Now I understand this is a typical very heavy English dinner.'

He was impressed by his bedroom and described in detail the mirrors on the wall, the chest of drawers, the spring mattress and the 'perfectly clean' duvet. 'I feel like a little tourist in an English good hotel. I feel like a little king, probably like a little John Major at the moment.'

We talked regularly. Peter turned high-tech, calling on a mobile from the goat pens. 'Please keep receiving. It's a line programme full of fun and voyages,' he bubbled into the mouthpiece. 'This is mighty England, a beautiful country with a lot to admire and learn and a lot to miss when I go back home.'

Things were on track. Thank goodness. I began to pay more attention to my own life: seeing friends, learning to rollerblade, going to the movies. I relaxed.

The Mowlems were warm and gentle, good solid English folk, but they liked their privacy. Peter was given his own sitting room in which to spend the evenings. It had a television, but he wanted to watch the programmes the Mowlems were watching. On their television. With them. The sitting room was cold, 'like a box', and he didn't like staying there on his own. 'It was a question of loneliness.'

This all came tumbling out over the phone one Thursday night. I had planned to spend the weekend with friends in Shropshire. It wasn't often I got out of town and I was looking forward to it. Yet Peter was miserable. He needed a bit of cherishing.

I rang my friends to explain why I had to cancel at the last minute, then made another call to Jonathon, a friend whom I suspected would be at a loose end. It was beautiful weather, would he like to go down to Somerset tomorrow to visit Peter? He thought that was a great idea.

When I woke up on Saturday a regatta of linen-white clouds was sailing past the church spires. In between, the sky was blue and strong. If the weather held, it promised to be the sort of day that decanted half of London onto the roads.

The flow of traffic along the motorways was lethargic. Long lines of cars moved over the gleaming black tarmac, pulling out to pass trucks and caravans and falling back into the same lane as if they were ribbons being wafted in the spring breeze. The day-trippers travelled with bare arms resting on wound-down windows and their radios broadcasting reggae and Mozart to the farthest fields. We should have known the drive to Nether Stowey would take much longer than usual. By the time we spotted the farm's weathered stone walls at the junction of two slender lanes it was nearly afternoon.

We pulled up in the courtyard and parked. The house adjoined a row of buildings which contained an office and work sheds. More sheds and an open barn stacked with the remnants of the winter's hay lined two other sides of the yard. A dog with a long silky coat basked in the sun by the kitchen door. It thumped its tail once at our approach and fixed us with coal-black eyes.

I was about to knock on the door when it gave way beneath my fist to reveal Alan Mowlem standing in a dim stone passageway. He had an open, sincere face. 'You're here. Come in.'

We made our way through several rooms, past cat bowls, sacks of animal feed, a baby walker, farming gadgets that held no meaning for me, a random sprinkling of plastic toys. Mr Mowlem came to a halt in the kitchen. We stood for a moment in uncertain silence.

'Drink?'

I took in the unscrubbed counters littered with bowls, plates and saucepans; the linoleum floor and rickety chairs set round a wooden table that didn't match; the one small carton of apple juice on a shelf above the table.

'Thanks. Just water, please. Jonathon? Water?'

To my relief, he nodded. Everything here spoke of hard work and little money.

Mr Mowlem handed us each a glass filled from the tap at the sink. 'I've put Peter in charge of the newborn kids. It takes them a day or two to get the knack of drinking. They don't like being separated from their mothers' teats.'

There are two things I know about goats. They cause road accidents but never get hit. They destroy the grazing for cattle but never starve themselves. Over the years I had seen thousands – hundreds of thousands – of the creatures ceaselessly tearing at leaves and grass, turning Africa into a dustbowl with their industrious teeth. Anything served for a goat menu – even plastic bags and bits of paper.

Mr Mowlem mistook my smile for a shared passion. 'You've kept goats?' he inquired. 'I know something about African ones myself. I spent two weeks lecturing in Ethiopia.'

We fell easily into discussion of a country we both knew. That was a relief. I didn't want to let the side down for Peter. There was more to being an adequate mother than wearing the right hat on sports day.

'I'll take you to Peter but first I want you to meet my wife, Leslie,' Mr Mowlem announced.

We followed in his wake to where she was busy herding nannies into the milking shed. She made small chucking noises to chivvy them on as the hawthorn walking stick in her hand landed on their passing rumps with a dusty thwack. Tied to her back was the Mowlems' ten-month-old daughter Emily.

The nannies filed obediently along two walkways which ran the length of the shed. When the lead ones reached the end, they thrust their noses into a feed trough. The ones behind them followed suit. Leslie rested her walking stick against a wall and stepped down into a central bay. It was lined with electric milking machines of the type I'd told Lankisa about. They made such a racket she hadn't noticed our arrival. She was singing softly to the goats as she milked them. The baby's head dipped towards a pink and grey backside as she bent to plug udders into a milking machine with practised movements and bobbed up again as she straightened and moved on to the next nanny. Emily was grinning at us.

The warm, pungent odour of fresh dung wafted into our nostrils. I glanced at Jonathon and wondered if his thoughts were similar to mine. All living things in the milking shed radiated harmony with the universe. Peter should be happy here. It was just like a *boma*.

Mr Mowlem led us into a shed which contained a line of stalls separated from each other by a low railing. Each stall held two or three creamy white kids and a bucket of milk. Peter was in the stall at the far end. We watched as he picked up a kid, placed it in front of a bucket and patiently held its head down so that its muzzle sank into the frothy milk. It appeared to be a fine line between getting them to drink and drowning them.

Sprigs of hair stood out from Peter's head in an uncombed tangle. His trousers were badly in need of a hot iron. He looked up and greeted us with a broad grin. The kid struggled free, leapt onto a hay bale and stood there on stiff, matchstick legs.

'This one has started drinking already. That one will, too, very soon,' said Peter with pride. He gave the impression he knew exactly what he was doing. He looked happy. At ease. The homesickness seemed to have evaporated.

'Enough of that. Show your guests round the farm.' Alan Mowlem spoke slowly but without a trace of condescension. He was used to having foreign students around. 'I'll leave you to it then.'

Peter was only too happy to oblige and led us back out into the sunlight. The tour of the sheds round the yard and the two fields behind them was a strong endorsement for the versatility of goat genes. There were Angora goats with shaggy coats, white dairy goats with unblinking eyes, and meat goats which seemed to have a premonition of their destiny and retreated to the back of their pens at our approach. In a field behind the barn we admired goats grazing beneath an apple tree which Peter said belonged to a threatened species. In another field we looked at goats of a very rare breed with low-slung bodies set on stumpy legs.

Back in the farmyard he leaned over a railing and fondled a Roman-nosed billy behind the ear. 'This one is Bonzo. He's very friendly. Mr Mowlem makes cheese. And he sells the milk to a dairy. It's for people who have allergies.'

Soon after that we took our leave of the Mowlems. The farm was only a few miles from the coast. An excellent place for a picnic. Men fished from the beach. Cows stood in a meadow enclosed by a tonsure of trees. We were on a cliff sandwiched between wheat-fields and the sea. The world was cupped in an up-ended bowl of grey haze – fishermen, cows, green wheat, the slaty waves – and we were walking inside it.

Peter besieged Jonathon with questions and listened intently to his answers. It was rare for him to be silent for such long stretches. But he was in a buoyant mood. He had shed the loneliness of the evenings spent on his own at the Mowlems'. He was living in the moment.

He drank in Jonathon's rambling discourse on nuclear plants, the British defence system and why the sea is salty, as we strolled above the rocks. Sometimes he laughed and sometimes he became grave and said, 'That is very interesting.' This was man-to-man stuff. Always in search of a father figure, Peter was captivated by Jonathon's eclectic knowledge. He was a wise elder.

'We have one of the largest naval fleets in the world. The British have always been masters of the sea.'

As he said this Jonathon stepped onto the cliff face and peered over. A rock tumbled onto the beach and Peter grabbed at his shirt to pull him back. 'Be careful! You will fall!'

Jonathon made a pretence of being annoyed, taking a gentle swipe at Peter's hand. 'You're such a fusspot.' He was in his forties but had no children of his own. He was enjoying the paternal role. 'Does Kenya have a navy?'

'A dozen patrol boats. Not a lot more,' I said.

'Can't do much with that,' Jonathon harrumphed.

Peter immediately came to his country's defence and said that the Kenyan navy was large by African standards. Then he added thoughtfully, 'Every bull thinks he is the biggest.'

Maasai proverbs were Peter's way of showing that he too was wise. When we spoke of corruption in Africa he pronounced, 'If one fly falls into the bowl, all the milk is spoilt.'

Jonathon listened attentively. 'What do you think of all this travelling, Peter? England is a very long way from Kenya.'

'If there is a journey to take, always be the person travelling and not the person waiting.'

I thought of Rosina, who was that person. She'd taken a *matatu* to Mike Eldon's house to say goodbye to Peter. He'd already left for the airport and the disappointment had made her swoon. She'd fainted in the hall.

'I don't miss her,' he'd told me, picking at a flake of paint on the wall as he stood by my desk. But during his first weeks in England Peter spent hours shut in his room writing her long letters on a notepad. He gave me the bulky envelopes to stamp and asked eagerly if there was a letter from Rosina when I went through the post in the mornings. There sometimes was.

Peter had instructed her in one of these letters to go to Mike's house on a particular Sunday so that he could talk to her on the phone. It happened to be the day we visited Bill Forse's farm. But Peter didn't tell me this even though the trip had been arranged well in advance. Had he forgotten about Rosina? Maybe he thought I would be cross that our plans clashed.

He'd casually mentioned the expectant Rosina as we were finishing a lunch of roast beef. So I'd asked Bill if Peter could use his phone to ring Kenya and he'd said yes. Peter made the call from another room. He wanted to speak to Rosina in private. When he returned a few minutes later, I couldn't read the expression on his face. 'She wasn't there,' he'd said and added, 'She'd gone but she had waited.' Since then he'd spoken of her hardly at all. If I'd been Rosina, I would have found Peter's long absence hard to bear. She, however, accepted it without complaint.

Africans have great patience. It is a different sort from ours. They can happily wait for hours. For the doctor, a friend, the bus. This might have something to do with the appalling state of the infrastructure. There are comparatively few phones and they rarely work. It is the same with the public transport. The *matatus* are infrequent and always packed. During the rush hour the passengers next to the window have their noses squashed flat against the glass. So business and social life is conducted on a hit-or-miss basis, rather like miracles. If there is transport, you turn up but not necessarily on time. If there is no transport, you can't ring to apologize. You 'bounce'. No one seems to mind being stood up.

In Rosina's case there was also something else. She was deeply in love with Peter. But she came from a traditional home. She knew that it was not her place to complain. If she did, she would lose him. Rosina was Kikuyu, and I wondered if she was the right girl for Peter. Among traditional Maasai, tying the knot across tribal lines is considered daring. Mistrust lies close to the surface, particularly between the Kikuyu and Maasai, who had been fighting to the death over land.

My mind wandered to the goat-herding Nanyokie at Engaruka. She was beautiful and dutiful yet had a curiosity which opened a window onto an above-average intelligence. Peter had taken a great shine to her even though she was only eleven. Not for the first time, my thoughts turned to matchmaking. In Maasai families the parents arrange the marriages.

'I wonder what Nanyokie's doing these days? She must be about thirteen now,' I ventured.

'I don't know.' Even if Nanyokie had been literate, it would not have been the done thing for Peter to write to her.

'Well, there's one way to find out. We should go and visit her when we're both back in Kenya . . . I wonder if she's married . . . Perhaps you could put in a bid, Peter.'

Peter took this seriously. 'Mereso's a councillor. He's a very big man. He would want at least three hundred pounds for her.' Then he added, 'She may already be married.'

Jonathon looked at Peter in disbelief. 'So I can go to Kenya and buy a thirteen-year-old woman for three hundred pounds?'

'It's not buying. It's compensation,' Peter retorted.

'Compensation?'

'For the loss of a daughter.'

'Hardly PC, this bride price thing. How many children would she have by the time she's eighteen?'

'One or two.'

'Three,' I said.

Jonathon was now truly astounded. 'Woah. In England it's illegal to make love until you're sixteen. Can you get divorced?'

'There's no divorce. It's against the rules.' Peter didn't see the sense in this question. 'If you don't love her, why marry her?'

'You can fall out of love,' Jonathon replied.

'You're talking about romantic love. This is . . .' I fumbled for the right word, ' . . . pragmatic love.'

'Natural love,' Peter corrected.

We had reached a promontory on which stood a small boxlike building surrounded by barbed wire. Jonathon said it was a Ministry of Defence aircraft-spotting station. On the far side the cliffs dropped sheer to the grey rocks below. Peter walked in the direction of the station. 'I'm going to make a telephone call,' he said over his shoulder and disappeared behind a concrete wall. Ever since the episode of bungled communication at the garage in London, this was how he referred to having a pee.

I could see that Jonathon was intrigued by Peter's unquestioning embrace of Maasai customs. When Peter reappeared, he asked him, 'What's the strangest thing you've ever eaten?'

'A jam sponge roll,' I said.

Peter ignored this. Our sense of humour was often at a tangent. 'I ate *paan* once.' Indians chewed *paan* – betel leaf, lime paste and crushed areca nut. It stained their mouths red. 'It made me drunk. And another time I went to a *nyama choma* place in the Mua Hills. We had chicken cooked with beer and mayonnaise. I had ten pieces. Whoooeee. I got drunk then too. But I have never been drunk again.' He grinned.

'Have you ever killed anything?' Jonathon went on.

'Of course.'

'I've shot a lot of plains game with my seven millimetre, but I've never used a spear,' I offered. I was enjoying idly listening to the conversation from the sidelines. It was just like lying in the grass under the thorn tree at Kipenget's and allowing the Maa to wash over me. I was content with the warmth of the day and Peter's obvious enjoyment of the outing. The loneliness he had felt at the Mowlems' had evaporated. Yet I should have known that this was a momentary happiness brought on by our easy companionship under a spring sun.

CHAPTER 19

'When I first came to England I had no activity. I just stared out the window wondering what to do. Now I am so busy, I have to plan everything and there isn't enough time.'

He came into the study and dropped the mail beside the printer. Then he stood back, loose jointed, relaxed. These days he didn't clutch the desktop while he was talking. He'd shaved his head for the hot weather. The bullet crop suited him, and I'd got used to the four gold studs in his ears. When he put on the navy-blue sweater he'd acquired for a dollar at a car-boot sale, he looked like the turnkey who had smuggled my cigarettes into the cells beneath the Nairobi law courts when I was being held on charges of currency-smuggling. It was mid-May and his tenure with the goats was finished.

'I've phoned Mr Mash. He wants me to start work on Tuesday. He has a neighbour – Mr Boughton – who's offered me a bed and breakfast and a sandwich for lunch and a bicycle so that I don't have to walk to work. I know how to get there. It's the last stop on the underground and then I catch a bus.'

'Well done! Things are really moving for you.'

He grinned with infectious pride. A metamorphosis had taken place since the wintry days when he'd sat on the couch in his overcoat, looking like a homesick Michelin Man. His new self-confidence showed in his face. He was growing more and more handsome by the week.

'I'm going to make something to eat. Then I'm going to my office (his bedroom) to write crazy letters. Can I boil you some carrots?'

I declined, saying I'd come down and fix something later.

'This afternoon I'm going to get my ears pierced again. I've got the money from the salary Mr Mowlem paid me and I know where to go. It's in Camden. And I need to buy more earrings. A goat ate one.'

'Great. See you later. I'm going out, but I'll be back late afternoon.'

'What time?'

'Fourish.'

'Then I'll see you before I catch the train.'

I looked surprised.

'I want to go and see Tara this weekend.'

I couldn't suppress the smile. He was behaving like any north London boy.

Peter phoned regularly from Buckinghamshire. Whenever he called, he said in a singsong sort of way that made it sound as if he was teasing: 'Hello, M. A. This is Peter here. Are you well? And are you happy? Have you heard from Tara and Petra?' The stylized greeting was consonant with the ritual Maasai one: *Kiserian inkera? Neserian inkishu?* How are the children? How are the cattle? After that he plunged straight in with news of what was happening on the stud farm. He spoke volubly.

'I'm looking after a bull called Fiston which is going to a show in Ireland . . .'

'On a boat?'

'On a truck.'

'Scotland?'

'Yes. I think so. I'm driving a tractor, M. A. Me, Peter Lekerian. I was terrified, but I did it! They tie Fiston on a rope to the tractor and I drive him round a barn. The driving is whereby he will not be frightened to be led in the ring at the show in Scotland. I'm sorry, I'm taking a very long time to tell you everything, but so much is happening to me. England is so exciting and wonderful.'

I listened and said little, just grunted in the parlance of the *boma*, and marvelled at how articulate he had become. His English had improved in tandem with his confidence. He was changing and growing rapidly. He seemed to be much more responsible, more like an adult.

'The Boughtons are such good people. Mr Boughton is like Mike Eldon. Just like a father,' he bubbled.

The Boughtons *were* wonderful. Mrs Boughton cooked him breakfast and dinner and made him a packed lunch. The bicycle lay idle. He was driven to work. They bought him a thermos and filled it every morning so he could have hot tea on the job. It sounded like he'd landed on his feet. Peter said he wanted to pay them rent. I said that seeing him happy was probably reward enough, but it would be nice to offer anyway.

In the evenings Mr Boughton and he sat by the fire and discussed the goat project. Mr Boughton was a retired farmer who was taking an avuncular interest in Peter's ambitions. He made detailed inquiries about the stock-carrying capacity of the land at Olorgesailie. He got Peter to itemize the incidental expenses of rearing goats and figure out how much they would cost him each year. I knew that Peter still expected me to give him the capital, but he didn't refer to it much these days. I had made it clear that while I would help him as best I could as soon as I had some spare cash, it was up to him to convince an investor that the project was worth sinking capital into.

Everything seemed to be coming together for him . . . so I thought. That was before Peter said he was having strange feelings. When I asked him to elaborate, he was evasive. He began to have violent mood swings. One day he was as happy as a sandboy, the next he complained that no one loved him. It was the onset of a journey which, as it turned out, left us both increasingly befuddled at every turn. Some process had been set in motion deep inside him, but I failed to read the idiom of his distress. Our notions of mental unrest, if not the disorder itself, are shaped by our cultural background. If Peter had been back amongst the Maasai, he would have said he couldn't get what he wanted because a curse had been laid on him. May you be warmed by lying with snakes.

The phone calls accelerated frantically. Soon we were speaking for half an hour almost daily. Sometime in the second week at the farm, Peter kicked off, as usual, with how his day had been. He'd led Fiston around, washed him down, mucked out stalls. There had been a lamb to feed from a bottle and a premature calf. He said he was exhausted, but it was more than that.

'Are you feeling sad?'

'M. A. , I think I'm going a bit crazy.' His tone of voice was mutely pleading. 'I have certain feelings that I want to write in a book. They may think it's sedition, but it's not. I'll write about corruption, bribery, sport, and the issue of *matatus* whereby they are dangerous. Normal, everyday life.'

Outside in the street a man about Peter's age walked down the road on crutches. He was swinging along at a rapid pace as if he was in a marathon. As I watched, he stumbled lowering the crutches off the pavement onto the road, recovered and pegged along over the zebra crossing. What was normal, everyday life? I didn't know any more.

'Why do you want to write this book?'

The young man I'd watched growing up hadn't a single iconoclastic instinct. He craved safety and security. Yet his mother figure was known for taking swipes at the establishment as she careered towards the edge. It was a puzzling act to follow. Peter was making a statement of sorts. It wasn't just his friend Joseph who could challenge the inequities the Kenyans had to put up with. Just as I wasn't the only one who could write books which debunked the system.

'I want to tell the world about Kenya. I'll find a publisher,' he said, defiant.

'Great. Well, I look forward to reading this,' I prevaricated, endeavouring to serve up some enthusiasm.

There was a pause, then he said, 'What are your plans for the goat business?'

'It's not my goat business. It's yours. What are your plans?'

'I need money. I have no time.'

Another pause.

'I miss you, M. A.'

'I miss you too.'

If you can mark these things, I'd say that phone call was the beginning of his descent into babbling madness. Put another way, he was having difficulty making the transition from boy to man. If he had been amongst the Maasai, he would have marked this rite of passage with ritual circumcision, which was deliberately delayed until boys reached the cusp of manhood. Even more damaging to his psyche, there had been no parenting when he was a youngster in the universally traditional sense, which is every child's right.

Mebikie, who should have been his important father role model, had never taught him about responsibility and self-discipline. He was adrift, rudderless, clinging to the role of the adopted orphan. He was the special boy who deserved to be pampered. He was sulking because I refused to indulge this image he had of himself. Here in England, far removed from his culture, I felt helpless and so I floundered. Yet I drew hope from the intuitive knowledge that a deep love coursed beneath the hostility. I would never abandon him. He was angry with me because I wasn't the mother he'd needed as a small child, but I couldn't be because I hadn't been there. So I braced myself for the flak.

It arrived a day or so later in the form of a nine-page letter. I made a cup of coffee, sat down at the kitchen table and began to read. It was ranting and incoherent. He said that he loved me and that I'd shown him the light. But, he went on, he had not come over to England to learn and work. If he'd wanted to do that, he would have gone to college and done it the formal way. He wanted to know why I hadn't given him a loan because who else could give him money in England. There followed a rambling metaphor about cows which cannot give milk unless they are fed properly. He pointed out I had promised to take care of him and set him up in a farming business on his return to Kenya. As I read on, my throat constricted; my chest felt tight. His confusion roiled up from the pages. He said he deserved to live on the streets and other things which were worse. He said that God loved him and, again and again, that he loved me.

We had each dreamed what the other could be, but our images of each other were false. I didn't even feel guilty. That's how bad it was. The exclamations and capital letters and question marks seemed to change the world. But when I put the letter down and looked around and saw the plants on the tallboy and the Ethiopian plates above the stove, I realized it was only me who was different. I was panicking.

I rang Mildred in Croydon. She wouldn't know anything about Maasai warriors and circumcision, but she worked for Parentline. It was worth a try. I imagined her with rimless glasses and blue-rinsed hair, a jersey that was in the process of being knitted placed on the sofa beside her so that she could pick up the phone. Mildred was no nonsense right from the start.

She said, 'How old was he when he came to you?'

'About thirteen.'

'That's too late to close the wound of being abandoned. You can only give him love and help him as much as you can. His rage and sadness will never heal.'

She was right. Nnee, his aunt, Paul the headmaster, his aunt's husband or boyfriend or whatever he was, Gabriel, Mike, the Fitzgeralds, Mr Boughton – we had all dipped in and out of his life, slapping Band Aids on his hurts instead of cleansing them. It wasn't his fault, but he'd been spoilt. This trip to England was the first time he'd had steady exposure to the dynamics of a Western family, which included discipline as well as love and support. I prayed he'd pull through and come out on top.

Mildred's next contribution was canny. 'What's the question that's bothering you?'

That focused the mind. What *was* the question?

'I guess I'm wondering if I should give him some money when he's still so immature.'

'What would you do with your daughters?'

'Easy. Tell them no handouts.'

'Yes. That would give them strength and help them to become adults.'

'So . . .'

' . . . so do the same for Peter.'

'You mean . . . treat him like one of the family.'

'Exactly. Now get on with it.'

Family first. Culture second. It was stunning in its simplicity.

Of course, a canyon lay between realization and implementation. Peter was hard at work stoking things up. He told my friends he'd been a street boy who'd had to beg for food. He phoned Tara to complain I was patronizing towards him. Tara rang to berate me. I cut her short by slamming down the phone mid-sentence.

It rang again. 'I don't like being hung up on like that,' she said. 'Just listen to how angry you get. That's what you do to Peter. It isn't fair on him.'

'Shut up!' I shouted and hung up again.

The phone gave a prim ring. I picked up the receiver, pressed the disconnect button and left it lying on the desk. The old python shifted and coiled, squeezing my braincase. Maybe I was going mad too. I was certainly operating on a very short fuse.

It had been quite a day. First the letter then Mildred then Tara. Everything was coming unglued. That afternoon the phone rang again.

'Hello?'

'M. A.' I heard the hollow monotone and could barely breathe.

'Yes?'

'Have you received my letter?'

'Yes.' It came in a whisper.

'I apologize if I have made you unhappy.'

'Don't worry. You're the one who sounds unhappy. What is it? We must . . .'

'I want to go home. Tomorrow.'

The python wrapped its tail around my tongue, making it hard to speak. 'It's your decision, but you're running away. This is an experience you'll never be able to repeat. Think of all the things you could still do and see in England.'

'You can't stop me.'

'I won't.'

'My family misses me.'

'It may be difficult to get a seat on the plane at such short notice. I'm going up to Liverpool to see John and Petra this weekend. Why don't you come with me? They'll want to say goodbye.'

'All right. Then I'll go home.'

That Friday everyone was more relaxed. I'd apologized to Tara. She'd rung Peter and told him that if he was going back to Kenya to rile me, he was cutting off his nose to spite his face. Petra had rung to get an update and was looking forward to seeing us. Peter walked up the stairs at supper time jingling coins in his pocket and looking as if he'd won the lottery. He dropped two bars of chocolate on the table and swept me up in a bear hug. Then he seized the broom out of my hands and began to sweep. His movements were alert and vigorous.

'I can do that! This morning I washed Fiston the champion bull at the Welsh Agricultural Show. Now I can wash up the kitchen!'

Later he waylaid me in the corridor and dragged me into his bedroom.

'I know I am a boy who talks, but I'll only talk for fifteen minutes. No, five! You'll have me for five hours in the car tomorrow.'

He wanted to make a point about Richard Leakey, a white Kenyan, who had recently announced his intention of forming a new political party which cut across tribal lines. I had known him for many years and admired his courage and beliefs. But Peter was concerned. If Richard succeeded in getting Safina registered, he would stand for election in Peter's 'home area'. For Peter, this was a dubious prospect. Richard was third-generation Kenyan. I, like other whites, thought of him as a native. Not so, Peter. Richard was not of his tribe. He was an 'alien'.

'He doesn't speak Maasai,' Peter said.

'He's fluent in Swahili.'

'We need someone who will bring wells and schools.'

'Richard's brilliant at that. You couldn't have anyone better. Let's talk about it in the car tomorrow. I've got to get supper.'

I moved towards the door, but Peter blocked my way, waving his hands. He was half crouching with eyes wide and mouth shoved forward. He was very excited.

'He might be president!'

'Great. That would be the best thing that could happen to Kenya. Now, if you want to eat tonight, I've got to start cooking.'

Politics served to accentuate the gulf between us. I was motivated by things such as democracy and corruption. Peter thought in terms of dams being dug where he could water his goats, and schools being built which his younger brothers and sisters could attend. He didn't care whether the money for these things was come by honestly or otherwise. This attitude exasperated me. We had lost our Nairobi home because I had spoken out against human rights abuses. Had none of this rubbed off on him? It was not until the aftermath of our heated discussions, when I had cooled down, that I would remember that was the very reason why he chose to vote for the party in power. For him, challenging the system was synonymous with loss. And he didn't want to risk losing another home or another parent.

We set off early for Liverpool the next day because we were stopping at Sheffield on the way. I was covering a training session of amputee athletes for a magazine piece. We drew up to the stadium and parked. I'd forgotten to pack spare underpants and had rushed back into the house to get a pair. They lay on the back seat where I'd thrown them. I now dithered over whether to leave them there or to open the boot, fish out my bag, open it up and pack them inside.

'Whaddya think?' I said to Peter. 'It doesn't look good to have your underwear lying around.'

He shrugged. 'Most people wear their pants under their clothes, but some people carry them.'

'Good point. Well, I'm wearing some already and I don't want to carry them so they'd better go into my suitcase.' Things weren't too bad if we could still discuss my underwear like this.

Down on the track the athletes were priming their muscles for the day's training session. The coaches watched approvingly and hunched into the sharp gusts that marked the advent of northern summers.

Robbie Barrett was doing a few silken warm-up circuits. He was a Paralympic gold medallist whose leg had been amputated below the knee. I introduced him to Peter and explained where Peter came from. Robbie immediately challenged him to a race. Peter grinned happily. This was the sort of action he understood. He took off his shoes and socks and lined up next to Robbie. He looked confident. It would be easy enough to beat a one-legged man.

Ready, steady, go! Robbie's legs pumped up and down like pistons. He left Peter trailing yards behind. It was decided to do the race again now that Peter had got the measure of Robbie's pace. But Robbie still beat him.

Peter fared better with the javelin thrower. Like Robbie, she was a champion in her sport. She was about Peter's age, had long blonde hair and high cheekbones. I could see the two of them deep in conversation on the far side of the stadium. When he came back, Peter explained he had shown her how to hold the javelin and throw it like a spear. He said she would be able to throw longer distances the new way. Later, the girl invited him to go and have something to eat. Peter said goodbye and hugged me twice, great all-embracing bear hugs.

'That's enough. You'll be back in two hours,' I chided. I had braced myself for a difficult weekend, but he didn't seem to have a care in the world.

I watched the two of them as they disappeared round the corner of the stands, walking close together and chatting easily. Tears came to my eyes. I loved him and hated to see him suffer. 'He's so innocent,' I muttered.

Robbie overheard me. 'No, African. He's natural. He comes from a place where you talk to people in the street and give a stranger a bed for a night.'

Things began to go downhill after that. When we were in the car Peter made it clear he was still determined to go back to Kenya. He'd said Mr Boughton was helping him to make the reservation. I knew this was true because I'd rung Mr Boughton and asked him.

Apart from anything else, I was worried about what would happen to Peter when he got home. He wouldn't be able to live with Mike on a permanent basis as Mike had remarried earlier in the year and was moving house. He didn't have a job to go to either. His salary at the Ostrich Park hadn't been enough to survive on anyway. And although he was being paid well enough on the farm in Buckinghamshire, he didn't seem to have managed to save anything. I'd already tried to find out where all the money had gone, but he'd staunchly refused to discuss it.

I tackled these subjects again as I drove. 'What are you going to do for work?'

'I will find a job.'

'And where are you going to live?'

'I can stay with Joseph.'

'But you haven't got any money. What are you going to live on?' Silence.

I asked a lot more questions, none of which he replied to. His face was like a stone. This aggravated me so much that I pulled onto the side of the road and braked. 'Talk to me!' Silence. I

shrugged and pulled back onto the road. 'All right, it's your life.'
Peter's response was to pull his coat up over his head, as if he was
on a mortuary slab. He stayed like that all the way through the
Pennines to Liverpool.

Things didn't improve once we got to Petra's digs. He shut himself
in one of the bedrooms and refused to come down to eat. After an
hour or so, Petra said, 'I'll go and talk to him. Poor Peter, he must
be feeling miserable.' She came back half an hour later, looking
bemused. 'He's really upset. He says he's not being treated like a
man. I tried to get it out of him, but . . .' She looked at me helplessly.
'M. A., he was frothing at the mouth.'

That Sunday we went for a walk in the cathedral gardens. They
were sunk below the level of the street and filled with gloomy trees
and mildewed gravestones listing at an angle. The Gothic feel of
the place expressed our own sombre mood. Peter's sulk had infected
what should have been a happy weekend. Everyone was on edge.

John let off steam by scaling a smooth wall which soared up to
the street above. The stones had few handholds but John was like
Spiderman. Rock-climbing was his sport. Peter watched, hesitated,
then launched himself at the dank stones. There had always been
an unarticulated energy flowing between the two of them. If they'd
been antelope, they would have ended up battling it out with locked
horns for dominant male. Peter climbed up, moving slowly as he
fumbled for footholds. When he'd gone about twenty feet, he got
stuck. He was spreadeagled against the wall like a squashed fly, not
knowing where to move next. I hovered below, watching anxiously.
When he looked down, Petra and I could see his flushed face and
pressed lips.

Petra said, 'He's not going to fall.'

'He might. He'll hurt himself.'

'No, he won't. Stop fussing . . . You really love him, don't you?'

'Yeah. I do.'

If Peter had heard me, he paid no attention. He began to inch
slowly upwards again.

'Look,' said Petra. He'd scrabbled over the top and was standing
next to John.

The drive back to London took an eternity. I'd decided I'd let

Peter be until he was ready to talk. The result was we didn't exchange a word. It was like being in a thunderstorm before the rain.

It was late by the time we got home. We'd eaten *en route* in studied silence. Peter went straight to his room while I went into the kitchen and switched the kettle on. A few minutes later I heard him clomping down the stairs and put my head round the door to see if he wanted a cup of tea. For a moment I didn't really take in what was happening. He was standing on the landing with his coat on, holding a duffel bag in one gloved hand. Despite the bullet haircut and the deliberate way he dropped the house keys at my feet, there was an air of wildness about him. It was his anger.

'I'm going back to Chesham to say goodbye then I'm taking a plane to Kenya. I'm not coming back. I'll sleep on the streets until I leave. I've done it before.'

Until then I'd been trying to gauge what I said, weighing my emotions and words. Now it was gut stuff, erupting from somewhere deep inside. Peter had lost his Maasai family. Now he was doing his best to lose his mzungu one. Perhaps he thought he didn't deserve to be loved and was running away before we pushed him out. Well, he wasn't going to get rid of us that easily. Like it or not, we were there to stay. 'How dare you walk out on your family! All the people who love you. Petra, Tara, me. You're going to leave us without even saying goodbye? How dare you!'

He ignored my outburst and brushed past onto the stairs, where he hesitated, then swivelled round to stare up at me. Everything about him seemed to have swelled: the muscles at his neck, his bulging eyes and bunched lips. He raised a finger and shook it at me.

'I'll call a press conference! I'll tell them how you treated me!'

'Don't be stupid. Who the hell cares how I treat you, except the family!'

He ignored this and turned away. His shoes thudded on the carpet as he descended the stairwell. The front door clicked shut, and the walls shuddered and sighed. I was transfixed by the fugitive sounds of his departure.

CHAPTER 20

Peter didn't go home, and he didn't live on the street. He just kept right on washing Fiston the bull and leading him round the barn at the end of a tractor. I knew this even as he was marching through the darkness to the underground with his duffel bag slung over his shoulder because the moment after the front door slammed shut, something occurred to me.

As soon as he'd gone, I dashed upstairs to his room, which was in its customary mild disarray. I could see his sturdy blue suitcase – it had belonged to my mother – shoved under the table. The Mills and Boon paperbacks – his literature – were stacked on the shelf on top of a sheaf of pamphlets of the type that are handed out in the street to passers-by. I walked over to the cupboard and opened it. There was his navy-blue jacket on a wire coat hanger. You don't catch a plane without your luggage.

In the following days there were many evening phone calls to the Boughtons' house from either Tara, Petra or me and sometimes all three of us in quick succession. Peter's *mzungu* family acted as a control tower. By the end of the week, he rang up to say he was coming home for the weekend. He was breezy, cheerful. 'I'm fine. Are you all right? Are you happy?' I said yes, I was, but I thought, *I'm wrung out. Not even fit for goat fodder.* The way he talked, you would have thought that nothing had happened.

Peter. Sometimes I liked him. Sometimes I wished he would dematerialize. Yet all the while we were weathering the spectrum of his emotions – the storm-cloud brooding, the thunderclap explosions, the catharsis followed by sunshine – I was aware that I loved him. Like my daughters, he was well and truly planted in my heart. I think he realized this too after my protest on the stairs that he couldn't walk out on his family. The spontaneity of that outburst had registered with both of us.

He didn't arrive until late Friday evening. It was about eleven o'clock, and I'd already packed it in for the day. He came into the bedroom with two mugs of tea, put mine down next to the alarm clock and sat nursing his at the end of the bed. He seemed relaxed and we were gentle with each other.

'What took you so long?'

'I missed the bus and I had to wait for nearly two hours before someone gave me a lift to the station. I've been working so hard on top of the silage. I've been putting old tyres on top of the PVC to keep it in place. The silage pile is so big. *Whoooeee.*' He swivelled his eyes to the spires outside the window, black silhouettes against a dark sky. 'It's as big as this church. I can even walk on it, sliding.'

'I haven't fixed supper for you. Sorry, I wasn't feeling so good today so I went to bed early.'

'I'll get something from the kitchen. Have you got an aspirin? I like the work, but it's given me a headache.'

'Nope. Not a one.' I gave an apologetic shrug.

'I'll get one from the *duka*. The Indians will have some.'

'It's nearly midnight. They're shut.'

'I'll knock on the door and ask them to give me some.' That was the Maasai way.

'This isn't Ol Tepesi. People here don't open up shop in the middle of the night. You'll just have to sleep it off.'

He leaned forward, a hand placed on the bed, his voice soft, conspiratorial. 'I have been thinking of my aunt Naserian and how she looked after me when I was a small boy at Naivasha. You have protected me like she did. When I go home, I will buy a mattress and keep it under my bed so that you can always sleep at my house. You are my mother, not an honourable member of parliament. You don't have to tell me you are coming.'

'Peter, why didn't you ever ever mention Nnee in your letters? You never said you'd found your real mother.'

He gave my feet a contrite look.

'Why?'

'You are my mother too, M. A. When you left your house I rode on Tara's bicycle and thought of you so much I fell into a puddle. Whenever I passed Kipenget's house in the *matatu* I thought of you and cried.'

203

'You never cry.'

'I cried in my heart.'

The night at the curtainless windows kept the rest of the world at bay. We were contained within the puddle of light thrown out by the bedside lamp. The room was warm and cosy, given to secrets.

'Before I came here, I had time with my mum and I told her I want to know who my father is. She was angry, but I made her tell me.' He paused, then expelled his breath in a short gasp and his eyes fluttered upwards. 'I have been with him.'

'You've met your real father?'

'Yes, yes.' His face burned with intensity. 'This man came to our home. He was very good to me. We were just talking nicely. When I knew he was my original father, he said he will give me a present.' He gave a short gasp of pleasure and said, 'A cow.'

I was filled with curiosity. 'So what's he like?'

'Very intelligent. Handsome. Very relaxed. He's my father's age-mate. He has sons my age. We used to play football together. What I like about him is that he can tear off his ears like this.' He slid his hands down the side of his head and made a motion as if to throw something onto the floor. 'He can be really crazy.'

'You like that?' He looked as if he was about to laugh but it petered out into a *huuh*. His voice became low and hesitant. 'No. I am really ashamed to know this man is my father.'

An image flashed through my mind: a dappled clearing deep in the forest where tribesmen dressed in leaf skirts are placing confessional offerings at the feet of a grizzled man sitting on a stool. Like some headhunter I was accruing the family's skulls and I didn't know what to do with them. It was an unsettling feeling.

I tried to reassure him. 'Lots of boys and girls have different fathers, don't they? He's your father's age set so that makes it quite socially acceptable.'

'Yeah, they do. Still, I would think that I am different because I am not tall like my brothers. My father is tall but my mother is short.' I didn't know if he was referring to Mebikie or his real father but nodded. 'My brothers don't have my bravery at all,' Peter continued, as if he was confronting some internal tribunal. He shrugged. 'On the other hand, I lead my own life.' As usual when he talked about his background, I was left with the feeling of not fully understanding what he was telling me. No wonder he was undergoing an identity crisis.

He suddenly switched tack. 'What will you say if I ask you something funny?'

'Tell me. I'm listening.'

'M. A., will you give me permission to marry?'

I hadn't been expecting that.

'Rosina?'

'Noooo, I am reading a book written by a Maasai that talks about the different clans. It is very interesting. But I don't want to marry a Maasai girl. That's too local. Too tribal. Maasai girls are dull.' He was articulating his thoughts carefully, addressing them to the lump my feet made under the duvet. 'I want a university dropout who can teach me. Who will be able to join our family. Rosina's English is not good. She is not a very educated girl.'

Poor Rosina. I thought of her fainting in the hallway at Mike's house when she'd gone to say goodbye to Peter. Peter had a point, but oh how pragmatic he was being.

'Well, if that's what you want.'

'Do you approve of a university dropout? I wouldn't want to do anything that would make you unhappy.'

'I approve of you making a sensible choice. Marrying a good woman who will make you happy. Does Rosina know how you feel? It will be hard for her. She loves you very much.'

'Nooooo.' He was pensive.

If Peter had been talking to Petra, at that point she would have told him to get on the case and let Rosina know what was going down. I should have known that he had something on his mind, but I was too tired to pick it up. I just said that I was glad we'd had such a good chat and that it was time both of us got some sleep.

Other clues slipped by me, too. He spent a lot of the next day sitting on his bed writing letters on a pad which he balanced on his lap. He could have done it at a table in the kitchen or the living room but he preferred privacy. He came down for supper, watched some TV and went back up again. When I went to bed, Peter's light still showed under the door as I walked past. I stopped and tapped on the door, 'You still up? Whadya doing in there?'

I heard him padding across the carpet in his socks before he opened it a crack. 'Writing letters.'

'Well, sleep well.'

The next morning, when I came in from tennis, he handed me the fruit of his labour and asked if I wouldn't mind posting it. It was a thickish manila envelope for a Mr and Mrs Wagaki in Nairobi. Peter caught me glancing at the address. He asked if I knew them and, when I said I didn't, launched unsolicited into a potted biography of his new friends. Mrs Wagaki worked for an insurance company on the floor above my old office in the Press Centre. He was surprised we had never met on the stairs or in the lift. We could have got to know each other. She was a very nice lady – so nice, M. A. – and about my age. The sort of woman who made a good mother. Mrs Wagaki and her husband were the only Kikuyu couple to live in Kisamis. This was very brave of them because the Maasai don't like the Kikuyu. What's more, they were very active in the church and had helped to organize a wedding he'd gone to just before he came to London. They lived in a house with a tin roof set back at the foot of the escarpment. Perhaps I had noticed it when I drove down to see Nnee? When I said I hadn't, he said he would take me there to meet them the next time I came to Kenya. I said they sounded like a nice couple and that they were obviously good friends judging by the weight of his letter and left it at that. I didn't give it another thought.

The subject of marriage came up again the following weekend when the whole family was gathered around the kitchen table: Tara, Petra, John, Peter, Jonathon, me. We also had two friends visiting from Kenya, Gillies and Fiammetta. The meal was finished but the wine was still flowing. We were sitting with our chairs half-pushed back, feeling mellow. Suddenly Peter stood up and gave a speech, and as he talked, his fingers resting lightly on the tablecloth, he kept on referring to himself as an elder. When he'd sat down again, Jonathon beetled his eyebrows and poked his glasses down to the end of his nose so that he could appraise Peter over the rim of the lenses. 'So you're an elder now. Down in Somerset you were a warrior.'

'I'm an elder,' said Peter.

'Get on with you, Peter. You're a bullwasher.' Playing the Maasai card didn't work with Jonathon. He was a naval man.

Gillies, who had been listening politely, changed the subject. 'How are you liking working on a stud farm and looking after a champion bull?'

'Fiston! He's a very great bull. I love him very much. When I am washing him, I say, "Fiston, you're going to a show," and he looks at me like this.' Peter's neck and cheeks swelled and he pushed air through his nostrils in a snort. He had metamorphosed into an arrogant Limousin. Fiston was so plain to see that we all laughed.

Gillies said, 'The Maasai talk to their cattle. They really notice them.'

'But never slaughter them,' added Fiammetta.

'Oh yes, we do,' said Peter. 'The Maasai don't eat food in packages from Sainsbury's. We like to slaughter because we want to know what we are eating. Like this,' and he poked his finger into my bowl of melted ice cream. Everyone laughed again, which encouraged Peter to continue. 'I went into the pub today because I wanted to make a short call but the man refused to let me. He said, "You can't come in here unless you drink our beer." But he relented. He lost because I was strong and I didn't care.'

'Tell Gillies and Fiammetta about the time you made a short call in Finchley Road,' said Petra.

Peter's eyes became very small and his mouth very big and he slammed his fist into the palm of his hand. 'My bladder was full!' he cried.

John said to me, 'Peter's always at his best when you're drunk.' I nodded. He was on a roll. There was no stopping him.

He had launched into a story about hunting lions. It was a textured riff of exposition and sound effects. 'The warriors wear jingle bells on their knees and stuff them with grass when they are tracking so they cannot make a noise. When they see the lion, they take out the grass and surround him whereby he is so frightened because of all the noise. The warriors with strong knees make a big jingle and the ones with no muscles make a weak jingle.' He rolled his eyes up into his head and thrust out his chin to the beat of his feeble trills and wild ululations.

'Jingle bells! Jingle bells! Jingle through the hay!' we chanted.

'M. A. has warrior's knees from climbing the stairs,' Peter observed. I put my foot onto the table and rolled up a trouser leg.

'See,' he cried, 'she has a muscle there, on the inside of her knee.'

Tara said, 'Tell us about Grace, Peter.'

I looked at her. 'Who's Grace?'

She was surprised, 'Don't you know? Grace Wagaki. His new girlfriend. Peter's in love.'

'Peter! You old sneak. Is this why you've been writing volumes to the Wagakis?'

'What does Grace think about it?' asked Petra.

Peter said, 'She doesn't know yet. I am courting her through her mother first. I talk to her sweetly from the phone in Mr Mash's office. Grace is very educated. She is studying art at college. I met her at a wedding in Kisamis, but I haven't really talked to her yet.'

'It would be a good start,' muttered John.

'If I marry her she can drop out of college and look after the kids on my farm.'

'She may want to get her degree before having babies,' I said.

Peter quickly corrected me. 'Not babies. Goats.'

'And what about Rosina?' Petra put in. 'Does she know about this?'

Peter slid over that one quickly. 'She's just a village girl.' He obviously hadn't given her a thought. We all looked a bit taken aback.

John was moving his cigarette pack back and forth across the table. 'When you're finished with a woman, you don't waste your time hanging around. Do you, mate?'

'Peter,' Tara began. She took a drag on her cigarette, folded her arms across her chest and cupped her elbow in her hand, then blew a jet of smoke up to the ceiling. Everyone fell quiet. Who better to put Peter straight than The Word. 'You've got to face the music and write to her. Better she knows it from you than hears it from someone else. That leaves her with her self-respect intact and gives her time to collect her feelings before you go back.'

Peter looked chastened. 'Yes, Tara,' he said, suddenly serious. 'You're right. I will write to her.'

The weeks went by and blossomed into summer. Peter learned how to swim and sat in the long grass and talked to the cows. Harvest time came and he was put to work in the fields hauling in the bales of hay. He became lean and muscled and smeared blobs of gooey white stuff onto his cheeks and forehead because he said he was sunburnt. I visited him on the farm and when I climbed out of the car, he exclaimed, 'M. A., you look so beautiful! I don't know what has happened to you. You must be happy. I'm proud to have such a mother.' I threw my head back and laughed with pleasure.

It was decided that Peter would go back to Kenya at the end of August. He was happy, but underneath he yearned to be amongst his own. I booked him a seat on Gulf Air and thought of what I could do to help with regard to the goat project. I made contact with a small aid organization which worked amongst the pastoralists who lived on semi-arid land. An appointment was made and Peter came to London. I gave him the letter they had written so that he could read it before the meeting.

While we were driving in the car to their office, I remarked, 'Nice letter, isn't it?'

Peter said, 'I haven't read it yet.'

'Well, read it before we get there so you know what they're all about.' He took it out of his blazer pocket, slowly unfolded it and stared at it as if it was a possession.

I reflected on this as we sat in a small room with Mr Wambua, another Kenyan. He was waxing lyrical about goats with high milk yields and wondrously small appetites while Peter listened with his hands wedged between his knees. I knew that he had planned to read the letter that night when he was alone, absorbing every word. For Peter, it was something to be done slowly and at leisure.

I made a few notes while Mr Wambua talked. Some of them were about goats and some a list of what I had to do. Nothing had changed in my life. That morning I had arranged for a phone line to be installed in the room Peter was about to vacate, sorted out a broken washing machine and written most of the piece the *Sunday Times* was expecting. My publisher was coming to dinner and I was wondering what to cook. I scribbled, 'Defrost Wambua.' No. Wrong. I crossed out 'Wambua' and wrote 'chicken'. Peter and I still had a lot to learn from each other.

As the departure neared, we became reminiscent, retelling the good things and beginning to feel sad that they would soon be behind us. He bade a wistful goodbye to Mr Mash and Mr Boughton and a sentimental one to Fiston and went down to stay with Tara in Brighton for a final weekend. He hugged me often and talked, apprehensively, of what he might do when he got home. 'It is time to prepare for the next journey,' he said.

Then two things happened. The first was a phone call from Mr Boughton. He said that he had planned to put a few thousand pounds into the goat project but had changed his mind.

I was astounded. Peter had never mentioned he was interested in investing. 'Why? What happened?'

'He has no money sense. He's irresponsible with finances.'

I didn't know what he was talking about, but he soon filled me in. 'He's spent nearly everything he earned. He's hardly got a bean left. Most of it on phone calls to Kenya. A hundred and fifty pounds.'

'But he should have saved such a lot. Where's it all gone?'

'I don't know. You'd better ask him.'

I was dumbfounded. That was Peter's investment for the future which he'd so blithely thrown out the window. Would he never learn?

I had planned the next thing. Peter was a hopeless spendthrift; had been ever since he was a little boy. He was incorrigible, didn't take any notice of all the advice that was given to him. As for all the times I'd urged him to live within his budget, I might as well have talked to a brick wall. He hadn't listened to me as a mother, so I decided to be a man instead.

Warriors are disciplined by *olpirron*, the firestick elders. Firesticks are fashioned from trees which grow by the riverbeds and have long, straight branches that run parallel to the ground. They are used to start fires by rubbing two of the sticks together until the friction creates a spark which falls onto a pat of dried donkey manure and sets it alight. The firestick elders are of an age set at one remove from the warriors. That makes them old enough to be wise and too young to be the warriors' fathers. This was important because fathers might be too lenient with their sons. When a warrior steps out of line, he has to face the firestick elders. They harangue him for several hours, and they impose a fine such as a cow or a sack of sugar.

I summoned Peter to my study and told him to bring a chair from the roof terrace and take a seat beside my desk. Then I started with my firestick elder harangue. I said he was a spendthrift and irresponsible and a disappointment. And when I'd finished, I said it all over again in a different way. Peter listened attentively, almost ceremoniously, his face covered with chocks of light and shade from the sun falling through the blinds. Then I asked him where all his money had gone and how he intended to support himself back in Kenya and get the goat project under way. Peter promised to look after his money from now on and vowed to make it up to me somehow and said he was sorry to have disappointed me. But he point-blank refused to expand on how he'd spent his money.

Then I harangued him a bit more for good measure and ended up by saying, 'And how can you marry Grace if you can't support her?'

He hung his head and mumbled, 'I cannot marry her.'

'No, I suppose not, at this rate.'

'I cannot marry her because I have spoken to her on the phone. She is not interested in me.'

That made me feel sorry for him so I decided to call it a day.

We stood up and Peter's eyes gleamed with admiration. He said, 'You are very smart, M. A. You know everything about me.'

When Tara and I saw him off at the airport departure gate, it was awful. He hugged me hard until my eyes misted up. Then he hugged Tara until she couldn't see too well either. And then he hugged both of us at the same time and put his head first on my shoulder and then on Tara's.

Finally, I said, 'You'd better get going or you'll miss the plane.'

He let go of us and took a step back and looked straight at me. He said, 'Come home soon. I don't want to stay with anyone else. When I am with you, I feel one hundred per cent protected. The matter of being a mother is not breastfeeding and giving food. It is one of respect and crying together when there is sadness. When I was in Liverpoool, I was tearing my clothes and did not understand this. How could I throw away Tara and Petra? When you come home it will be my time. I will take you to my family. I will give you a community. Even if I'm not there, they can't turn you away. You're my mum. You'll have roots in another place.'

Later, as we headed for the M4 in the car, Tara said, 'Look at it this way, M. A. He'll never starve. You've done all right.' That was the African way – a pragmatic recognition of victories, no matter how small. Peter had travelled and seen the world and he knew where his heart lay – amongst his own. I didn't mind that he hadn't come to grips with agricultural technology or that he would probably never be a Big Man. That was the lesson I had begun to learn. Allow your children to create their own destinies. Despite the rows and the madness, England had been a success. For all of us.

I thought it would be all right with Peter gone, but somehow it wasn't. I missed him. A few days later I was walking along the street behind a guy in cycling shorts and found myself looking at his legs. I edged up next to him and said, 'Excuse me, can I ask you what sport you do?'

He wasn't fazed by that. 'A bit of cycling. Some rollerblading.'

'I just asked because of that muscle on the inside of your knee. It makes the bells jingle when you're hunting lions. You've got a warrior's knees.'

'Yeah? Is that right?'

We walked on in silence for a bit, side by side. And when I came to my turning, I said goodbye.

'Hey,' he said, 'I'm proud to have warrior's knees.'

CHAPTER 21

The girls wore blue gingham dresses; the boys, grey shorts. The clothes ballooned around their small bodies. Hand-me-downs or bought a few sizes too big to save money. They clustered together, clasping each other's hands, the teachers' knees a tidemark for their still heads. I stood at a discreet distance, clutching my arms to me. The day was grey and drizzly. In England we would have said how warm it was. But it was cold for Nairobi. Peter had been back at the Ostrich Park for a couple of months. I had taken time off work to fly out and make sure he was properly settled back into Kenyan life.

'Ostriches lay eggs in batches of up to one hundred. But they only cover and hatch about two dozen of them. I'm going to show you how they grow inside the shell.'

Peter threw a switch, lighting bulbs inside a row of eggs. Shadows flared against the creamy white shells, growing larger and larger, like the children's eyes.

'This is the early stages of an embryo. You see how it gets bigger. The ostrich is growing inside. Here it is almost ready to be hatched.'

Peter had acknowledged my presence with a friendly nod. He presided over the kindergarten class with the authority of a man well versed in his subject, but his voice was laced with gentleness. He loved small children.

I had arrived unannounced, having first stopped to look at the two tortoises in the pen behind the ticket booth. Peter had been keeping a close watch on the eggs the female had laid ever since 'Indian boys' had stolen two. He was fascinated by the tortoises. He'd had to sit a written exam on ostrich behaviour to get promoted, but learning about tortoises was his own idea. He'd studied reference material from the zoology section of the Macmillian Library on his day off and tracked down a tortoise expert in the back rooms of the Nairobi Museum.

From there I'd walked up a shrub-lined path to the education centre. It was a large, open-sided room filled with displays of ostrich arcana. There were photographs depicting the ostrich life cycle from fuzzy chickdom to fearsome maturity. But most of the items were of an anatomical nature. Ranked along a shelf were large jars of formaldehyde in which floated oddly shaped rubbery things the colour of bruises. One was a bisected heart; another, a liver. There was also a bluish orb surrounded by what looked like cotton wool: an ostrich eye. The children had clutched at each other more firmly as they peered at it.

It was Peter's job to demystify these strange, ugly birds. Most bits of an ostrich can be used, he explained. The meat is good for your health because it is low in fat and cholesterol. It is as white as chicken meat and tastes like very good beef.

The skin – there was a bobbly hide stretched batlike against a wall – is tanned into supple leather. It is used to make handbags and belts, even shoes. The feathers – he pointed to a fluffy bunch of them tied together at the quills – are made into boas. Maasai warriors made headdresses with the plumes. I had a rather moth-eaten one at home. I was always pestering Peter to pluck some feathers for it from the ostriches' tails.

'And *now*, what would you like to see?' The children's eyes were glued to his lips. 'I am going to show you an *ostrich*.'

He walked through a door at the back of the room. The teachers chivvied the children along with little flicks of their hands against their backs.

The ostriches were kept in corrals to the left of the education centre. There were more than a dozen of them. Their names were written in yellow on green boards nailed to the fence – Greedy, Hardfoot, Dude. Appropriate appellations. Ostriches weigh 200 pounds and can kick a lion to death.

Anthropomorphizing the ostriches by giving them names may have been an attempt to make them more appealing. An uphill task. There is none of the cuddly cuteness of a panda or the awesome majesty of a tiger. They have bulging, florin-sized eyes and scaly, two-toed feet.

Peter liked the ostriches. He said their muscled necks were like pythons. They sometimes bit him hard with their beaks as he leaned against the fence, expounding on their attractions. '*Whaaa!* I nearly lost my tits!' It amused him.

Peter had created a new life for himself on his return from London, and the Ostrich Park was at its epicentre. He was back on the payroll as manager of the education centre and was responsible for showing the visitors round. He even had two assistants working under him, Irene and Patrick. He referred to them as 'my colleagues'. During the week most of the visitors were schoolchildren who arrived in large groups in buses. On the weekends the park filled up with tourists and parents with their kids in tow.

Not only was he gainfully employed, he was earning nearly $150 a month. It was far more than the large majority of Kenyan men his age were able to bring home. In fact, most of Peter's contemporaries from Oloopolos Primary hadn't even found work yet. Compared to them, Peter was doing very well.

The ostrich pens were the highlight of the tour, an occasion for audience participation. This was the moment when he produced a plate of *sukuma wiki* and handed each one of the group a single green leaf. He then urged them to hold it between thumb and forefinger and proffer it to Dude, Hardfoot and – heaven forbid – Greedy.

'Be very still. If you jerk your hand, they might bite.'

The children held the leaves above their heads, soundlessly, tentatively, and the birds slithered their beady heads over the fence. Peter called to Irene to take over and slipped away so that we could talk.

'You look settled in here.'

'Oh yes, M. A. I really love it.'

'So it's not so bad being back in Kenya? You've got a job and a place to live. You've done really well.'

'I think of you with your family apart. I'm with my mum and dad, but we struggle too.' He screwed up his mouth and looked pensive. 'You know, M. A., when you left me behind in Kenya, I was complaining that you hadn't taken me with you. But when I was in England, I was very homesick. Then when I got here, I missed you and Tara and Petra very much. I wanted to be back with you. All those things we did together. They were very interesting.

Comparisonwise, Kenya is different from England but both places are good. It is an issue of wanting to be in the place you have left.'

I smiled. 'You mean, the grass is always greener on the other side of the fence. So did you enjoy your time in England?'

'Very much. I learned a lot.' He became serious. 'I was very confused when I went to England. I thought I was going to sit there and you would give me lots of money. But no one likes to be parted from their money. Now I realize that it was good I had to work. I learned valuable things about rearing goats. Mr Mowlem was wonderful. Just like a father. And so was Mr Boughton and Mr Mash.'

So all the anguish had been worth it. The rationale behind his farm apprenticeships made sense to him at last. I thought back to how hard he'd held on to Tara and I at the airport. That young man had been bewildered and lost, afraid of the uncertainties that lay ahead. This one was in command. The change was there to see in his reserved demeanour. In front of others he greeted me with a perfunctory kiss on the cheek. He no longer needed hugs.

'Let's go down and see your family. Get into the sun. I can't stand these grey skies.'

Peter nodded, enthusiastic. 'My mum really wants to see you.'

The following week we were crawling along behind a battered old pickup filled with potatoes and cabbages beneath the knuckles of the Ngong Hills. For the Maasai, travelling between the market at Kiserian and Oldonyati on the far slopes of the hills was like moving between your apartment and the supermarket. Ordinary. But as far as I was concerned, a magical alchemy went to work as soon as the car crested the lip of the escarpment and the vast *Out of Africa* panorama of the Rift Valley snapped into view. Nairobi's crumbling streets, the shifty-eyed people and barred houses were blown away. Looking down onto the flat thorn trees and bruised volcanoes was like standing naked on a mountain with your arms lifted up to the sun. Freedom.

Peter had arranged to take his annual leave so that we could spend time together. We were on our way to his *boma*, but there was an obligatory first stop: at the home of my old Maasai friend Kipenget.

She was out. Collecting firewood. Narasha, her second eldest son after Meriape, imparted this information with a shy simpleton smile, his earth-dark eyes unclouded by ambition. He had been keeping an eye on the goats as they grazed higher up the hills and had abandoned them to come running helter-skelter down the slope when he saw the car bumping towards her house over the tussocks of grass.

Now that he was as tall as Peter, his slowness was more apparent. The other children said of the gentle Narasha, *Hana akili*. He's not so smart. He has no brains. His birth had been prefaced by a drawn-out, painful labour in a mud hut. Poor Kipenget. Traditionally, it was the sons who looked after the mother because the daughters left home when they married. Out of eight children, there were three boys but only two could be useful to her: Meriape, and Lepapa, the baby. He was still in primary school. Yet Narasha was happy enough in his circumscribed world. A boy in a man's body.

I had brought food for Kipenget and asked Peter to get it out of the back of the car. Small children materialized from nowhere – Kipenget's was the local hangout for the neighbourhood – and began ferrying the packets of tea, *posho* and sugar, the cabbages and biscuits and cooking fat to her lean-to kitchen.

As we were doing this, Peter said, 'Look who's coming.'

I turned and saw a silhouette against the horizon. His face was in shadow and I could only see the outline of his dark figure and his halting movements. I was puzzled by the sense of something different yet startlingly familiar. Then I realized. It was the limp, slight yet noticeable, like that of a man one of whose legs is an inch shorter than the other. A cloud moved overhead and the sun fell on his black bomber jacket and trousers and gumboots, his wispy moustache and lined forehead. The sudden brightness had the effect of making him look blacker than ever, naked and exposed. The children stood frozen in their tracks, clutching packets to their pigeon chests. I watched and sensed the effort of his stride as he walked down the hill. It was as if he was limping across my heart.

There was hesitation in his eyes as he stepped into my embrace. We kissed on the cheeks and he whispered into my ear, so softly it was barely audible, 'Mary Anne.'

'Isaac.'

'Yes.'

'So.'

'You have come, Mary Anne.'

'Yes.'

Peter said, 'He was let out of prison last year. In an amnesty.'

Isaac stepped back and stood by the car, supporting himself on the bonnet with one hand, like a man in shock, and stared at the ground. It is not the done thing for men to show their feelings.

I hadn't thought much about Isaac; in fact, couldn't recall a lot about him. Paul the headmaster had expelled him from school twelve years before for stealing. I remembered this because it was the day I had first met Peter. I knew that he had been imprisoned for something particularly nasty and that he had been recently orphaned. Without the dubious support of Baba Isaac, Mama Isaac had died within a week of her husband's burial. I'd given Isaac money for food, clothes, school fees, the bed which had promptly been appropriated by his father. Sometimes he'd come with us on the picnics and outings to the movies. He was the light-fingered, irresponsible boy, the one we'd said would land up in jail. Isaac was an identikit of the men we fear: the burglars who break into our houses at night. His face was tight, middle-aged, hollowed out from within by brutality and loss. I looked at his cheerless features and felt a surge of love.

'I'm going to sit down,' I announced. Tara and Petra would have recognized the thick, exuberant timbre. It was my departure voice. Women keep their emotions hidden too.

The bare patch of earth outside the shack that was Kipenget's kitchen – her living room – was untidy with the meagre rubbish of the very poor: torn snippets of cloth, dried-out corn cobs, a battered tin pot with a hole in it. Chickens pecked about our feet. A skeletal dog lay in the dirt, not even bothering to pant.

'When did you get out?'

'Last October. My parents were already dead.' His eyes misted and he bent his head to fiddle with the crude metal bracelet at his wrist. 'It was my father's.'

'I'm sorry. Hard times. Where are your three brothers?'

'At school. They stay with an uncle but I must buy their food and clothes. I'm a shepherd for a Maasai man. He pays me one thousand a month. I keep two hundred for myself.' Just over three dollars. He was so thin his trousers looked empty. I longed to squeeze a leg to see if there was a shin bone and flesh inside the folds tucked into his boots.

'Are you eating?'

'Yes. It's things going round in my head.'

'What were you in for?'

'Assault.'

'And?'

A short silence fell. I could see the lie rising in his eyes then retreating.

'It was outside a bar. An argument with another boy. I attacked a girl with a stick and cut her head. Her mother brought charges.'

'You were drunk.'

He hesitated. 'Yes. I was drunk.'

'It must have been very tough.'

'It was not too bad. There were forty in my cell. I cooked for one of the political prisoners. The warders feared him and brought him food from outside. He paid me with sodas and bread.'

I thought, *He probably ate better inside than he does now.*

'I was inside, too. Just for a bit,' I said.

Isaac lunged forward and shook his finger at me. His eyes were gleaming with excitement. 'That's when they called you Mother of Two!'

'What?'

'The newspapers. They called you Mary Anne Fitzgerald, Mother of Two Girls. *Mama ya wasijana wawili!*'

I roared with laughter and Narasha laughed too, glad to see that everyone was happy again.

At that moment one of the children began to do an impatient little jig in the dust to get our attention. 'Kipenget! Kipenget! She's coming!'

I drove the car back onto the road and got out to meet her. She was bent double by the three-foot branch strapped to her back. She stopped and eased it onto the ground, the weight of it pulling her backwards as she did so. We kissed twice on the lips. Then her face crumpled and she turned and pressed it against the side of the car. She made no effort to contain her sobs and they burst wetly through her nose and her mouth.

I was there when her husband Kili had been so drunk he'd slashed her skull wide open with a *panga* and she'd had to be taken to the Kenyatta Hospital. I had retrieved her from the verge of despair when she'd buried her savings in the earthen floor of the hut and Kili had beaten their daughter Segenun to make her tell him where it was hidden. I'd heard her complain about her back aching from carrying firewood and water every day. Meriape had related how she'd run through the night, yelling like a banshee to chase away thieves who'd thrown a rock through the wooden shutters of the house. I'd seen the desperation in her eyes when the cows died in the drought. But I had never seen her with tears on her face. My heart sank.

'What is it? What is it?' I wanted to hug Kipenget but couldn't because her body was glued to the hot metal of the car door like a child burying itself in its mother's skirts. So instead I stroked her back. 'Is it Segenun?' I knew she was pregnant. Perhaps something had gone wrong. The baby was in danger.

'*Hakuna. Hakuna.*' Nothing.

And then I realized. It was everything. The whole damn shitload of life had got to her. We soldier on through adversity heroically until someone is nice to us. Then we fall apart at the seams. Men don't realize that what women want is to be both triumphant and coddled. I'd been there. And not just the day Peter hugged me in the living room in London.

I heaved the log into the back of the car, eased behind the steering wheel and opened the passenger door. 'Let's go home,' I said, and as she sank into the seat with a sigh, 'It's okay. I'm here now.'

Kipenget was adamant I wasn't going to carry the firewood. She dragged it out of the car and held it under her arm in a clumsy fashion. The leather straps were dragging in the grass. Peter and Isaac were sitting on stools, leaning their backs against the kitchen wall. When they saw Kipenget staggering towards them with the tree branch, they stood up, greeted her politely then sat down again. They made no effort to help. Firewood is women's work.

We all had a mug of tea after that and Kipenget pulled out a survey map of the area to bemoan how Kili had sold off a parcel of land and they had been cheated in the demarcation. I knew that would liven her up. She bent over the map and stabbed at it with her finger, exclaiming volubly in Maa for the benefit of Peter and Isaac. The paper was so worn at the folds it was about to fall apart. Kipenget was having trouble locating her plot.

'You've got it upside down,' I said but no one was listening.

'I've got fifty acres but I wouldn't live there,' said Isaac. 'It's terrible land. No good for grazing. Anyway, there's too much fighting. The other clan is very aggressive. The other day they attacked a settlement and killed three people with arrows.'

'Where is it?'

'Next to Peter's land.'

Peter had been full of gossip about the clan wars. It was almost the first thing he'd mentioned when I arrived. But he'd never told me they were being waged right on his doorstep. I was interested to hear Isaac dismiss the area's ranching potential. He had unwittingly confirmed what I'd already seen for myself. Peter's land was a desert.

'Kipenget's not going to get anywhere. I've seen the demarcation for her plot down at the Lands Office,' I said.

Isaac shook his head and clicked his tongue against his teeth. 'These people are wasting their time. They're always arguing over land. They should get on and develop what they have.'

'What do you think, Peter?' I asked.

'It is an issue of inheritance laws. The allocation must be settled by a judge.'

'Maybe Peter will become a lawyer.'

'A what?'

'He's a Bintou Yookay.'

I looked puzzled.

'You know, England.'

Poor desolate Isaac. Anxiety had aged him but jail had made him wise. A charity had built him a small cinder-block house and a cement water storage tank, Isaac said. They had left the floor unfinished. It was a jagged rubble of stones and cement. The charity had told Isaac he must lay cement on the floor himself and nail gutters to the roof to catch rain for the tank. Not much chance of that. Gutters beaten out of recycled cooking-fat tins were on sale at the Kiserian market. They would have cost $15, five times his monthly food allowance. And there was certainly no way he could afford to hire a cement mixer to drive the twenty-five miles from Nairobi to do the floor.

The bare, floorless rooms were a corpse, not a home, because Isaac could not breathe life into them. So he slept in a hovel next to his employer's cows while the handout house crowned the valley like a mausoleum. And the rats that sent up motes of dust as they scurried into its cracks were the ghosts of a future as bleak as the present.

By the time we reached Kisamis the sun was at its zenith, leeching the sky to a pale transparent blue. The wooden shacks danced in the heat thrown up from the road. It had pushed the men into the tea-houses and the mongrels into needle-thin shadows beneath the eaves. I had a private agenda. I wanted to meet Mr Wagaki. He was Grace's father.

Peter didn't say as much, but seen in the cold light of Maasaini, his lovesick assault launched on Grace from England was embarrassing. He wanted to put it all behind him. 'Grace was very frightened to see me when I came back. But I just decided to be myself. Now we talk normally,' he confided.

Meanwhile a gentle revival of his romance with Rosina had taken place. At first it was lunch, followed by another. Then it was the occasional evening. Now they saw each other three or four times a week. This in itself was proof of their mutual affection. Rosina was still teaching at the Shining Falls Church Kindergarten at Ongata Rongai. On the weekends, when she was free, Peter was working at the Ostrich Park. It was difficult to find the time to be alone together.

Yet Grace remained a sticking point in their relationship and Peter wanted my advice.

'Rosina is very strong. I never want to hurt her. But she is giving me a problem over Grace.'

'In what way?'

'She nags me to tell who the other woman is.'

'You mean she doesn't know it was Grace?'

'I can't tell her. If she finds out, she will stab her. It is the Kikuyu tradition.'

I thought of the gentle, doe-eyed Rosina, who taught little children and went to church every Sunday. She could barely bring herself to say hello when we met. 'Rosina wouldn't do a thing like that.'

'She might. She gets very angry when I am late and says I have been fooling around with my friends. She's very strong.'

'You say you never want to hurt her, but that's what you're doing. Keeping Grace secret is a way of saying you don't trust her. I'd want to know too if I were in her shoes. You'd better tell her.'

He pondered this for some time, then said, 'I like Rosina a lot, but I am not ready to marry.'

Mr Wagaki's shop looked identical to the other two-room buildings except for its blue facade. It was raised off the ground and had a wooden verandah where the customers stood as they made their purchases. He sold groceries and household goods – paraffin, biscuits, cigarettes sold by the 'stick' – from behind a scuffed wooden counter protected by a grille.

I said, 'I was behind you on the road this morning. Before the escarpment. You were going very slowly.'

'So it was you! When you didn't pass, I thought it might be someone trying to hijack me.'

'A *mzungu*?'

'You never know these days. One can't be too careful.'

He had white hair and a greying moustache and was dapper and courteous; a man whose standards are immutable whatever the circumstances. Peter had introduced me by name without explaining our relationship. I got the feeling Mr Wagaki was unaware of the background which connected the two of us. Peter had surely not told him that he had been living with me in London, that it was I who had posted the heavy manila envelopes bearing the Wagakis' address. That as Grace's father, he and I might have been in-laws if Grace had so wished. This deliberate oversight on Peter's part left me thirsty for intimacy. I wanted to refer to Grace in some way to give the stamp of reality to those expensive telephone calls from Mr Mash's farm. By remaining silent, Peter was trying to banish his lovesick folly.

Mr Wagaki was very sorry, but he had run out of sugar. A pretty girl in Western clothes appeared through a door at the back next to the shelves of aspirin and powdered baby milk. She volunteered to see if one of the other shops had sugar in stock. Peter gave her a studied hello but did not introduce us.

'You must be Grace,' I said.

'Oh no,' she laughed, 'I'm her sister Mary. Grace has finished her arts course. She's working in Nairobi. Painting leopard and giraffe designs onto belt buckles and napkin rings. They're on sale at the Ostrich Park.'

While I was waiting for Mary to return, a battered white *matatu* wheezed to a halt in a plume of golden dust. Definitely not a *manyanga*. I crossed the empty road to where the driver sat with his back to me. He was unaware of my approach. I tapped him on the shoulder, and as he turned, his face lit with recognition. I leaned through the window and gave him a smack on the lips. He opened the door and unfolded himself.

'So! Meriape! *Habari ya siku nyingi?*'

Kipenget's eldest son was in his early thirties. He had thinned down, grown a goatee and pencil moustache. Che Guevara, like John. His eyes were focused, alive. He had a job driving this *matatu*, he said, resting a proprietorial hand on the bonnet. He covered the ten-mile route between Kisamis and Kiserian ten hours a day, for which he was paid 200 shillings. I made a quick calculation. He earned half Peter's salary. I asked if he was helping Kipenget with money. He nodded and I believed him.

'My father's here too,' he said.

The old man manoeuvred his way past the *matatu*'s bumper on slow, deliberate feet and teetered to a standstill an inch from my face. He poked me fondly in the chest. He looked as if he'd been drugged. The sour, rank smell of *muratina* enveloped us. If I'd lit a match, we would have ignited. 'Merianna. Merianna.' Poke. Poke. '*Mimi natoka London.*' I'm from London. He was smiling in a silly way.

'Great, Kili. Another Bintou, yeah? Bintou pub by the looks of it.'

And so the soap opera ran on, unfolding the petty dramas of life behind the Ngong Hills. Kili was back to pickling his liver. Meriape had shaped up and was helping to support the family. Heaven knows where he'd got the money to bribe the driving instructor for a licence. Lepapa was doing well at school and the doltish Narasha was content herding the goats. The heavily pregnant Segenun was the wife of a man considered rich by Oldonyati standards although in England or America he would have been eligible for welfare benefit. All the other daughters were married too and producing offspring almost as quickly as Kipenget's rabbits. They were off her hands, which might have been why she was having a breakdown. When we mothers don't have children around to harass us, we implode with the grief of being left alone to enjoy life. Isaac the ex-con was battling his way through a renaissance: the joy of being free offset by the sorrow of being orphaned and the worry of supporting his brothers with no money. And Peter? He was just fine. He was a worldly Bintou Yookay.

CHAPTER 22

Peter and I left Kisamis and continued on our safari to his family's *boma*. It was already late in the day, and a swiftly sinking sun was brushing the horizon with copper rays. I had been driving for nearly an hour. My hands were sticky on the steering wheel, and I wanted to stretch my legs to make sure they still worked. Then we crested a ridge and there it was – the Kepaeka's home. Nothing had changed in the intervening months since my last visit. From the rocky bastion of the ridge above, the mud and dung huts looked like upturned coracles. We could see the enclosure where the heifers and goats were kept and the acacia tree whose spreading boughs gave shade when the sun was high. There was a man sitting beneath it. It was Mebikie, swishing languidly at the still air with a giraffe-tail fly whisk. Crouched down on legs as thin as spears, he looked like a grasshopper poised to land on some lesser insect. He didn't move when the car appeared.

In the shanty towns, there is the sound of laughter and squealing children, women shouting to each other and the nearby rumble of traffic. Here in the bush, where you could have set up an infernal racket without fear of disturbing anyone, an end-of-the-day lethargy had taken hold. The *boma* was silent, becalmed. No one, not even the children, spilled out of it to welcome us.

Peter said, 'They remember you. When the children are naughty, my brothers say, "Watch out. Mama Kali will get you."'

I stopped close by the thorn fence, but Peter said it wasn't a good place to put the car and pointed to the far side of the *boma*. It seemed exactly the same as the spot we had just left, but it must have held some special significance or he would not have asked me to manoeuvre the car over the lava rocks. The code of conduct which held true in Nairobi, even infiltrated Oldonyati, was not valid here. A woman couldn't eat with men, but a man could drink tea with women. Yet under no circumstances did an elder join in the happiness and praise songs of the boys. A woman could though, if she was married. Above all, a woman never – ever – told a warrior to carry a water *debe*. Somewhere between Ol Tepesi and Kipenget's place, amidst the tumbled basalt scarps and stunted acacias, lay an invisible fault line. Normal behaviour on the other side – our way of behaving – was here greeted with consternation or laughter. It was a mirror image of what Peter had experienced in England. To function without disgracing Peter, I had determined to suspend judgment. Well, up to a point.

A large branch blocked the way. I asked Peter to get out and move it.

'It's taboo for a man to carry that. Very rude.'

I gave a small shrug and clambered out of the car. The branch was heavy. It was a struggle to move it. He must have detected my exasperation and wanted to make amends because he came up and pulled it easily to one side. But the parking problem wasn't over. Nnee appeared and said something to Peter in Maa.

'My mum says you should put the car inside.'

I was about to refuse but checked myself. 'Fine, if that's what she wants. Do you think the car can squeeze through that narrow opening?'

Nnee produced a stick and we walked over to the entranceway and placed it horizontally against the opening to measure its width. Then Nnee spat onto her thumb and carefully smeared her spittle onto the stick to mark the length. She handed it to me. I walked back to the car – by now all the women and children had gathered to watch – and with great show laid the stick along the front bumper. It was there for all to see. The damp mark on the stick fell short.

'Well?' I inquired,

'It is better to leave the car here,' Peter pronounced. The women murmured their agreement and the children, who had been solemn and silent, began to prance about the car with little exclamations of excitement. They pressed their hands and noses flat against the windows and peered at the *mzungu* things inside. They stared at their reflections in the side mirrors, bending their heads to the left and right like birds at a window, until Peter shooed them away. I had successfully negotiated the first hurdle. The decision where the car 'slept', as the women called it, had been made by the group.

'I'm going for a short walk.'

'I will send my brother with you,' Peter said. Again, I was on the verge of protesting but thought better of it. A skinny boy of about seven slipped his hand in mine and we set off to where the land began to descend to the valley below.

'You wait here. Back in a second,' I told him in Swahili. There were no generous bushes, but I was soon concealed by the rise and dip of the land. The red earth, the colour of lobster roe, was dry and non-porous. My pee splashed up and splattered my ankles. Midstream, a man appeared over the crest of the scarp a few yards away. I rose and stood clutching my trousers.

'Sopa.'

'Sopa,' he replied and strode on.

I squatted again, twisting my head round to see if anyone else would appear over the horizon. There was a brief glimpse of the upturned soles of two leather sandals, a snatch of dark skin, the hem of a red-checked *shuka* caught in the breeze, as fleeting as a gazelle gone to ground. And why not? It was inevitable the boy would want to see how white women do it.

His name was Tumpeni. We were able to talk to each other because he had started school the year before. The classes were held in Swahili, which had been a new language for him. By the time they graduate, students are supposed to be fluent in three languages: their mother tongue and the national languages of Swahili and English. That was the Kenyan system. Mebikie had no faith in scholastics, but World Vision had sent representatives round the area to persuade the heads of family to give at least one child a formal education. Mebikie had chosen Tumpeni. He was the youngest and was not yet needed for herding.

Tumpeni was one of several children who all looked similar until I came to know them better. Together we played telephone with the little plastic sieve Nnee used to pour milky tea from the cooking-pot into our mugs. My idea. And extracted rhythms from my pills by shaking the bottles. Theirs. The Maasai have few possessions. Certainly not toys. The games delighted them.

Peter, of course, had his own agenda. In the early evenings – the Maasai said 'when the sun goes red' – bleats and grunts rose above the swirling dust as the herd was driven home, and he said, 'Do you mind if I go and look at my goats?'

Each one had a special name. It reflected some physical characteristic or described the circumstances of its birth. I could see his still head over the fence, staring at them with concentration.

Later, when 'the cowhide covers the land', was my time with the children. I sat on a stool and they huddled round me in the darkness, the torch throwing a puddle of light onto my notebook.

'What are you writing?' asked Tumpeni.

'About everything that's around me.'

'Like that?' He pointed to the new moon. It was a luminous crescent in a snowstorm of stars.

'Exactly.'

Outside the hut, away from the fire, we were alone in a vast blackness which contained lions, hyenas and perhaps bandits. I liked him for seeing the night's seductive beauty.

'You have big hair. You should take it back from your face.' He stroked my temple with soft fingers, then ran them through my hair. It was contained in his small fist. He opened his fingers. 'But if I left it go, it will fall down again.'

The children's voices floated through the night like falling leaves. They were trying to teach me Maa by naming the things around them. Stool. Stick. Gourd. *Lorika. Sobua. Mala.* I toiled to mimic the words.

'*Lakira,*' said Tumpeni and raised his finger to the stars.

They took their turns with the pen, transposing the commonplace onto the unfamiliar paper. The head of a giraffe which had no eyes. A stick man. A series of joined-up circles which might have been a tortoise. The drawings were very small, composed of frail, agonized strokes. Then I asked if they could write their names. More tortured concentration. More wiggly, barely decipherable lines. *Mure. Median. Ntangenoi. Mbele.*

Seen through the prism of life in the *boma*, I was constantly redefining Peter. One revelation in particular realigned the co-ordinates for parenting my Maasai son. The expositor was Nnee.

She was less shy on this visit and didn't call on Peter to translate. We spoke together in Swahili, hers far more halting than mine. With this newfound means of communication came the stirrings of genuine fondness that was, I believe, mutual. Nnee was a small sturdy tree in a large forest. She didn't make a show of her presence. She was rooted, peaceful.

She wanted to know if I drank wine and whiskey. Peter said that sometimes I took a little wine. She wanted to make a stew for me with the potatoes and vegetables I'd brought but didn't have any fat to cook it with. She only had fat from a dead cow.

'I don't think you'd like it,' she said. 'I can drink a mug of sheep fat straight down. After giving birth, I'll have two or three mugs of fat. Just like that. Fat gives you strength.'

'Myself, I am sick,' Peter interjected.

I asked him what was wrong.

'I was kicked in football above the umbilical cord. I even received first aid. I may have to go to the doctor.'

'Why didn't you go to the doctor before you left Ongata? You don't think ahead,' I said.

'I thought about it, but I didn't want to waste money.'

'Well, there's no doctor here so there's not much we can do about it.'

Nnee nodded in agreement. Peter screwed up his mouth and ostentatiously massaged his ribs. He didn't like the way the conversation was panning out.

'The pain is coming from everywhere. I am even sweating,' he groaned.

'Then it can't be your stomach. That wouldn't make you sweat.'

Peter said, 'What will you eat tonight? Nnee is making *uji* for me with milk.'

'Aren't you too sick to eat?'

He took in a deep breath. He was about to launch into a circuitous explanation which would encompass his desire for food while still acknowledging his very sore stomach. Then he decided against it. 'The short answer is no. I will probably die afterwards.'

'That's the way to go. With a full stomach.'

Peter's mouth curled and we both laughed.

I began peeling two carrots with the blunt knife Nnee had lent me. It seemed the easiest solution for supper. I'd found them in my bag. The tiny flames from the cooking fire gave the knife a dull sheen as I hacked away and the peelings dropped onto the dirt. Nnee said something to Tumpeni and handed him a tin plate. He brought it across.

'Nnee says to put them on here. She'll give them to the goats.'

A silence fell. From the next hut came a rhythmic, leathery gasping. The warriors were singing. Nnee and Tumpeni sat watching me with a gaze that was both dreamy and attentive. Tomorrow it would go round the neighbourhood that *wazungu* lived on a diet of raw carrots – goat food – and wine. I wondered if I did the same to Peter, made snap judgments about his culture.

Tumpeni suddenly stood up and told a story in Maa accompanied by a lot of animated flourishes. When he was very small he was asleep under a bush. He was awoken by the sound of people approaching. They were *wazungu*. He was frightened and ran away.

'Would you do that now?' I asked.

He straightened his shoulders and said casually, 'No. I am not scared now.'

'There have been a lot of lions prowling around. They're very dangerous,' Nnee remarked.

'They're a long way away. They don't come near the *boma*,' Tumpeni retorted, dismissive of the danger. Mothers. They were always making a drama out of nothing.

'Lankisa was bitten. Here.' She lifted a hand and indicated the half moon of flesh between thumb and forefinger. 'It wasn't serious. We took him to the dispensary. Another warrior was attacked badly. He had to go to the hospital.' She was calm, unruffled.

This seemed like a good opportunity to give her the present I'd brought. Peter had helped to choose it. It was a length of thick red and blue material. Just right for keeping her warm at night. Nnee made small exclamations of appreciation as she unfolded it. She put it on the bed. '*Ashe, Merienna. Ashe oleng.*'

'She likes it. She says it is better even than the blankets given by a man at marriage to his mother-in-law,' Peter said with approval.

He picked the material up and with one hand tossed it to the back of the hut.

'Don't do that! Be careful with it!' Nnee and I said it in unison.

I had noticed this about us. We listened to him when he rambled on, indulging his soliloquies. We fussed over what he should eat. We found fault in the same things. Nnee had given him a scolding the day he had kept me waiting for over an hour.

Nnee and I treated Peter the same way. This realization that we operated within remarkably similar frameworks of social and moral conduct had a liberating effect on me. It confirmed what I had suspected all along. Peter's self-justification for his sometimes graceless behaviour was baseless. It wasn't 'an issue of being a warrior'. There were ground rules which ran deeper than the traditions of different cultures. The common denominator that binds us all is normal human decency. Peter's two mothers had united.

Later, when Peter had gone to sleep in another hut, Nnee said prayers. She was a Baptist, but she believed in the Maasai god Nkai, Peter said. 'She's not very Christian. She's only practising Christian morals,' he explained. This studied qualification was made in light of Peter's own religious experience. At his church in Kisamis members of the congregation swayed on their feet and raised their eyes to the corrugated-iron roof, giving testimony to how they had seen the light of Christ. Peter said he was 'more cool'. He believed in Jesus, but he wasn't one of those people who had been saved.

'Thank You God for guiding us through the day, for giving us food, for helping us to have the right speech to people. Thank You for looking after relatives who aren't here. And please make Tumpeni's tummy better,' Nnee intoned.

Tumpeni and I sat on the opposite bed, heads bowed. The firelight glowed on our clasped hands. I was sucked back into childhood: knees hurting on the hard floor; head buried in the blanket; eyes screwed tight; chanting parrotlike with a show of mock piety. Nursie Pursie was supplanted by Nnee's soothing presence. It was cosy and safe. Peter hadn't been here as a child to know that nursery feeling of security.

Afterwards, I took some water behind the hut and washed in the dark. It was only a plateful. Water was scarce. I'd dropped the soap on the ground and it was covered with dung and bits of dirt. My trousers were too big – they were borrowed – and a turn-up got in the way when I peed. There was no privacy in the hut to change into something dry. It didn't matter. I'd sleep with them wet. I thought, *I'm happy exactly as I am.*

Tumpeni snuffled and squirmed like a puppy, nestling into the curve of my hip with his head tucked beneath my out-flung arm. And he pushed, nudging as a dog nudges its bowl towards you with its nose, moving me inch by inch across the expanse of cowhide. My forehead rubbed against something hard. The warm smell of goats wafted above the odour of ashes and animal fat. I was wedged against the upright sticks that separated the bed from the newborn kids on the other side. The fire had gone out and the hut was enveloped in blackness. It was cold. I fumbled for my *kikoi* and wrapped it around me.

I lay there in the dark, warm again, listening to the night noises of gentle sniffles and snorts, and I was suddenly presented with a vision of Euston Station in the winter. Its bleak facade. The decanted passengers being chased by a bitter wind. London. I didn't want to go back.

From Tumpeni came a mutter, a sleepy smacking of lips. His breathing was soft, rhythmic, like the tide sighing back into the sea. It was the sound of all children tucked up in their beds.

But how many children would have accepted me so unquestioningly, cuddling against a stranger like this? His trust was tangible. I felt it as surely as if it had been placed in my cupped hands. That thought, his warm body, my desire to protect, unearthed a neglected sensation. I'd talk to Nnee tomorrow about a packed lunch for school. Tumpeni wouldn't eat the corn they gave them. It was ridiculous he should walk the eight miles there and back on a mug of tea and a few scraps of *posho*. The poor child was all skin and bones. How could he concentrate on his lessons? No wonder his tummy hurt.

I had vowed not to get involved with more children. Too late. Love had intervened.

So each day I did the school run, delivering Tumpeni in his postage-stamp shorts and blue-checked shirt to the dilapidated corrugated-iron building on the plains. He perched on the edge of the passenger seat and gripped the dashboard with both hands, as if he was negotiating a minefield. Then one morning the car wouldn't start.

Rescue lay to the north in Nairobi or to the south at Lake Magadi. Nairobi was distant, maybe forty miles; Magadi, slightly closer. But there was nothing there except the houses, offices and workshops built by the company which dredged up soda from the oozing water. It was inhospitable territory. A baking inferno of heat where you travelled with plenty of petrol and water and hoped you didn't break down. There was little passing traffic so I decided to take whichever vehicle stopped for my upturned thumb, regardless of the direction it was travelling in.

I told Peter and Nnee not to worry, I'd be back by nightfall, and started walking to the road. A troop of baboons soon fell in alongside, casually keeping pace while pretending to look in the dirt for interesting things to eat. Their tails curled up and arched over their pink, hairless rumps. Baboons were vermin. One had grabbed a baby goat when Mebikie had left the kids untended to have tea in Nnee's hut. 'He just munched it. It was a nasty incident,' Peter said. I picked up a rock and threw it at the largest male. The troop lolloped off and swung their way up into the thorn trees. They sat in the branches, giving little barks and watching me.

The Maasai complained of chilly weather, but already it was well above eighty degrees Fahrenheit. The sun had bleached the land and covered it in a golden haze. From down on the plains, where Tumpeni was squeezing himself onto a bench between the other children, came a foghorn bellow followed by the sight of a weighty bull diminished to the size of a toy. It was pale yellow, like sand or a labrador, plodding across the road. As I watched, fifty yards away a lone impala stepped out of the bushes on hesitant feet. It paused, lifted its head to look around and scented the air. Seconds later a herd of russet females appeared and noiselessly followed the male across the road. They were etched with a vibrant light. Watching their graceful progress and knowing that I was invisible to them, I had the strange sensation that an ethereal energy was at work. I stood transfixed. Then they were swallowed by the bushes on the other side.

Not long after that three men in a white Suzuki rumbled past, slowed down and then reversed. I told them about the four-wheel-drive Toyota that had died on me. It was back there, in the *boma* where I stayed, I said. Meaningful glances were exchanged inside the car. A white woman living with the Maasai. But they said they would give me a lift. I squeezed into the back seat.

My companions were Kikuyu, born in the verdant, rain-fed highlands. They worked for the National Social Security Fund and had been assigned to discuss pensions with the workers from the soda company. They had never been to Magadi before, they said. And when the man in the front passenger seat remarked on the barren landscape, how deserted it all was, his voice was suspicious.

White clouds rode the hot sky. The sun burned through the shut windows, ironing the energy out of us and leaving us limp and exhausted. The men were uncomfortable in their suits and ties. Sweat glistened on their necks and foreheads. The two who were passengers took off their jackets and sat with them neatly folded in their laps. Their shirts were stained at the armpits.

From time to time we passed ochre-robed figures and herds of goats or cattle wrapped in sparkling plumes of dust and then a military camp where the General Service Unit underwent survival training. A herd of zebra danced in a mirage beneath a jagged ridge. The men gazed on it all with grim resignation.

They didn't ask why I was living in the boondocks, dressed in *kikois* and beaded bracelets, my hair stiff with dirt. We chatted about politics, and they realized I was *au fait* with current affairs. I made one or two remarks which made them laugh. That brought me back from beyond the pale. I wasn't a complete bozo after all.

Magadi was prefaced by a khaki scarp. At its foot there was a barrier across the road and a large sign which said something to the effect that we were entering the property of the soda company and that if our car had broken down, under no circumstances whatsoever should we seek help from the mechanics at the work-shop. The men looked relieved at having reached some sort of civilization, but I think the sign set them back a bit. Over the last hour they had become proprietorial about my misfortune. A uniformed company employee stepped out of a pillbox and asked the driver to put down his vehicle registration number in the book and sign his name. Then we drove on.

The lake was extraordinary. Not cool, refreshing water but a silver and pink expanse which refracted the sun in wild prisms of light. It gave off a caustic, abrasive odour. The smell, which was like a chemistry lab, came from the soda which surged up from the subterranean belly of the Rift Valley. It was so thick that the workers – they were called miners – could stand on it. They were sweeping the stuff up into hillocks of snowy crystals.

The lake was flanked on both sides by miniature escarpments, the result of ancient volcanic turmoil. In the depression on the far side was a collection of one-storey buildings of the negligible number that rural Africans reckon constitutes a town. The bank and the post office were shut but the store was open. Maasai lounged in the shade of the verandah, the women sitting on the concrete floor with their legs stretched straight in front of them. The men propped themselves up against the wall. They stared at me as we went inside to buy some sodas. They weren't sure what to make of this culturally androgynous white woman, either. Next we went round the corner to the butcher, where flayed carcasses hung from meat hooks. The NSSF men wanted to put in an order for lunch – goat stew butchered and cooked on the premises – before discharging their hitchhiker.

There was another barrier on the perimeter of the workshop complex and another book to sign. I had not wanted to be a burden to them, been at pains to make it clear I was prepared to fight my own battles, but they were adamant. They couldn't leave me stranded. They were going to make sure I got help. More to the point, they knew, as I knew, that the workshop manager would almost certainly be a fellow Kikuyu.

The furthest building was a clattering cavern of trucks and heavy machinery. Men in white overalls crawled over them like worker ants. Mr Mbugua, the manager, sat at one remove from the oily clamour in a glass-fronted office. Introductions were made and the NSSF men took their leave. With a certain relief, it seemed. There were bowls of greasy goat meat to attend to.

I launched into my tale of woe. I hated to impose, but my car wouldn't start and, as he knew, it was difficult to find a mechanic in these parts. I had no alternative but to turn to the Magadi Soda Company. I was living in a *boma* up the road. Was it at all possible that someone could drive me back to the car and take a look at it?

I didn't tell him I had no money.

Mr Mbugua's response was guarded but polite. I didn't fit the customary mould of visitor: a tourist or a day-tripping Nairobi *memsahib*. Was I working with the Maasai? he wanted to know. You could say that, I replied. Well, he *had* just said it. His face softened. Company regulations didn't allow him to send his mechanics on outside jobs, but he would make an exception this time. I was doing good work for the community and that was admirable. I smiled in a self-effacing way and thanked him.

The mechanic had playboy good looks. He wore wraparound sunglasses and gave me appraising sidelong glances as he drove. He was called Isaac but I could call him Miti, which was his nickname. He was working out here because of the pay. He partied in Nairobi every weekend. Otherwise he would die of boredom.

He had brought another mechanic with him, called Moses. In case we broke down and someone had to walk, I presumed. Moses was flung out on the back seat with his head thrown back, snoring.

'Is your car before or after the military camp?'

'After.'

'How many miles?'

'Hard to say.'

'Not too much further on, I hope.'

'I really appreciate this. You must be very busy.'

Stunted trees and powdery earth rushed by. Somewhere around here was Peter's land.

'What would you do with country like this?'

'Farm giraffes.' His voice was amused, disdainful.

I was beginning to see everything with double vision: the *mzungu* world I had always known and a new, Maasai world. I looked at the tassels of tiny leaves on the bushes and saw food for goats which could survive drought. Useful. In fact, precious. Before, I would have glanced at the vegetation blindly. Not even noticed the leaves. I said nothing. Miti's wry, easy-going manner made me uneasy. I couldn't relax with him. He was a sophisticated Kikuyu. A townie. I was a country bumpkin. A Maasai.

When we eventually reached the *boma*, Peter came up followed by Nnee, who looked at once concerned and relieved. Nalotu-esha, Peter's sister-in-law, drifted into view with her baby Salaiyo bouncing on her hip. The children and other women appeared after that and a couple of men who were visiting Mebikie. Finally, they were all there. Except Mebikie, who sat at a distance in the shade of a tree. No one said hello to the mechanics.

They opened the bonnet of the Toyota and got out a wrench or two. The sight of the tools excited Nalotu-esha. 'The doctor's going to give the car an injection!' she cried.

Miti's mouth twitched and he sneaked a look at Moses.

While they were fiddling with the engine and running round to the driver's seat to press the accelerator, I pulled Peter to one side. 'Got a bit of a problem here. Do you think you could quietly do a whip-round?'

Peter gave a little snort through his nose. I knew why. Getting cash out of the Maasai is like extracting blood from a stone. There isn't any. All the money was out amongst the lava rocks, chomping its way through the vegetation,

'What about your aunt? The one who has a *duka*? Mama Safi. I'll pay her back in a couple of days.'

Peter shook his head. 'M. A., to get cash from these people is very difficult.'

'So what are we going to do?'

'We'll give them goats.'

'Peter, these guys are Kikuyu. From Nairobi. They've probably never slit a jugular in their lives.'

'We'll put two goats in the back of their car and take them up to Kiserian. I can sell them immediately. Just like that. But we'd better hurry. Before it's dark.'

'Pee-eter. No goats in the back of the car. We've got to keep face.'

Eventually Miti and Moses got the engine revving, and I offered refreshments as they were packing the wrenches and things into the toolbox. 'You must be hungry. Would you like something to eat? We've just slaughtered.'

The two men exchanged a complicit look and said they were fine.

'Some tea, then. Surely you're thirsty. It's right there.'

Miti and Moses politely shook their heads. At that moment I caught sight of a dog lapping away at a yellowy mess under the tree next to the car. Miti and Moses noticed it too. A nanny had dropped a kid there earlier in the afternoon. It was the afterbirth.

'Well, in that case I'll just bring some water to wash with. No . . .' I raised my hands to fend off further refusals, ' . . . I insist.'

Nnee and Nalotu-esha weren't too happy about sharing out the water, which was the most precious thing around, but I overrode them. Miti and Moses rolled back their sleeves and I dribbled some over their hands out of a small plastic container. Then I handed them the soap with the dung and straw on it and they scrubbed away, even getting rid of the grease from around their fingernails.

'Now, let's sort out the payment. How much do I owe you?' I said it in a hearty, no-nonsense sort of way. I wanted to be a Nairobi *memsahib*. But suddenly my nerve failed me. I rushed on before they could answer, babbling, 'I'm sorry. Look, I can't pay. I just can't pay. We have no money. What about goats? We can give you two goats. Or if you want, we can put them in the back of your car. Run them up to Kiserian. They'll sell. Just like that. How about it?'

A little gasp of air escaped through Miti's nostrils. He had a strange grin on his face. 'It's not a problem. The next time you're down at Magadi, you can bring the money.' They drove off.

Peter looked at me, puzzled. 'Are you all right?'

'They never said how much.'

It was getting late, but in a way, the day had only just started. I'd been profligate with the water, poured the last precious drops over Miti and Moses' hands. There was work to be done.

Everyone disappeared into their huts to gather their containers and loaded them into the car. Then they loaded themselves in too. I told them all to get out. A long discussion ensued over who could come and who stayed behind. This all took half an hour. We eventually trimmed back the passenger list to a manageable size. Peter and Nnee were going to help draw water. Nalotu-esha felt a bit out of sorts and wanted to get some *dawa* from the dispensary. And Tumpeni had to come because he had been cheated out of his ride to school in the morning.

Diesel engines have a distinct noise pattern. There is the low hum and tick as the engine warms up. The click of the key in the ignition and the eager rumble as the engine turns over and flares into life. Tick. Hum. Click. Whine. I tried again. Tick. Hum. Click. Whine.

I turned to the expectant audience. 'Sorry, guys. Everybody out. It's back to the donkeys. They didn't manage to fix it.'

It had been another typical African day. Much exertion and nothing to show for it. Tomorrow I'd hitchhike to Nairobi.

CHAPTER 23

Peter may have been keen on his career, but he was gravely delinquent when it came to managing his budget. I was staying with friends, writing a magazine piece that had been commissioned in London, but we saw each other regularly. He still cadged off me mercilessly. 'I have no money to get to work or buy food for the rest of the month. Can you lend me fifteen hundred shillings?' When I suggested I get him a new pair of shoes, he said slyly, 'It would be good to buy me three pairs. That way they will last a long time.' He said he was going to buy tea and *posho* for Nnee, then pulled me into the shop to pay. He made me feel like an Amex gold card.

Sometimes he said he couldn't pay the rent for his room in Ongata Rongai. Ongata, as it was known, lay just beyond the city boundary and for that reason had long been a prime site for fencing stolen goods. Stacked balconies hung with washing stood cheek by jowl with bars, brothels and Day and Night Clubs. It wasn't a shanty town like Kibera, where nearly half a million people were jammed into two square miles of shacks. But even by Nairobi's yardstick, it had an exceptionally high crime rate. Beyond Ongata on the road to the Ngong Hills, red-roofed stone villas leavened the back-alley sleaze with bourgeois prosperity.

It seemed strange to think that Peter had a home of his own for the first time in his life. He was proud of it. 'It's the best plot in Ongata even though it's a very small room and I have to keep everything there. There's a day- and night-watchman. And electricity and water. You just go to a tap outside when you want to wash. There's no hot water. Whaaa, it's cold when I take a shower in the mornings.'

I was looking forward to visiting it. Tara had told me he was expecting me to sleep there, for at least a night, but the invitation hadn't been issued yet. Instead, he waited to be picked up at the end of the dirt road where the *matatus* collected their passengers.

Whenever I dropped him back there, he sauntered off with his hands stuck in his pockets. He never looked back. I got the impression the white woman in the smart car was bad for his street cred amongst the *bhangi*-eyed touts in knitted rasta hats.

If Peter wasn't earning a king's ransom, by Kenyan standards it was definitely enough for a comfortable life. But he was habitually skint. The strange thing was, when I wasn't in Kenya he seemed to make do on his salary.

Budgeting to live within your means is challenging, but Tara and Petra had got the hang of revenue and expenditure, more or less. At least they never asked me for loans. Tara had been holding down three different jobs to underwrite a course on counselling. Petra was on a university grant but worked in the holidays to cover her other expenses. It was time Peter, too, became versed in the fickle nature of petty cash.

I brought the subject up one overcast day when we were driving to see his friend and neighbour, Joseph Simel, who was still heavily involved with litigation over what had been unlawful government allocation of Maasai land. The Toyota was climbing steeply, pointing its nose at the Ngongs' cloudy peaks. Joseph and his wife Anastasia had moved away from the family *boma* to Oloopelos Secondary School on the windswept plains above the Rift Valley. She was the school secretary.

Peter itemized his outgoings as we bumped over the rutted track. He gave Nnee money to buy *dawa* for the goats when they were sick and to spray them against ticks. She kept a meticulous record of what she spent, he said. Then there was the stipend for the brothers who looked after his herd. They had to be fed and so did Nnee and Tumpeni. And Nnee had needed a new pair of shoes that month.

I thought of Peter's father and his herd of goats. *Why couldn't he sell some and use the money to provide for his family?*

Peter pre-empted the question before I could open my mouth. 'I know you don't agree with this, but it is the custom for the sons to support the family.'

'So what about your elder brother?'

'He can't. He's married. He must look after his wife.'

'And your younger brothers? The ones who are going to be warriors soon?'

'They are working for me. They look after the goats.'

For a moment he had me, but I rallied.

'Okay, I accept all that stuff about your brothers. But why don't you keep the goats separate from your Ostrich Park salary? Look, the goats are a business. Businesses should make enough to run themselves. Think of your family as members of the goat project. Sort of employees. Finance the *dawa* and food and everything from the profits.'

'There are no profits.'

'Yes, there are. What about the kids you fatten up and sell at the market?'

'It is not the season.'

'But it will be. You've got fifty nannies who are going to drop fifty kids. Fifty bundles of money on the hoof. Sell them and there's your petty cash for running costs.'

'My herd is too small.'

'You're doing far better than most young men your age. Goats. One hundred and sixty acres of land. A job that pays well. You've got more than most people ever dream of having.'

As I said this, the reality of it hit me. Peter *was* doing well. So well, in fact, that in many ways he was better off than Tara and Petra. I empathized with their ambition to be independent because they were behaving like . . . well, like me. Peter was born a Kepaeka not a Fitzgerald, which was why I could intuit my daughters' foibles and moods but not his.

I wrestled the car past grazing herds of zebra, gazelle and cattle and parked outside Oloopelos Secondary's front door. Its dour grey edifice of cinder blocks, capable of withstanding a blizzard, was more suited to the bleak landscape of England's industrial north than this breathtakingly beautiful setting of undulating plains. The school was empty inside. There were no students or teachers. Not a single stick of furniture. Electric cables crawled along the ceiling and walls but there were no light fixtures, no switches. The place had an abandoned air even though it was in use. It felt as though it was waiting for someone to come and occupy it. Oloopelos may have been one of the better schools in the district, but it was plain as sun on a spear that the money had run out during construction.

The sun through the windows cast a daffodil light onto the sign above the door. God Help Us Grow. Peter stared beyond it onto a flattened patch of grass that was the football pitch. He had his hands in his pockets, eyes fixed on the tree trunks which served as goal posts.

'They are good. Very wide and strong.'

'You should put the goat money into a separate bank account. Use your salary for the rent and food. So you don't run out in the middle of the month.'

He looked contemplative, pursed his lips. 'I'll do that,' he said.

I walked down the corridor and poked my head round an open door. The room was bare except for a solitary table and chair. It was hard to imagine Joseph's wife Anastasia here. With her collars of beads and *rubega* the colour of madder, she was more suited to the mud and dung of the *boma*. Not like the young woman who sat behind an ancient manual typewriter. Her hair was pulled back into a neat goat's-tail tuft. It accentuated the fine line of her cheekbones and wide-set eyes. She looked demure in her little jacket and purple dress, straight out of secretarial college. But when she pushed back her chair and came forward to shake hands, the strongly muscled calves betrayed her. 'You have come. Where's Peter?'

Two plovers wheeled up from the grass on the football pitch and gave their haunting skirling cry. From the classrooms came the low hum of voices. Anastasia strode out on her athlete's legs past thorn trees abloom with the students' washing hung out to dry. We turned the corner of her small stone house and came upon a barefoot girl pummelling some laundry. She was bent over a plastic bowl set on the grass, her legs stiff and splayed wide like a giraffe at a waterhole. When she saw us, she hastily adjusted her blouse, which had slipped off her shoulder. 'This is my girl,' Anastasia said in passing as she rattled the key in the back-door lock. It was a sure sign Anastasia had gone urban. She had a maid. I took the limp offering of sudsy fingers and shook them. The girl looked square and dumpy next to Anastasia. She was about fifteen.

Joseph was in the tiny living room, looking solemn in a macintosh he had put on against the chill. We sat on a wooden-legged sofa and chairs with crocheted woollen doilies draped over their backs. A couple of religious homilies hung on the wall. Anastasia brought us lukewarm orange sodas. She set them down on a little wooden table with both hands so as not to spill a drop then perched in a chair, demurely smoothing her skirt over her knees. The couple seemed so serious and mature compared to Peter. Was Peter a late developer or was Joseph exceptional amongst Maasai young men? Observing them from the vantage point of another culture, it was hard to know.

Joseph's court case against the government had placed him in a certain amount of danger. Peter told me he kept his movements to himself as much as possible. Sometimes he slept in other places. There had been strange men asking his whereabouts down at the *boma*.

Joseph had become a fledgling politician. He'd been elected the location KANU chairman. Peter belonged to the ruling party, KANU, too. He didn't see beyond the roads and piped water which appeared after the election to the corruption which provided the money for development. Our heated arguments on the subject left Peter baffled rather than enlightened. But Joseph was a man after my own heart. He was a dedicated iconoclast. His alliance with the old guard didn't make sense. I had asked Peter about it. 'Joseph knows the Maasai will only vote for KANU so he must change through KANU.'

Joseph had been making something of a name for himself. Land allocation was very topical. Kenyans considered land ownership their birthright, and they were keenly aware that there wasn't nearly enough of it to go around. Tribal clashes over land had been in the news for several years. Thousands were homeless, hundreds more had died in the fighting. Loodariak, Peter's and Joseph's 'home area' as the Maasai liked to call it, was in particular turmoil. Fights had erupted between rival clans using bows and arrows and spears to dispute the ownership of group ranches and individually owned plots: persuasion by means of projectiles. Joseph had opted for change through more formal channels and his chances of success were looking as promising as they had ever been. With the support of Survival International, a London-based human rights organization, he was preparing the legal groundwork to challenge the verdict that had been found against him in the high court. This was a major feat in Kenya, where the ordinary citizen was usually brushed aside early on in the judicial process. It was a two-pronged attack. Joseph was also seeking recourse through parliament. He was working on a white paper to annul the adjudication. If it was tabled and enacted, there would be no need for lengthy court procedures.

'How are things with you, Joseph?'

'We are well.'

'And your case?'

'I have been to see the D. O. about the border dispute.' He said this in the low tones of a cellar revolutionary. There was a warning note in his voice. Peter looked uncomfortable. It was not a suitable forum for politics.

I quickly moved on, 'And the baby?'

'Very well. It is sleeping next door.'

We continued the pleasantries. They were polite but stilted. Joseph was a different man from the one who had expressed surprise that the British people were monogamous. He asked me nothing of Peter's trip. He was too busy visiting lawyers, writing letters and petitioning officials to be interested in such frivolous pastimes as going to raves and browsing in the Camden shops. He had become resolute, a man devoted to a cause.

Peter didn't volunteer to relive his English experiences either. I had been looking forward to excavating memories and reliving them through Joseph's eyes. Peter's short call at the garage. Washing Fiston the bull. Even the time Peter went mad and frothed at the mouth. It was to have been a good old get-together. Instead a screen had been placed between us.

Beneath Peter's composure coursed . . . coursed what? Hostility? Confusion? Maasainess? I couldn't quite put my finger on it, but the dynamics had shifted. I felt like a guest, not a friend.

Peter and I had forged a connection in London which had been soldered when I'd behaved like a Maasai firestick elder and given him a dressing down in my study. After that we had been able to look into each other's hearts. Yet since my arrival in Kenya, I'd sensed that he was holding himself in check, keeping something back. The distancing was so subtle it was barely noticeable. At first I had taken it for a newfound maturity. But as the days went by, I looked at him differently. He had become wooden, was floating beyond my reach. I was tormented by it and fell prey to the curse of all mothers. Where had I gone wrong?

It took some time to divine the reality. Peter still bore childish traits. Self-absorption paraded as self-assurance. Deceit marred the generosity. I had spoilt him. Given too much too easily. In the headlong rush to change Peter, I hadn't allowed time for his mettle to take hold. Trapped inside this man was the uncertain soul of a small boy. This revelation came to me a few days later when we were back at Peter's *boma*.

It was early morning and the herds were streaming out to forage amongst the lava rocks. The sheep and goats were fat and eager, full of vitality, the bells at their necks playing mezzo-soprano riffs. Their snorts and jingling somehow sounded livelier during the day. Peter's father Mebikie was sitting on a black stone drinking tea and communing with the still-shadowed Boulder Mountain. He ignored the animals because he was expecting a patient. Mebikie was highly regarded for his healing powers. In fact, he was reputed to be one of the three finest herbalists in Kajiado District along with his brother and a relation of Kipenget's. This was no small claim. The catchment area for his surgery was several hundred square miles.

Soon enough the sick man appeared with a friend in tow. He was lean, with skin the colour of an eggplant. He wore plastic sandals. The friend wore shoes and socks and a silver-coloured watch which glinted above his bead bracelets. Someone of considerable means. The two men had looped their ear lobes above their ears to avoid the thorns of low-hanging branches. They must have walked a long way.

They greeted Mebikie and squatted on the rocks. Their pink-flowered *rubegas* were hitched up around their knees and their *rungus* lay in the dirt beside their feet. A warrior brought them mugs of tea. They drank it with noisy slurps in a way that made it seem their lips weren't touching the rim of the mug. Mebikie became voluble and gesticulated with a whippy stick cut from a thorn tree. The patient and his friend nodded and grunted and sucked away at their tea.

In due course one of Peter's brothers passed between the men and the *boma*, leading a white nanny by the ear. It no doubt had a presentiment of its fate because it bleated as it was being pulled along. The men ignored it and continued talking and drinking in the amphitheatre of Boulder Mountain's dissolving shadow. Then Mebikie said something and they rose and followed the goat.

I was keen to see Mebikie practise his herbalist skills. Peter had said there would be no problem about us watching but, as we approached, we could see through the leaves of the bushes that the patient was slipping his cloth over his loins.

Peter said, 'Wow, he is naked. He won't want you near. You'd better not risk it.'

We stopped where we were and sat down on rocks. We were some fifty feet from the four men. The patient was crouching on his heels. He had his back to us. The dark knots of his spine reflected the sun.

The heat had brought the flies out. I kept swatting at my eyes, but Peter wasn't bothered. He said, 'I had malaria when I got back from London and was teased because I took the pills I'd got from the Ongata clinic. There were so many sick that day and the pickpockets were working hard. I was ready for them. I had a knife in my pocket. When I came home, Mebikie said they would do no good. He slaughtered a goat and gave me herbs to make me vomit the poison. It was a crushed root from the *esumeita* tree. He boiled it until it foamed, whereby he sieved it. I really vomited until I thought my gullet was coming out. It was bitter medicine.' He prounounced it *biter*.

'Did that cure you?'

'I felt very strong after that. Mebikie said it would teach me some manners to know that his *dawa* works.'

'It's confusing, this swapping back and forth between worlds. Do you feel different now that you're a Bintou?'

'Not really.' He smiled.

'Travelling between London and Nairobi was difficult. Now it's just Nairobi and Ol Tepesi.'

'I love my job at the Ostrich Park. I want to stay there.'

'You really love it?'

'Yes.'

'Not like the first job you ever had. The one at the tourist hotel.'

'Oh no. Not like that one.'

This was a trainee position Mike Eldon had wangled for Peter in a game lodge at the foot of Mt. Kilimanjaro. Peter had quit within the week. I had heard different versions of the story but had always wanted to know what had really happened. While we watched the goat being slaughtered, Peter told me.

Peter said he'd got malaria and retired to bed, by turn drenched in sweat and shivering with cold. Things hadn't been too bad until then despite the ten-hour workday. He didn't like the sweeping, but he envisioned himself working behind the reception desk quite soon. That's where he should be, not cleaning dirty rooms. He liked to be with people, talk to them. He was miserable with the malaria so he asked another cleaner to bring the manager. He knew he would feel better once the manager came to see him with the doctor. But the manager didn't come. Peter was outraged. He was ill. How could he ignore him? It was terrible to treat your staff that way. The man had no feelings. He decided to go home to Mike's house.

Truculent with fever, Peter rose from his sickbed and packed his few clothes into the Alitalia bag he had been given. He'd show the manager. He'd show the lot of them. He was 'footing' down the road to find a *matatu*, vomiting and dragging his bag in the dirt. A man came towards him on a bicycle and Peter waved him down. He was last seen by the lodge staff, wobbling pillion past a disinterested herd of zebra.

'I think I must have been so sick I was a little bit crazy.' Peter laughed and wrinkled his nose. The black cloud of flies that had settled onto the dead goat was spilling over onto us.

We watched as Peter's brother and the man with the watch lifted its slack body above the patient's head. Mebikie was facing us. He had bent over from the waist as women do when washing clothes in the river. His hands were very busy.

'He's giving him a bath with the goat's blood,' Peter said. 'He will take herbs afterwards.'

'Would you do that now?'

'Take herbs?'

'Run away just because the manager's too busy to see you.'

'Oh no!' He drew his chin to his neck. His mouth made a reproachful O. 'I was very crazy then. I was just a young boy. It was a very bad thing to do.'

'Guess so. But we all do crazy things once in a while.'

Peter's brother and the man with the watch came past, carrying the goat, holding it upside down by the front and back legs. The head lolloped down. They had taken out the stomach contents and it swung loosely like an empty hammock.

The patient had stood up and was tying his *shuka* at the shoulder. Peter saw me watching him. 'He won't take alcohol or fat. Mebikie will speak to him. Do's and don'ts. Some people have psychological problems and trouble with the family.'

Purification with a cleansing bath of goat's blood followed by a good talking-to. The medicinal prescription followed by counselling. There was a shadowy correlation to Western practice. It was that sense of being totally cared for. Peter would have been halfway to recovery from his malaria if the manager had taken the time to come and see him.

It suddenly struck me that what Peter needed more than anything else was Mebikie's attention: not as a herbalist but as a parent. He had two mothers – Nnee and I – fussing over him, but in many ways his father was still absent. A mother nurtures her son. It takes a father to make a man out of him.

Peter sat with Mebikie and listened to him as he talked, punctuating his monologues with flicks of his stick. He in turn related to Mebikie the things he had done in Nairobi and, on his return from London, in England. Not being able to understand Maa, I wasn't able to eavesdrop on their conversations. But I could intuit them. Peter and Nnee hummed together. There was no electricity between Peter and Mebikie. Was Peter salt in his wounded pride? Given their aborted beginnings, there was perhaps little chance now of a proper relationship.

Mebikie was impossible to read. He certainly looked as inscrutable as ever as he supervised the butchering of the goat carcass. Physician, heal thy son.

CHAPTER 24

'This is a strange country. It's a question of slowness. I'm more used to the way they do things in England than here.'

Within days of saying goodbye to Nnee and Mebikie, Peter and I were on the road again; this time, to Tanzania. Despite having been here before when he had joined me on assignment for the Audubon Society magazine, Peter was experiencing a touch of culture shock.

There was a purpose to our travels. For years I'd been exposing him to a Western lifestyle, my values, in the hopes of giving him a better life. I'd been looking in the wrong direction. He needed to come to grips with what had been floating on the periphery of his awareness all along: the culture he was born into. There were no firestick elders at Mebikie's *boma* to lick him into shape so I had determined we would pay another visit to Pashet Sengeruan, the chairman of Engaruka. Unlike Kenya, a country that has been staunchly capitalist for decades, until recently Tanzania was a socialist state. Like Eastern Europe before the fall of the Berlin Wall, it had been fairly isolated from the rest of the world. As a result, Maasai tradition was still intact. Not only that, it would be a chance to meet Nanyokie once more. Perhaps he would do better with a traditional wife. Peter was involved with Rosina, but he hadn't made any long-term commitment. I said nothing about the importance of finding his tribal roots. It was something he had to discover for himself.

So here we were in Tanzania where the familiar, though still there in the unpaved streets, the cigarette kiosks, the serious black faces, had been shifted out of focus. Arusha, a four-hour drive from Nairobi across the border, is a frontier town. A place to get supplies, get the car repaired, get laid before melting back into the bush for another three months. It once provisioned colonial coffee-farmers, hence the avenues lined with yellow cassias, red flamboyants and purple jacarandas. For twenty years under Julius Nyerere's socialism it slumbered like Rumpelstiltskin. But with the advent of capitalism, it is a hub for professional hunters and for tourists embarking on safaris into the game parks.

The tourists are driven past the clock tower, packed shoulder to shoulder in Land Rovers and Landcruisers. They wear khaki hats pinned up at one side and look through the windows at the Maasai men methodically pedalling bicycles with their *rubegas* hitched up around their knees, the cows grazing dark mounds of garbage in the ditches. They are on their way to the game lodges.

The hunters walk about as if they own the place. They wear very tight, very short shorts that show off their muscled wrestler's legs. They drop in at the Discovery Club (members only) for a quick one at the bar while the differential is being fixed. They drink beer from a glass mug and pinion the bottle between arm and chest to leave the other hand free for a cigarette. The ash drops onto the dogeared briefcases propped at their feet. Their fingernails are encrusted with engine oil.

Peter and I were travelling as locals, mixing with the men in purple and pink shell suits, the women who strolled sulkily through the dust swathed in brightly patterned *kangas*.

We were dining in a side street on the insect-blitzed verandah of Mr Khan's store. He sells diesel injector pumps to the hunters and tour operators, as the sign on the wall advertises. Next to it is a board bearing a hand-painted reminder, 'Customers who takes their bites to their vehicles are requested to make sure they return their utensils.'

Mr Khan's place is known as Chicken on the Bonnet because in the evenings he trundles out two halved oil drums filled with slow-burning coals and thus converts his store into a restaurant. His cook serves up plates of greasy French fries, slender shish kebabs and succulent chicken hunks accompanied by small plastic bowls of chillies. You eat these with your fingers sitting in your car or, if you arrived on foot, on a bench at a trestle table.

The corpulent Mr Khan has a thin moustache and sits by the braziers on a straight-backed chair. He surveys his domain like a slit-eyed Buddha, rising only to accept the customers' money. His young sons flutter around him: resting a head on his knees, tugging at each other's clothes and flicking rubber bands at the waiters. Their T-shirts have *Zubeda's Auto Spares* printed on the back.

One of the waiters slapped glasses of passion-fruit juice in front of us. He had a head shaped like a soccer ball and kept looking at Peter aggressively the way kids eye each other on the playground. Both were dressed in Western clothes. He wasn't sure if Peter was a fellow tribesman. Peter drew his elbows close to his ribcage, glanced down at his shirtfront and mumbled something in Maa.

Switching from the lingua franca of Kiswahili to their mother tongue had the effect of transforming the waiter. He was smiling and relaxed. 'If you're Maasai, why didn't you say hello to me?' he said cheerily. He was also speaking Maa.

A lizard scurried along the wall and froze. Moths thumped softly against the neon strip light. It was encased in a metal grille which was secured with a padlock. A legacy from the socialist days of scarcity when light bulbs were a hot item on the black market.

'Tomorrow we'll go down to the market and get some food. Some fruit and vegetables and biscuits. And tea and *posho* and stuff to give to Pashet. Don't want to sponge off him and Mary.'

'We can buy food in Engaruka,' Peter replied from behind a midden of chicken bones.

'Last time we were on starvation rations. I seem to recall it was a teaspoon of peanut butter for breakfast and a carrot for lunch. I was like a rake by the time we got back to Arusha. You know I hate *posho*. There's no reason to think we can find any food there this time.'

Peter accepted this with equanimity. 'Okay.'

Not for the first time, I wondered why he always assumed things would work out for the best. The hunters criticize Africans for living in the present and having only a flimsy concept of the future. They never plan ahead, they say. It has been suggested that it is because Africa has no seasons. Europeans have been stocking up for winter since fire was dragged into caves. The African way is to pluck a banana from the tree when you are hungry. Neither culture is particularly right or particularly wrong. It is simply a different approach to life. You can only understand why people behave in a certain way by living as one of them.

I wanted an early start. It's an African habit. Narrow the distance between you and the horizon while the sun is still low. Friends were putting us up for the night: Peter, on the verandah; me, in a tent in the garden.

'Shall we go back? I'm quite tired.'

Peter nodded obediently. As far as he was concerned, I was in charge. When we got to the bush, I planned to let go of the reins. It was time for Peter to take over. I wanted to be led.

We walked down to the dirt plot by the petrol station where the taxis were parked. The haggling began.

'How much to the Greek Church?'

'Two thousand.'

'We're not tourists. The local price.'

'One thousand eight hundred.'

'*Wananchi*, brother. Would I wear shoes like these if I was a rich *mzungu*?'

'All right. For you, one thousand five hundred.'

I tutted and made as if to walk off.

'Wait! Petrol is very expensive now. They raised the price.'

I said nothing.

'How much, then?'

'One thousand.' Less than two dollars. The taxi driver sneered at this risible sum and fell silent. I turned away and would have moved on to the next taxi but for the froggy croak of an ancient engine turning over.

'Get in,' he said. It was always the same.

The car lurched and dipped over the potholes. Our headlights scraped Orion's belt, then swooped downwards to impale a sleeping dog curled up on the tarmac. We were driving down a road that looked as if it had been strafed with rockets. This was where the tourists passed. It was the highway that led to the game parks. We bumped along, veering this way and that to avoid the similarly lurching and dipping oncoming vehicles.

When we had approached the driver to open negotiations, he had been sitting in the passenger seat with the innards of the car's radio in his lap and a screwdriver in his hand. He had carefully stowed these in the glovebox, which was now secured shut with a padlock. The taxi's interior spoke of diligent maintenance. A few wires had sprung loose from below the dashboard and around the ceiling light. Masking tape, applied over rents and tears, kept the rest at bay. There were no door handles missing.

'Nice car. How old is it?'

'It has twenty-five years.'

'That's older than you, brother.'

'It is my father's.' Unlike Kenyans, Tanzanians drive cautiously. It was another aspect of the slowness Peter had been referring to. Things were not built to last, but they were made to last.

A dark blue Mercedes drew up beside us – another drunken car jolting over the battlefield. Behind the steering wheel was a middle-aged Sikh. His features were pockmarked and pudgy beneath his turban, a pineapple wrapped in a napkin. He smacked his lips. I looked straight ahead.

'He is talking to you, mama.'

'I know.'

'You must greet him.'

'Certainly not. *Wahindi*.' I said it with feigned disgust, knowing this would strike a sympathetic chord with our driver. Africans dislike Asians, as they call them. They mimic them in whining falsetto behind their backs. *Chunga mwizi*. Watch out for thieves.

'Tell him you're my bodyguard.'

The taxi driver thought this was very funny and roared with laughter. He leaned across the passenger seat and shouted through the window, '*Mimi ni bodyguard yake!*'

I could see out of the corner of my eye that the Sikh was still leering. 'He wants to talk, even though you are with your husband,' cried the taxi driver, his Adam's apple bobbing with excitement.

This embarrassed me. 'He's my son.' And to Peter, 'That would give you a very old wife.'

'Yes, M. A.,' he said, polite, inscrutable.

I could poke fun at myself but for Peter it was out of the question. Maasai elders are accorded respect. They are at one remove from the age groups below them. Their pronouncements are accepted unquestioningly. Even if they make little sense. This aura of sanctity extends to the personal too. It is not done to inquire if an elder is happy or sad, on top of the world or out of sorts. This was at odds with the easy-going companionship I revelled in with Tara and Petra. We discuss what we've seen, what we think, how we feel. The girls pass judgment by balancing love with blinding directness. 'You look like a *memsahib* in that shirt. What's got into you? Go and change.' Peter was perplexed to hear them talking like this.

The innuendos had bypassed the taxi driver too. 'Tell him you are married,' he insisted.

'Why should I? I don't like the look of him. That's why I won't talk to him. I don't have to hide behind excuses.' The taxi driver was puzzled. He fell quiet. I had been enjoying the cut and thrust of the gender war, but it meant nothing to these three men.

This was a country where genital mutilation and wife-beating were orthodoxy. Taking a stick to your wife, now and then, made it clear who was boss. Of course, if there was provocation – an illicit affair – women were treated more harshly. Husbands had been known to gouge out their wives' eyes so they wouldn't look at other men again. Or they chose a final solution by pouring paraffin over them and setting them alight. These cases of assault and murder were brought to court and you read about them in the papers. But rapists were rarely charged and convicted. Men were the legislators. In Kenya, only 3 per cent of the members of parliament were women. Rape and battered women were not their concern. A few years previously, there had been a notorious case of mass rape. It had begun as a prank and ended in tragedy. The boys at a mixed boarding school had raided the girls' dormitory. The girls had panicked and rushed to the doors to escape them. It became a stampede and nineteen girls were trampled to death. The boys raped seventy-one of the survivors. The headmaster said, 'The boys meant no harm. They only wanted to rape.'

I speculated on the infinite possibilities for defining our moral universe and tried to parse the meaning of being man or woman, old or young, English or Maasai. It was confusing, to say the least. Yet again I debated on my status and Peter's. Mother or elder. Family or foreigner.

A friend, Chris Marshall, had volunteered to drive us to Enga-ruka. The following morning we set off down the cratered road. Tanzanian towns have no suburbs. The cardboard shacks give way to coffee bushes and, shortly after that, empty savannah. Soon we had abandoned the tarmac road for a narrower rutted one that set free great clouds of dust as we drove. Crumpled hills and mountains sat on the horizon. The view stretched for perhaps fifty miles and there was not a building in sight. The landscape was scorched but majestic.

Occasionally we met herders trekking cattle. They wore denim caps and flipflops and had daggers tucked into their belts. Some carried multicoloured golf umbrellas. They encouraged the cattle to plod through the dust with shrill whistles and thin-wristed stabs at the air with their *rungus*.

We stopped by one group and Peter asked their news. He was solemn and – was it my imagination? – faintly superior as he talked through the car window. The herders had come from Shinyanga and were heading for the market at Arusha, a distance of over 200 miles. The men's shirts and shorts were in tatters. The cattle were sleek, still plump despite the journey.

At Mto wa Mbu – Mosquito River – we turned right to drive in the lee of the Rift Valley's wall. Baobab trees clung to the foot of the escarpment. The bark, in the diffused sunlight, appeared to be the colour of a bruised plum. Francolin and sand grouse flighted up from the long yellow grass. I recalled one of the professional hunters telling me this was good country for black-maned lion. Lion or not, it was wilderness and superb: Maasai country.

'What impresses you most about this place?' I asked.

Peter replied without hesitation. 'The cattle and the goats. The herds are so fat.'

Fertility is of prime consideration to the Maasai. Livestock breeding livestock breeding livestock. Prestige comes with bountiful herds. The tribe believes that the first cattle on earth descended a ladder from heaven to be given to the Maasai. They are God's custodian of all cattle. Those which appear to belong to other tribes are merely on loan. Livestock are not just the tribe's lifeblood, they are physical manifestations of the spiritual aspect of the life cycle. To have livestock is to be blessed. To be denied livestock is more than bad luck. It is to be cursed.

We came upon Engaruka in the late afternoon. Pashet was standing on the verandah of his house, leaning against one of the support posts of the tin roof, his legs crossed at the ankle and his *rungu* tucked high up under his armpit. He watched without surprise as the Land Rover shuddered and stopped. We climbed down, wiped the dust from our trousers and stepped forward.

Peter said, 'Pashet!'

Pashet shifted his shoulder to move it into a more comfortable position against the pole. 'So. You have come back,' he said in Kiswahili. 'I have just come myself too. I have been in Arusha for a week at a government meeting for chiefs.'

Like the cattle, Pashet was sleek with fat. He wore jeans and a black bomber jacket. His chubby face was framed by a black Homburg and the large loops of flesh swinging from his ears. The effect was raffish: the local cowboy. I remembered our visit three years earlier when Pashet's face had contorted with anxiety at the suggestion of visiting Arusha. Then he was a down-home boy. A sojourn in the big town was a prospect laden with anticipated disaster. He would get lost, get robbed, lose face. But now he imparted this news with negligent assurance. 'There is a conference twice a year,' he said.

'Mary *iko*?' I inquired, asking after his wife.

He nodded and turned to lead us through the passage which separated the two rooms in the house. 'She's in the back.'

Little had changed in the compound. The grove of banana trees with their black malacca-like trunks, the mud kitchen hut, the shady mango tree were still there.

However, there was building in progress on the opposite side of the courtyard – a floor of beaten earth, and a tin roof supported by walls of open-weave saplings. It was the new guesthouse. At some stage between now and our next visit in another three years, the walls would be filled in with a mix of mud and stones. Mud on its own doesn't bind. It crumbles under the blitzkrieg of termites and ants. Play a hose on the wall and it melts. You need stones to glue it together.

Mary was equally phlegmatic about our arrival. Displays of wonder and delight when unexpected visitors drop by is a Western thing. I kissed her on both cheeks and made a show of unloading the food and asking the best place to put it. I wanted to make it clear we wouldn't be freeloading.

While I did this, Pashet pulled up two round stools and invited Chris and Peter to relax. They were seated with their back against the kitchen wall where they could survey the marketplace in front of the house. An old Somali, the shop owner next door, sauntered up to exchange news with Pashet. Peter stood immediately and offered his seat.

I brought out the presents: a handbag for Mary from London, as had been agreed upon at Cecilia's circumcision; a shirt for Pashet.

Mary held it up. 'He can't wear this. Look how big he's got since last time.'

It was true. Pashet had been transformed from David to Goliath. He laughed it off, 'Mary's in luck. She can wear it.'

Later she led me into the narrow room where Lori and I had slept on the floor. She had converted it into a *duka*. Some Sportsman cigarettes, a row of brown paper bags containing sugar, a few small packets of tea huddled together were caught in the copper light of the kerosene lamp as it toured the rough-cut wooden shelves. A pair of scales stood on a rickety wooden table in the middle of the room. There was nothing else.

'What do you think?' she whispered, her eyes like glow worms in the darkness.

Mercantile aspirations in the Middle East turn to car showrooms and pastry shops. In the States it might be a pizzeria or drycleaner's or beauty salon. East African pastoralists, however, set their sights on becoming purveyors of tea, maizemeal, sugar and cigarettes.

The previous year I had written a story about Samburu warriors serving as UN peacekeepers in Bosnia. By the Samburu yardstick the wages accrued by the end of their tours were so bountiful they were equivalent to winning the lottery. Was there a drycleaner or pizzeria or pastry shop to be found in the entire district? No, not even a tannery for hides, let alone a cottage industry in sandal- and bag-making. But *dukas* selling basic foodstuffs sprang up like mushrooms.

'Mary, I don't think there's much profit in selling this stuff. You want a big profit, don't you?'

She nodded, excited. 'What should I do?'

'What about selling something that no one else has? You can set the price you want as there's no competition.' After all, economics wasn't that difficult. Buy low. Sell high.

Mary's eyes glowed. 'And make a big profit instead of a little one?'

'Yeah. That sort of thing,' I prevaricated.

The conversation continued in the kitchen. We sat on low stools with tin mugs of perfumed tea by our feet. We were telling stories and giggling while we peeled potatoes and carrots for a vegetable stew.

'What should I sell?' Mary asked.

'Well, what can't you get here?'

'Maasai things.'

'Like *rubega*s and tyre sandals and tin mugs and plates?'

She was nodding eagerly.

'There you go, Mary. You can become the Woolworths of Engaruka. Go for it.'

She didn't know what she was doing. Neither did I. Culture can diffuse and distort fact into an unrecognizable shape. As it turned out, my attempts to be a good friend were misguided.

CHAPTER 25

It was just after dawn. From the other side of the wattle poles came the swishing sound of Mary's seven-year-old daughter, Jekleen, sweeping the compound with a bunch of sticks. Her energetic collection of carrot scrapings and potato peels released miniature tornadoes of dust into the air. My nostrils tickled. I opened my eyes.

There had been anonymous scurryings in the darkness and cicadas shrilling and buzzing. The wind had soughed in the giant mango tree so persistently that I had been convinced it was raining until Jekleen's endeavours had proved otherwise.

Sometime after midnight I had heard the leering yip of a hyena prowling the streets for food. Hyenas will have a go at cooking pots, drunks who have passed out on the way home or anything else which is left outside. At another early-morning hour something had landed with a soft thud on my stomach and woken me up. I had grunted – 'oomph' – and fumbled to switch on the torch. A marmalade kitten was preening itself in the far corner of the hut. I felt enormously snug inside our wooden bower.

Chris was oblivious to the noisy trilling of the birds. He lay on his back in a sleeping bag, his right ear a few inches from a chewed sheep's knuckle. The kitten's. Peter lay on the dirt floor shrouded in the green *shuka* he had packed in his knapsack. Even his head was covered. He looked ready for burial.

The previous evening he had been brimming with chatter. Chris was leaving us at Engaruka to return to Nairobi. We had been debating our means of return. Since our previous visit a *matatu* service had been introduced. I had been prepared to walk to Mto wa Mbu, a village astride the nearest road to Engaruka. It was forty miles away, only a two-day journey. I saw little reason to alter the plan.

Pashet had scoffed. 'You can't with *your* legs.'

'I'm going to release some information,' Peter retorted. 'M. A. is known as Mama Land Rover.'

He had arranged a folding chair with a slatted wooden seat under his head as if it was a pillow. 'I'm going to be battered and beaten tomorrow' were his last words before falling asleep.

His corpselike form didn't stir when someone called my name. I stumbled guiltily to my feet and peered through the poles. The man on the other side was incredibly black: face, shirt, trousers.

'Do you remember me?' he asked.

'Yes . . . of course . . . Moses?'

His teeth flashed white. 'I've come to see Pashet. I can't stay. My wife is sick. She's passing blood.' He smiled again. 'You are back. Come later to my *duka* for tea. I am selling these days.'

I got up and decided to go for a walk around town. The line of *dukas* where men in purple and red robes squat in the deep shade of the verandahs. The donkeys flicking flies from their ears. The fields of maize bisected by irrigation ditches. The dilapidated clinic with its health workers and dog-eared posters: a warning against AIDS, an advertisement for Malaraquin.

It was on sale at the *dukas*. The government supplies the clinic with chloroquine but had not provided any drugs for over two months. There were only a few tablets left. Malaria was epidemic here. Pashet said he was suffering from it. Moses' wife probably had it too. People complained about it with the same resignation with which the English moan about winter colds.

By the time I got back, Chris was fiddling with the Land Rover but Peter, in his green shroud, still looked like a corpse. I called over, 'Wake up, Peter. It's Sunday. Don't you want to go to church?'

He sat up and blinked, stuck a finger in his ear and wiggled it. 'Oh yes, M. A.! I'm coming!'

Peter was a pious churchgoer, attended regularly. God and sport underpinned his social life. But he had only sampled our church across the street in London once. 'It was very sad, very quiet. The trouble with Catholics is they have no music.' He liked a bit of action on Sunday mornings: foot-tapping hymns.

The one-room church stood at the top of the town, at the base of the escarpment, not far from the clinic and just beyond the school. It would have been a feature of architectural prominence if it had not been obscured by trees – mangoes, cassias and red flamboyants – and choked by the dormitories that were hard on its front steps.

We milled about outside with the congregation. Several young-sters were taking first communion that day. The girls were tall and lanky and wore white: dresses, ankle socks, gloves, bonnets and eyebrow-skimming Jackie Kennedy veils. They carried little white handbags the way the Queen does. The dresses were very fussy. Ruched tops, sleeves that would have looked good on a lamb chop and crinolines under the skirts. The boys were in long-sleeved white shirts and grey flannels. One wore very black dark glasses, even at the altar. I debated which decade had been sartorially resurrected here. I decided it was Florida 1950s or Zimbabwe 1980s (the same thing) with antecedents in the plantation houses of the American South.

I chatted to Willy Richard, a teacher who had ridden up on his bike. He greeted me in the Tanzanian way, 'Poleni safari.' Expansively translated, it meant sorry for the hardship and tribu-lations you inevitably must have experienced on your journey. He spoke in English after that and told me he had once been to Nairobi, in 1987.

The school chef greeted me. He was a cheerful man in his fifties who wore shorts and a ripped T-shirt. He was barefoot and had the sort of lean, perfectly muscled body which would have taken months to build in a gym. He was stirring Sunday lunch over an open fire in a cauldron the size of an oil drum. It was kidney beans, the regional staple.

The gathering began to flow into the whitewashed interior. I took my leave of Peter. The service would last at least two hours. Moses – now in green shirt and pale jacket – appeared at the head of the steps and grabbed my hand. He ignored my lame protests and maintained a firm grip as he sliced through the press of people. He whispered a command to two men and they rose from their bench. Peter and I had been allotted a prime position in the front row. There were no pews.

The congregation shifted and stirred to make room for other

latecomers. They did not look particularly Maasai. The women were swathed in colourful cloth of bold prints. The men wore trousers. But some, like Moses, had looped ears which stuck out from their chess-piece heads like jug handles.

The shepherds for this flock – a pastor and two deacons robed in white – stood in the sanctuary with their hands clasped in front of their chests. One of the deacons had a thin face and pointed beard. Like an apostle, Peter whispered. Behind them was a raised altar bearing two lit candles, vases of yellow cassia and a cross. The cross was draped with green and gold tinsel. Streamers of green, red, silver and gold were strung from the roof beams too, and a few paper cutouts of Santa Claus. The Christmas decorations had been up on our last visit. Everything about the church spoke of care and attention.

Two choirs sat between the clergy and the laity, facing each other across the chancel. On the left, ranked in three rows against the wall, the choir from Lower Engaruka. To the right, against the opposite wall, the breakaway Upper Engaruka choir.

The contenders from Upper Engaruka opened with a mellifluous hymn accompanied by the slithering rattle of seeds and reeds. The *kayamba*. They sang watching the choirmaster, who held his arms out to the side and thrashed them up and down. The women in the front row wore orange and green dresses made from local cloth and white headcloths fringed with golden beads. Their sandshoes were fastened with fluorescent laces.

A few prayers were said and then the old guard from Lower Engaruka rose to its feet in the self-assured way of reigning champions. The men's shirts were fastened at the neck with diagonally striped ties. The women wore gold ear-studs and necklaces of white plastic pop-it beads and their hair had been raked into tight cornrows. The choir stood. And waited.

A breeze wafted through the mosquito netting nailed to the window frames. The Christmas decorations rustled. A chorister from Upper Engaruka untied her baby and put it to her breast.

'Another very tough choir,' Peter confided in my ear. 'Comparisonwise it will be hard to know who is best.' I hadn't heard him use that tone since Manchester United played Liverpool.

At a signal, the choirmaster's assistant pressed the button on the ghettoblaster in his lap. The machine began to thump to a steady metronome beat. The choirmaster was moving his arms about expansively in time to the thumping. He had the pop eyes and fixed smile of a mime artist. I recognized him from last time. He was young for a man with such weighty responsibility but disguised his youth with a small goatee. He wore black slacks and a white T-shirt which bore the image of the local member of parliament. He continued to conduct while the congregation sat in silence. This was hardly a fitting performance for a virtuoso.

Just as I was beginning to fidget with embarrassment, he tilted his head back and lifted his arms, the forefinger and thumb of both hands forming an O. He opened his mouth. Another large O. A hush descended. Then, at a flick of his hands, the choir exploded into a riff of perfectly pitched tenors overlaid with soprano descants. Ants of pleasure crawled along my forearms.

Some minutes after this *tour de force* Moses approached Peter and murmured in his ear. Peter nodded and Moses crossed the nave between the choirs to step up in front of the altar. He seemed to be the master of ceremonies, commanding people to begin doing this or stop doing that with a nod of the head or a swift horizontal slash at the air with his downturned palm. Peter said he was the church warden.

Moses cleared his throat and announced to the congregation that there were two visitors amongst them today. They were special visitors because three years ago they had given generously towards the construction of the hospital. And now, he said, he was going to give the floor to Peter Lekerian, who had come all the way from Kenya.

Peter strolled up to stand by the lectern. Moses withdrew into the wings. It was a low-key entrance: no drumrolls, no studio applause. Peter carried it off with impressive self-assurance. He has an instinct for speaking in public. He told the congregation that he had come here with his foster mum, who had put him through school and who hadn't forgotten him when she left Nairobi. 'When she goes here or there, she takes me with her,' he said, 'even though I have a job in Nairobi.' He told them how he had travelled to

London to see his mum. And he said how glad he was that the hospital was nearly finished.

The congregation listened in rapt attention. As far as Peter was concerned, talking was as natural as breathing. I had a vision of myself – a white woman modestly covered from head to foot in *shukas*, surreptitiously dabbing at the corner of one eye – and liked what I had imagined. I liked being proud of my son.

Peter then waxed lyrical. He said his friends had listened to the tape we had made of the Engaruka choristers on our last trip and his friends had said it was some of the sweetest hymnsinging in the world. Even though, he pointed out, the choir did not come from a well known place. The audience was transported. They clapped and laughed and the women gave shrill ululations to show their appreciation of his oratory.

As the applause died down, Moses stepped forward. The heat and activity had made him slightly dishevelled. I longed to straighten his jacket and smooth his shirt collar over his lapels. He spoke in Swahili and I caught my name. Then he looked at me and gave a smiling nod. It was my cue. He wanted me to speak too. My worst, as the girls used to say.

I walked up to the lectern and said a few words of greeting in Swahili and explained that Peter would translate for me as I preferred to speak in English. I said that I was glad that we had been able to help with the construction of the hospital and that I was glad that soon it would be serving the needs of the people. I finished with something to the effect that I hoped the community would prosper as a result. A ripple of polite clapping, not more than that, broke the ensuing silence. Then Peter and I returned to our chairs.

The service dragged on for two and a half hours. Some time between the second and third collections, or perhaps the first and second, Moses signalled the communicants to come forward to receive the Eucharist. This was the cue for Upper Engaruka to give voice. They sang with their choirmaster inches from their open mouths to allow the communicants to file up to the altar. The boys and girls stood in a line with their tongues stuck out like giraffe browsing a thorn tree and the pastor bent towards each one, murmured, passed on. After they had all been administered the sacraments, friends wreathed them with garlands of shiny tinsel, an event punctuated by the popping light of a camera flash. It was Willy Richard the teacher. He fluttered his free hand this way and that, arranging them through the lens for a group photo as they stood solemnly to attention.

As they filed back to their seats it was the turn of the Lower Engaruka choir. Perhaps emboldened by the lavish praise of Peter's speech, the choirmaster ranged across to the other side of the chancel and stood with his bottom in the faces of the now seated Upper Engaruka choir. But he had overplayed his hand. His Cheshire-cat smile and saucer eyes were eclipsed by the communicants as they shuffled back to their seats and he had to raise his hands above his head. The choir never faltered, led by disembodied, O-shaped fingers dancing in the air.

When the service was over and the congregation had disappeared into the town, we fetched Chris and went with Moses to the edge of the plains to see the hospital. It was a grey cement-block shell with weeds growing where the floor should have been. The open roof and empty window frames seemed like wounds. The hospital had five rooms: a central reception with two rooms on each side. A baboon had deposited a large turd just inside the doorway.

Moses said they had the galvanized tin for the roof but the wood for the beams had been left outside for so many years that it had warped. They needed cement for the staff rooms, he added. The funds were short 1 million shillings. I listened to what he was saying and wondered at the faith of Africans and the hopelessness of Africa.

Afterwards in the Land Rover Chris asked why they hadn't simply renovated the existing clinic. I said I didn't know. I couldn't for the life of me figure out why they hadn't.

One evening I was sitting in the compound on the back step of the house helping Mary get supper ready. Night falls on Engaruka like a cloak once the sun has set. It is a thick, impenetrable darkness. There are no streetlights; no lamps twinkling between the cracks of curtained windows. Light – a wick in a tin in the *bomas*, a kerosene lantern in town – is a luxury. I was peeling carrots beneath the thin beam of a penlight torch. It was attached to a Velcro strip fastened around my head. My new toy. I was thrilled with it. It was much better than the old way: preparing food and writing in my notebook holding the torch in my mouth. The headband was the sort of invention I could master without breaking the thing. I moved about behind this beam of light like a car. Half the vehicles in Tanzania had only one working headlight. Mama Land Rover.

I knew Mary hadn't quite been won over by the torch-headband combo or she would have said that she wanted it. As for the children, it aroused both excitement and mistrust. They either fell to their knees and shielded their downcast eyes as if receiving a celestial message or squealed and scampered off. Sometimes they asked if they could borrow it and I would hand it over.

Peter appeared through the back door. He had been sitting on the front verandah with Moses talking *mambo ya wazee*. Men's business. He was excited and pleased. 'There's a Maasai man here from Kenya. Come and meet him.' I wiped my hands on my jeans and followed Peter through the house. I could sense the bulky presence of men, heard their droning gossip. There was no moon that night. My eyes told me nothing.

Silhouettes swelled and flattened as figures moved about. Pashet's friends dropped in to hear the news and give it and just to hang out. I could make out Pashet's sandalled feet by my shoulder. They were wedged against one of the poles supporting the roof. He must have been sitting on a chair, rocking it back on its rear legs. He was talking in the slow, relaxed manner of men who have been passing many hours at a bar. They were probably conjecturing who was sick, who had sold goats for a good price, who was sleeping with another man's wife. It was an inference reached after years of eavesdropping on men's conversations on various continents. They are the same, whatever the tribe. Western men show their appreciation of an all-male social gathering by laughing heartily, all together. Maasai men laugh rarely. They certainly never guffaw. In the pastoralist lexicon, laughter is a spontaneous reaction to a humorous remark, not a social semaphore. British farmers and stockbrokers, on the other hand, never foam at the mouth, never lie rigid and panting on the floor and never turn somersaults when they are excited.

Our notions of social response are shaped by our cultural backgrounds. This was as valid for me as it was for Peter. What hope had either of us of readjusting the way we looked at the world? Both our egos were already well and truly formed. Fold a fish when it's wet or it will crack. That's a Samburu proverb.

'M. A., this is Paul. From Kenya. He works in development.'

'Pleased to meet you. I gather you're here for a short visit.' His spectral Oxford voice didn't seem to be attached to anything. Then he shifted on his feet and I discerned the outline of draped cloth.

'Yes. We dropped in to say hello to everyone. Back to Nairobi before the end of the week. And you?'

'I'm from a small little place near Kajiado. I'm sure you wouldn't have heard of it. I've been here for about three weeks, but I've been down with a very bad go of malaria. This is about the first day I haven't felt wonky. I'm hoping to feel well enough to get moving soon. I've got some goats with Mereso.'

'We're going to Mereso's tomorrow. We stayed there once before. About three years ago when I was on assignment for an American magazine. Writing about how the Maasai protect their environment. Is Mereso a friend of yours too?'

'We're agemates, you know. And relatives. I'm driving the goats to Kenya to sell.'

'Past Ol Doinyo Lengai?'

'Mmm-hmmm. That's right.'

My thoughts turned to the last time I had seen the Mountain of God. I had walked that way with a caravan of camels. An image flapped across my mind's eye. One man, blood red, standing like an ancient anthill in a plain of primrose-yellow grass. It stretched smooth as glass to the horizon. And on the horizon was the inverted cone of Lengai.

'I'll probably hand them over to some herders after I've crossed the border. They can do the rest of it,' Paul continued.

'How long will it take to walk to the border?'

'About ten days, I should think.'

'I wish I could come with you. That's God's own country.'

He murmured some pleasantry and we left it at that. In my thirties my passion had been ignited by the prospect of cattle-rustling with Samburu warriors. Now the thought of walking goats with a middle-aged man was sufficient to give it a flutter.

We were leaving the following morning. The plan was for Chris to drive us the five miles to Mereso's *boma* on his way back to Nairobi. If we left early, he would reach home before nightfall. It was 150 miles as the crow flies.

While we were packing the car, Pashet summoned me to his room. He was lying on a pink-and-white flowered sheet. He turned to look at me, then turned back to throw the window open. A lozenge of sunlight fell onto his legs and I could see that his red-and-white checked *rubega* was twisted up around his knees. The effect was both louche and disconcerting. I had never before seen a Maasai man reclining on a bed.

'Can you help Mary with her shop?'

I was ready for this. 'I can't help with money. I have none. I'm very poor. I have no job.'

Shortly after that he came into the compound, wrapping his *rubega* around him in the absent-minded way men adjust their flies on leaving the urinal.

'Mary is coming to Arusha.'

'For her shop?'

'Yes.'

'Great. She can go with Chris. He's leaving today.'

'She'll wait and go with you.'

'That's fine,' I said.

CHAPTER 26

We were walking out so we were travelling light: a small knapsack and a cardboard box containing a grapefruit, the leftover carrots, some biscuits, a jar of peanut butter and *posho*, tea and sugar for the wives.

Mereso watched as Chris drove away leaving Peter and I standing in the dust with our luggage. He was over six-foot tall and possibly the fattest Maasai I'd ever seen. He was encased in rolls and rolls of fat marked by black creases where they folded over each other. When he smiled his eyes changed to slits. In Maasaini, where scarcity is a fact of life, there isn't a centimetre of excess flesh to be pinched. Maasai men are built like herons. Fatness says: I am rich so I can afford to eat as much as I want.

Mereso's physique was a manifestation of his stature within the community. He was well heeled in the Maasai way: thousands of head of livestock and numerous children. Six of them went to school. He may have been illiterate, but he had vision. He wanted them to become members of parliament. He was, in every way, a man of substance. He chuckled the chuckle of a rich man and said, '*Karibuni*.'

The English welcome you into their homes by taking you on a tour of their gardens. Complimenting the flowers is an oblique way of admiring your hostess, which in England is not a feeling to be expressed openly. The Maasai like to show off their animals. Mereso did this straight away by leading us across to his goats.

They were jammed together in a circular thorn enclosure which in turn stood inside the large elliptical fence that embraced the huts. It was the symbolic heart of the *boma* just as the altar is the stage for ritual in a church. The goats were white and brown and grey, dusted with black or brown speckles, splashed with patches or pure in colour. Their dark eyes glistened moistly. They craned their necks and gave sharp little tinderbox coughs.

Peter changed when he was looking at goats. His body was both taut and relaxed and it assumed an athletic intensity. He held his arms by his side and pulled in his chin, counting with his eyes while pretending not to. Goats made him look serious and adult. *Mambo ya wazee*.

'This is very interesting. They are like Mr Mowlem's. They keep the nannies and billies separate. And it's the same size herd,' he noted approvingly. 'These kids are only one and a half months old and some of the nannies are pregnant again. They're in very good shape.'

The conventional wisdom – which Mr Mowlem undoubtedly would have handed out in his lectures in Ethiopia – counselled against allowing nannies to give birth more than once a year in case they lost condition. Peter's breeding herd dropped kids every six months. He was in a hurry to expand. Mereso was obviously of a like mind. He too saw to it that his nannies stayed pregnant the year round.

'I don't live to be in a town. I live for my cattle and goats. I prefer it here on the plains to Engaruka,' he pronounced.

Peter hummed an affirmation in the back of his throat. He was in thrall to Mereso's intellect and his patriarchal manner.

'Isn't he a charming man?' he whispered. 'He's very handsome. Very big and strong. Like a leader.' He had found another father figure, this time in a man who lived according to pastoralist values.

A girl pulled aside the branches which protected the opening to the nannies' pen and stood in their midst making shooing sounds. The animals milled about and she shouted at me, 'Get out of the way! They're frightened of you.' I was a pink-skinned alien with an alien's smell. I stepped back and the goats burst forth with an explosion of bleats and raspy snorts. They stopped to look about them and scent the air, then trotted past a hobbled donkey and out the *boma* gate.

One of Mereso's sons herded them onto the plains. His eyes were kohled with ochre dust thrown up by their sharp hooves. He couldn't have been more than seven, but a warrior's spear soared above his head. It was not an affectation. Maasai youngsters are used to contending with the elemental forces of nature. Death by jaw, claw and horn is a common way of departing the world. The battle between mankind and wild animals has been waged on these plains ever since our Australopithecus ancestors inhabited them millions of years ago.

During the day lions preyed on any animal that wandered off on its own. At night they prowled along the *boma* fence looking for sections that were low enough to leap over. Other dangers lurked in the tangled vegetation that choked the slopes and ravines of the escarpment. When the goats left the interminable space of the open plain to follow the ragged game trails through leafy woodland, passing from the sunlight into secret shadowy tunnels, the herders were on the alert. The crack of a twig signalled a solitary bull buffalo or a short-sighted rhino startled by the passers-by. A quivering branch overhead launched a leopard on the hunt. The young boys who herded the goats and cows were expected to protect them from these attacks.

But it is the warriors' job to avenge the theft of clan property. They track down the lions which have taken livestock and kill them with their spears and stabbing swords.

It is a fairly even contest. Warriors are often mauled by lions which, like all cats, rake with their claws as well as bite. Lions' claws secrete traces of putrefying meat from their kills so a blow from one of their paws means being infected with lethal bacteria. Mereso's warriors had no access to antibiotics. Their infected wounds were packed with herbs instead. Some survived. Some didn't.

Once the goats had been dispatched to the war zone for the day, I made my excuses and disappeared into the grove of acacias behind the *boma*. I needed a pee.

'Where's she going?' Mereso asked.

'To look at the woods to see if there are any changes,' Peter replied.

'Is she looking for anything in particular?'

'No just going into the woods.'

Mereso accepted this philosophically. '*Laisungu* are always very curious. We'll let her just get on with taking a look at whatever it is that she's so interested in.'

By the time I got back, Mereso and Peter had retreated to the shade of an *enchani pus* tree. Mereso was sitting on a stiff cowhide with his legs to one side, resting his weight on his right hand like a girl at a picnic. We talked in a mix of Swahili, Maa and English with Peter translating for either Mereso or me when prompted.

I asked about Noonkepa, whose hut we had slept in on the previous visit. In my mind's eye I saw again The Breaking of Water at Birth lying beneath the stars alongside her lover Ololokidomo, in the very same place as we were sitting now, and roaring with laughter. It was the only time I had seen two Maasai flirting outrageously. On the whole, women are treated with indifference. I hoped Noonkepa would be my hostess on this visit too.

'She's away,' said Mereso, dismissive. He lifted a large hand to swat at a fly and his imitation Rolex caught a spear of sunlight.

I scrunched my face into disappointment. 'Darnit. I wanted to greet her.'

I gave Mereso the travelling clock I'd brought for him. I wanted to show how much respect we accorded him. He held it this way and that, turning it around in his fingers as if deciding whether or not to make it his friend. Peter had read the instructions with meticulous care the previous evening. He made a great show of demonstrating the function of each button and switch.

Mereso asked how much it had cost. 'Eighteen thousand,' I said. In Tanzanian shillings it sounded like quite a lot. He grunted and continued to stare at the green plastic thing in his palm.

The clock must have been satisfactory because soon after that he said in Maa, 'It's no good when visitors come unannounced and we are not prepared. Shall I slaughter a goat for you?'

'What do we say?' I mumbled to Peter.

He ducked his head and said to me in a low voice, 'We are only two. If we are five it would be different.' He was speaking in English.

'There is a drought so I can't offer you milk. We can only offer you meat to take on your safari,' Mereso went on. Peter translated this as 'canned meat' instead of 'butchered meat'. Mereso fixed his dignified gaze on a donkey which was flicking flies off its ears. He was waiting for his generosity to be digested.

I looked to Peter for a cue. He said, 'We must be humble and show we are strong by saying no. If we were drunk, we would say oooo-eee yes.'

'Tell Mereso that it's a very kind thought to slaughter one of his rams. But we have so much food with us already that it isn't necessary. His hospitality is generous enough as it is.'

People came and went. Old men wrapped in blankets, women who stood with feet braced and a fist on hip. They chattered and shouted and murmured sentences that were both rock hard and singsong. I kept on nagging Peter, 'What are they saying? No, tell me *exactly* what they're saying.'

We were without a vehicle, without sleeping bags and the other inexplicable accoutrements of the *laisungu*. This put us on an equal footing with this isolated community of Maasai. I wanted to be stitched into the fabric of their daily routine and become a part of it. There was only one reality – this khaki globe of cracked earth contained by extinct volcanoes and an overcast sky riding hard atop the Ngorongoro escarpment.

We were downwind of the animal enclosures, which were sending along tangy whiffs of goat droppings and the more pungent odour of donkey manure. In the great outer silence of the plains the breeze sounded like distant traffic approaching through the acacia glade. Here amongst the smells and insects and the chirruping starlings, I was seeking the epiphany of my relationship with Peter.

A man with a wrinkled goblin face joined the gathering. He had dropped in from another *boma*. He stood over us with his hands clasped on the knob of his walking stick. He scrutinized me with clouded eyes. We exchanged greetings. *Sopa, ipa.*

'She knows Maa well,' he observed. 'She has a soft tongue.' This was addressed not to me but to Mereso. To Peter he said, 'Is she married? Does she have children?'

One of Mereso's wives walked over and pointed at a plastic container at Mereso's feet. It had an old corn cob as a stopper. She exchanged a few words with Mereso then shouted at another wife who was standing outside her hut on the far side of the *boma*. The other wife answered with a string of vowels oi-eee-aaay. It was impossible to tell whether they were having an argument or a friendly chat. Peter said they were discussing whether this was the *debe* that had been run over by a tractor and if it was all right to carry water in it.

This seemed as good a time as any to discover whether our secret mission had any chance of success. 'Ask about Nanyokie. Find out whether she's married yet,' I urged Peter.

Peter said something to Mereso in Maa and he said something back. No one seemed at all interested in the exchange.

'Well?'

'She is married. To a warrior. They live near by. Over there.'

Whenever I really wanted to know what he was thinking, Peter managed to look inscrutable. We had expected she might be married. After all, she was probably fourteen already. Still, there was no trace of disappointment on his face.

Mereso must have read my thoughts because he said, 'I will send you with a young girl to show you her *boma*,' and patted the accident-prone *debe* to show how small the child would be. In less than a minute a young girl appeared. She stood impassively, her belly protruding slightly under her ragged *shuka*. 'Take this mama to see Nanyokie,' he instructed. 'The young man will sing to her like a warrior.'

Peter threw back his head and laughed. It was sharp, almost like a bark. Then he tucked the side of his face against his shoulder and looked at Mereso with one eye shut. The flattery pleased him, but he didn't want to show it. 'I am not very young like warriors, but those are very charming words,' he said coyly.

Mereso eased his considerable bulk upright. 'I have to leave you now. I have a meeting.' He said it in an offhand, furtive way and wandered off with the goblin man in tow.

I stared after the two red figures wavering in a column of golden heat and reflected that I didn't know these people at all. Least of all, Peter. What did he mean, he was not as young as a warrior? In England he'd talked endlessly about being a warrior. When he met people and described his life back home to them, he repopulated his schooldays with lions and spears and men pitting their strength against wild beasts. Perhaps he'd moonlighted as a warrior in the school holidays. I couldn't recall him recounting how he'd herded cattle or hunted lions, over Christmas. He must have told me about it and I'd forgotten. I felt thwarted. After all these years, this young man was still a stranger to me. I was determined to know my son better. As Peter would have said, it was an issue of The Truth.

The little girl was about fifty yards ahead, steaming across the plain and ignoring us entirely. We trailed behind, our feet sending up plumes of dust. There was no grass and the vegetation was sparse – just the occasional stunted tree or straggly bush.

I said, 'Would you like a biscuit?'

'No thanks, M. A. I can't eat in front of women.'

I rushed into the chink of opportunity. 'Is that because you're a warrior?'

'Mmmmm-mmmm.' It was neither a definite yes nor a definite no. A sort of maybe.

We continued walking through the dust, looking serious.

'So are you a warrior or an elder?'

The reply was ambiguous. 'I am too young to be an elder. And I am not a warrior.'

'You said you were a warrior when you were in England,' I pressed.

Silence.

'What do you feel you are?'

Peter ruminated on this as we scrambled down a shallow gully and up the other side. He was walking with his head down and pushed forward, staring at the ground. He stopped and lifted his eyes to the clumps of grey cloud pressing down on the skyline. 'It is hard to know yourself.'

Nanyokie's new home, we had been told, was just next door. This could mean it was anything up to ten miles away. But we must have been getting close because after a mile or so we came across her mother-in-law taking two donkeys to fetch water. She wore an ankle-length black cape offset by white beads. She had no shoes. She was somewhere between child-bearing and old age, still vigorous but no longer robust. Her hair had been shaved. It was grizzled, but her elegance had not dimmed. She had cantilevered cheek-bones, generous lips and a sculpted nose.

We greeted each other in Maa. There followed an exchange that sounded like dice being rattled in a tin. 'I have told her that you are from England. And that I am not Maasai,' Peter said.

He had been indulging in aliases ever since we had arrived in Tanzania. At Mto wa Mbu he had told the petrol station attendant he was Ugandan.

Mamma-in-law gave Peter a shrewd look. 'Well, you're certainly not English,' she harrumphed.

I liked this spirited woman. She was a bright counterpoint to the blighted surroundings. Peter seemed to think so too. He had been quietly appraising her.

'Comparisonwise she was terribly beautiful before her time,' he observed. Then he repeated it to her in Maa, that she must have been a great beauty once.

This pleased her. A touch of the coquette came to her voice. 'If I'd known you were coming, I would have dressed up. Then I would still be beautiful.' As she spoke, she leaned on her stick so that she could scrape a burr off the side of one foot with the big toe of the other. Her feet were cracked and grey, like the land.

She turned her attention to my hair. I doubt that she had seen a blonde before. 'Is it grey?' she asked Peter.

'No.'

She moved her head back, peered at me down her nose and tentatively pulled at a few strands as if inspecting merchandise.

'Is it a hat?'

'No.'

'It flutters.' She shook her hand from side to side to illustrate what she meant, then tsssked through her teeth. 'It's a lion's mane.'

I had brought more presents with me. I dug into a pocket of my fishing jacket, extracted one and handed it to her. 'This is for you.' It was definitely appropriate.

The round mirror was shaped like a tiny compact. It was backed with plastic and had a plastic lid so that you could shut it against the dust. I had bought it a few years before in an Eritrean bazaar. It was a lovely baby blue and just the right size for slipping into a pocket or the folds of a *rubega*. It had been my travelling mirror.

She palmed it and fluttered her hand again, more slowly this time. She hadn't gazed at her reflection yet. She was clearly in awe of the mirror, but coveted it. 'My son should have this. Warriors like to make themselves look beautiful. They're always admiring themselves. I'm old and don't need it.'

'I insist.'

'You mean I can be proud of myself?' I nodded. Encouraged, she launched into a shy confession, 'Actually, I do look at myself sometimes.'

I asked after her son and his bride, Nanyokie. She said her son was at the *boma* and Nanyokie was taking the goats to drink at the stream. There ensued a discussion as to what to do next. It lasted about fifteen minutes. Should we first make ourselves known to the husband, who might 'set Nanyokie free' to talk to us? Or should we veer off in a different direction to catch Nanyokie on the way to the watering place? Peter thought we should greet the warrior and ask his permission to talk to his wife. It was the courteous thing to do, he said. I was in favour of heading straight for Nanyokie. It involved less walking. Besides, it went against the grain to treat Nanyokie as if she was a chattel without a free will of her own.

As it turned out, mamma-in-law made the decision for us. She spied Nanyokie in the distance and shouted to her, 'You have some guests! Take the goats that side and wait for them.'

She hadn't filled out at all in the intervening years that had seen her through puberty. She was still tiny. The coils of copper which snaked from wrist to elbow seemed far too heavy for her fine-boned arms. The broad collar of beads at her throat emphasized the fragility of her stalklike neck. Her married woman's adornments – *isurutia* and *emonyorit* – made her look as if she was dressing up, pretending to be an adult. She was still as slim-hipped as a choirboy. She stood there, so small on the plains, and watched us with wide eyes. Her delicacy made her seem vulnerable.

When she recognized us, she covered her mouth with a ringed hand and giggled. She greeted me but said nothing to Peter, who was staring at a stone a few yards in front of him and looking rather bored. This wasn't easy for him. She was exquisitely beautiful.

I gave her packets of tea and sugar, which she handed to mamma-in-law for safe keeping. When I took out my notebook and jotted down a few impressions, she hovered by my shoulder and watched.

She was as curious as ever about how writing was done. A vision of Nanyokie at a school desk shimmered and dissolved. I felt a momentary pang. She would have made a fine daughter-in-law.

We started walking and I found myself on my own with Nanyokie. It was a good opportunity to give her the other presents – a string of cowrie shells to sew onto a gourd or hide skirt and another mirror. I wanted her to keep it for herself and not give it to her husband. She probably had no idea what she looked like in all her finery.

We were strolling side by side, our bodies brushing against each other. The goats had bells hanging from their necks, some carved out of wood and some fashioned from old cooking pots. They clonked and tinkled as the animals meandered along, their eyes patrolling for any tufts of grass. Nanyokie's eyes sparkled as she chattered in Maa. I couldn't understand much of what she was saying, but she appeared delighted to see me again. She took one of the rings from her fingers, lifted my left hand and tried to put it on my ring finger. It stuck at the knuckle, but she forced it over, smiling triumphantly when she had done it. 'You are like a mother to me,' she said.

At that moment a brown nanny moaned and keeled onto its side. Peter and Nanyokie both rushed over. She pinned it to the ground by kneeling on its neck while Peter was pulling at something under its tail. The nanny bleated in protest. It seemed a strange way to minister to a sick animal. Then I saw that Peter's hands had disappeared up her backside. He yanked and a pair of viscous legs appeared. It was a breech birth. Seconds later a little brown kid plopped onto the dirt and the mother began to lick it free of the yellow foetal sac.

'Look at her kissing her young one!' Peter cried. He was exuberant. He had been an efficient midwife, knowing exactly what to do. I felt a surge of pride, just as I had when he'd addressed the congregation at the church in Engaruka.

It took ten minutes for the kid to wobble to its feet and stagger to safety between its mother's legs. It stood there uncertainly while she delivered vigorous licks to its soggy coat. Then its legs splayed and it fell flat on its face. The nanny yawned. Her eyes were soft with contentment. It's the only time I have been able to say with certainty that I could read what was in a goat's heart.

Peter had been teasing and pulling at the nanny's udder to get her milk going and by now it was squirting onto the ground. He picked up the kid and put it to the teat. 'I think this chap was so hungry he wanted to come out just to get at the milk.'

While he was doing this, Nanyokie held the nanny by the ear so it couldn't move away. The two of them worked so smoothly as a team you would have thought they had been delivering kids together all their lives. But they didn't exchange a single word. They never even looked at each other. Peter was beyond Nanyokie's reach and Nanyokie was out of bounds for Peter.

As the kid was feeding, a man in his twenties strolled up and joined us. He had fleshy lips and a giraffe's long silky eyelashes. He thrust his spear into the ground and leaned against its quivering length with his legs crossed at the ankle. It was a symbolic statement. His double-edged *simi* was already sheathed and threaded on the belt at his waist. A very serious-looking nut, stolen from a seven-ton truck, topped his *rungu*, but he tucked the club high up in the V where his legs met his crotch.

His weapons were at rest, but it was a startlingly phallic pose. It was all the more bizarre because he exuded a gentle, almost effeminate aura. He had planted his spear to his left and wrapped his right arm across his body to hold it. He put his other hand flat against his cheek.

Peter and the man strolled behind us, deep in conversation. Every so often he giggled at what Peter was saying. Peter was carrying the baby goat in his right hand. He had grasped it by the hind legs so that its head was bouncing around a few inches above the ground. It was giving out a string of pitiful bleats.

He held it aloft and said to me, 'This is how warriors carry kids. If I hold it like this' – he cradled it in his arms – 'it's too comfortable. It doesn't make a noise and its mother won't be able to follow.'

Nanyokie shouted something in Maa and pointed. Peter dropped the kid and ran over to a bush and bent down to peer under it. Nanyokie picked up the kid and continued walking. I noticed she was holding it by the hind legs too.

'M. A., there's a snake!' Peter was crouched down, bobbing his head back and forth to see where it was hidden. He was very excited. I don't know what he thought he was going to do if it attacked. He didn't have a spear. Not even a stick. But he was enjoying himself immensely.

When he couldn't find the snake, he joined me and we walked together. Peter said, 'This guy is called Ole Materr. He says he remembers when we were here before. It was during the last great drought. He's Nanyokie's husband.' Peter imparted information if and when he felt like it. Sometimes he didn't bother to pass things on at all, even though he knew I was hostage to his translations. Seeing that I was interested in Ole Materr, he added, 'He's been with Mereso's family for about nine years. When we were here last time, he was up in the hills with the cattle.'

'Oh? I don't understand.'

'He had to work for Mereso to get Nanyokie's hand.'

'You mean . . . instead of paying a dowry?'

'It's still a custom for poor people who can't afford to pay with cows.' As he said it, I thought of how we had speculated on the size of Nanyokie's bride price when we were walking on the cliffs in Somerset. Three hundred pounds over nine years worked out as an annual sum of . . . hardly anything at all. We must have undervalued Nanyokie's worth.

Another thought occurred to me. 'Nanyokie must have been five when he chose her.'

Peter shrugged this off. 'Maybe. He can't count well. Maybe it wasn't nine years.'

'Whatever. But it means that when we were here last time, Nanyokie was already betrothed. Ole Materr was her fiancé even when she was eleven.'

Peter nodded in agreement. 'Yes, I asked them last time we were here if she had been chosen and they said yes she had.' He looked slightly smug.

'You knew all along?'

A Boeing 747 purred overhead behind the clouds, which were a fluffy white overlay on the gentian sky. I was suddenly aware of the heat, which made me realize that we had been walking for several hours on our quest for Nanyokie. And this caused me to reflect that we had made a special journey to Tanzania, driving over uncomfortable roads for two days, in order to find her.

'Why didn't you tell me all this?'

'You never asked that question.' Peter had become sullen. He hated it when I was logical.

'But you liked her so much. You said you wanted to marry her. We talked about it all the time. Even in Somerset.'

'It might not have been true about Ole Materr. Sometimes these people change their minds,' he said slyly. These people. They were *his* people.

'Why didn't you let me know the last time we were here? Then we could have decided whether or not to find out if it was true. We're on the same side, you know. I have your interests at heart.'

'I never liked her,' he said with disdain. 'Anyway, they told me yesterday at Engaruka that she was married.'

'What is it with you? You do this to me all the time. You never said anything last night about her being married.'

'Why should you know these things?' he replied. The inference was that I was not Maasai. But it was not that which perturbed me. It was his stony look which always appeared during our confrontations.

I shook my head in exasperation and glimpsed Nanyokie standing behind my left shoulder. She couldn't understand English but she knew by the tone of our voices that we were quarrelling.

Peter glanced at her then back at me. 'It is not good to talk of these things now.'

It was too late. I had worked up a fine head of steam and couldn't stop. 'Sometimes I think I just don't know you at all.'

His gaze was cool. 'You don't know me.'

Swift. Deadly. We all know instinctively where it hurts the most. I walked off, hurt at being excluded from his world; angered by his lack of respect; wanting an apology; knowing I would never get one. I was in despair.

Down at the stream there were women bent double, pounding their clothes in the brown water. My arrival cast a silence on their chatter. They twisted their heads round to get a look at the alien and stared. I wasn't in the mood for socializing so squatted by a bush. The shade it threw out was the size of a handkerchief.

'Hello! I thought you'd be too old to walk by the time you came back here. But you look good! Still strong!'

It was Noonkepa, preceded by a phalanx of goats. As they plodded past, satiated from taking their fill of water, their thimble hooves coated me with a fine dust.

I thought, *If I have to look at one more of these damn goats, I'll scream.*

CHAPTER 27

By mid-afternoon the heat had begun to subside. Two of the wives were sitting in the swelling shadow of the hut, with their legs stuck out straight in front of them. One was threading beads onto wire to make a necklace. The other fielded a fat baby at her breast. Languid clonkings and tinklings floated on the sun-stricken air: goats in the ceaseless pursuit of sustenance. They were still around, albeit at one remove on the plains. Peter, however, was standing next to me. I scanned his face for evidence of my recent barracking. There was none. He said hello and asked if I was ready. We were expected at Nanyokie's for tea. His nonchalant manner was his way of coping with conflict. No one watching us would have suspected we had scratched at each other's flaws until they had been laid bare.

Peter's convenient manipulation of the truth was so engrained in Maasai culture that over the generations it must have become embedded in the tribal DNA. I thought as a Westerner and wanted to pin down that same truth with logic. As far as I was concerned, failing to mention at any time over the past four years, particularly when we were making arrangements to visit her, that his putative bride was already engaged and that her fiancé was sufficiently serious about his intentions to indenture himself to his father-in-law, was more than an oversight. It was proof beyond reasonable doubt that Peter never gave much thought to anyone except himself.

There was one problem with this line of argument. I knew that Peter didn't subscribe to it. As far as he was concerned, my behaviour was unreasonable, incomprehensible and unacceptable. It was our only common ground. I held the same opinion about him.

My desire to be patient and even-handed had shrivelled. In fact, parental ambition seemed to have vanished altogether. I said as much to Peter. I told him that now that he was a grown man, it would be better if we were just friends rather than mother and son because, by his own admission, I didn't understand him and he didn't seem to want to know anything about me. As we retraced the route across the plains which we had taken a few hours earlier, I explained that Tara and Petra genuinely cared about what happened to me, which was an expression of their love. That sort of consideration was also the basis for friendship. And, I added, friendship was two-way traffic. Friends reciprocated. He should try it sometime.

I pointed out that he never asked me what I thought or felt, and he looked a bit contrite and said he did think about me and he even missed me when I wasn't there. Then I heard myself complaining that not once since we had known each other had he given me a present. It was a churlish remark that made me feel bad even before it was out of my mouth, but I said it anyway. Besides, it wasn't true. Nnee had made me a white bead bracelet with my name worked into the design with red beads, and he had once given me a pair of bead earrings. In my anguish I began to twist Nanyokie's ring round and round my finger. Peter looked a bit shaken and said he would give me a present as soon as he was rich. 'But the issue of Nanyokie is a cultural thing.'

'What's a cultural thing? Not to talk to each other? Is it culture or Peter Lekerian who's doing these things?'

We had stopped to face each other. Peter looked down and appeared to be contemplating the grey earth at his feet. The sun glanced off a sprinkling of rock chippings and alchemized them into fool's gold. 'It is our culture, M.A.'

'What is? To show lack of respect to your elders? Don't tell me Maasai don't talk to each other. They do it all day. You, of all people, love doing it. Chat away.' I took the stick he was carrying and used it to trace a circle in the dust. 'Culture?' The stick made another circle. 'Or Peter Lekerian?'

Peter hesitated, then exhaled. 'Peter Lekerian.'

'Aa-all ri-ight!' I grinned. He was taking responsibility for his actions.

This talk was interrupted because we had arrived at Nanyokie's place. It was simple, even by the yardstick of Enchani Pus Plain. The huts were small and low and inadequately plastered with dung. There was not a single object in sight except for the water *debes* and two donkey panniers which were so moth-eaten they looked like a horse's lunch.

Tea was served in tin mugs. The women sat in an informal half circle and watched us drink it. Nanyokie was beside me, perched on a *debe*. She sat with her hands in her lap, turning her rings round and round. She looked happy enough, but she didn't join in the conversation. The women were relaxed, listening quietly to Peter, smiling. During lulls in the conversation they were not embarrassed by the silence.

Nanyokie's mother-in-law busied herself sewing beads onto a leather headband. It was for her son to tie around his warrior's locks. He was away in a meat camp. I imagined him secluded with other warriors somewhere in the thick forest that descended like a waterfall down the sides of the escarpment. They would spend about ten days there, perhaps longer, living in the open while they ate their way through a slaughtered cow or bull. There would be little girls, too, to wait on them. Any possibilities of lovemaking were ruled out because the elders made sure these girls were on the safe side of puberty. Pregnancy outside marriage is a strict taboo.

Mamma-in-law said the warrior was her youngest. He followed Ole Materr, who 'would never put on ochre again' because he was a junior elder. Her eldest son was Mereso's age, she added. Mamma-in-law must have given birth to her firstborn when she was about fifteen. That was what was in store for Nanyokie.

I took a tube of sunscreen out of my pocket, squeezed some onto my finger and rubbed it onto my lips.

'What's that?' she asked.

'Fat,' said Peter.

'Why doesn't she give you some?'

'Old ladies know how to look after themselves.'

This pleased her. A white bead earring caught on the edge of her black cloak as she endorsed Peter's quip with a nod of her head. 'That's true. You boys are useless. We can't trust you to look after us.'

Peter let out a sound like a happy hyena to show that this amused him. His mouth took on the shape of a heart when he did this and displayed his buck teeth. I should have had them strapped into braces when he was a teenager, but it didn't matter. Maasai men are judged by their wealth not by their looks.

'Do your boys give you trouble like this one?' I pointed a finger at Peter.

She took the question seriously for she was a widow and relied on her sons to give her food. 'Sometimes we quarrel but then we make up. They look after me. Particularly the married one.'

I took note of that. If married sons looked after their mothers, what about Peter's family? Why couldn't Lankisa help Nnee? Mamma-in-law was Ilaiser, the same clan as Kipenget. This was reassuring. It made her familiar, one of us. The conversation gradually painted a picture of everyone's place in the social firmament of the Rift Valley as surely as if they had been discussing schools and neighbourhoods and where they went on holiday. The network of relationships is of paramount importance to the Maasai.

Peter, the only man present, negotiated the shoals of etiquette with practised ease. A compliment here. A quip there. He was assured and dignified, if a touch pompous. This was a different persona from the defiant young man of that morning. He had assumed the personality of an elder. I watched him and thought, *You could wash bulls in Buckinghamshire until they get foot rot, but you will always be a Maasai.*

I surfaced from this reverie because I felt eyes brushing over me. The covert glances were a sure sign I was the subject of discussion. They were curious about Peter's mothers. Why did he have two? They understood about his father giving him away. That was their custom too. But how did I come into the picture? Why had he been given away by his aunt as well?

'Is she really your mother?'

'Yes.'

'But you are Maasai.'

'My mother bore me but she raised me.' He avoided meeting my eyes as he said this.

'But she is white.' Their laughter was tentative, filled with respect. They lowered their voices further. Wasn't he afraid to go into a *laisungu*'s house? Did the *laisungu* speak Maa? Did she know they were talking about her?

I looked at these women, whose constricted universe revolved around udders and pregnant bellies and thought, *Is it fair?* I can go on safari and dip into Maasainess, come home again, soak in the bath and emerge as an Englishwoman. When I tell people I have a Maasai foster son, they say, Really, isn't that interesting? Peter had to explain how this white woman fitted into the complex but precisely ordered spider's web of clans, age groups and age sets. I didn't conform at all. I made his younger brother carry water. I argued with him in the open where the women could hear my hot words. I should have referred our disagreements to the elders, who were the ones who disciplined younger men.

Sometimes Peter was offhand and embarrassed when introducing me, particularly to his friends in Nairobi. Lately, 'This is my mum', said with a heart-shaped smile, had degenerated into a mumbled 'This is Mary Anne'. When I heard this and saw his eyes sliding away in denial, I resisted the inclination to think he resented me. I wanted to believe that in some way he was proud of me.

At this point *gogo*, the grandmother, emerged from the Stygian depths of the hut behind us. She was curved over with arthritis, and her palsied hands groped their way along the flaking mud wall. She stopped smack behind me and stood there like a question mark. Then she peed down her legs. No one paid any attention. When she had finished, she did a shuffling St Vitus's dance sideways and painfully lowered herself onto the ground at my feet.

Her cloudy, mushroom-soup eyes turned in my direction. 'I have a cold and a headache. Give me *dawa*.'

The women tittered.

'I have no *dawa*.'

I pressed the one coin I had in my pocket into her palm and closed her fingers over it. Five shillings. 'Here. Tell one of the young girls to buy you *tambac*.' I would have liked to have given her a mirror but there was none left. Besides, she had no use for it. She was blind.

'*Ashe. Ashe. Ashe.*' She intoned it like a priest at the altar and spat at my feet to seal the blessing. The coin trembled in her twisted fingers.

Peter watched this exchange with detachment. It is difficult to discern the standing of women in relation to men. The men make the important decisions, like when to decamp to new pastures, whether the warriors should go to war against another tribe, the auspicious time for the *eunoto* that signalled the beginning of a new age set.

Men are born with authority. Women do all the work. They milk the herds, build the *bomas*, fetch water and firewood on their backs. It's not done for a man to demean himself with manual labour. Women give birth and rear the children. In their spare time they make jewelry, decorate the milk gourds and fashion the warriors' belts and headbands. Did they extract respect as compensation for all this drudgery? I wondered. And how does a son behave towards his mother? Sons may honour their mothers, but whether or not they stuck around to get a piece of their mind was another matter.

The women wanted us to wait until the goats came home so that they could give us milk to take back in gourds. They trotted in on thimble hooves, their necks nodding, and the dove-grey light softened their coats. The women stood there watching them, calm in the encroaching dusk. The kids, now reunited with their source of food, butted udders and sucked greedily at the teats.

That evening we met up with Paul, the Maasai man we had met on Pashet's verandah who spoke English with an Oxford accent. He said, 'Would you care to have dinner with me?'

'Dinner? Love to. I've got some carrots and potatoes.'

'Good, I'll get someone to prepare them.'

'That's okay, I'll do it myself. Peter, can you ask somebody if we can borrow their knife?'

We were sitting on the cow skin. There were no stars because it was *Oloirujuruj*, the drizzling season. The night was moonless, still. Grey shapes stamped and stirred beyond the perimeter of the hide, and the warm scent of milk and dung cloistered us from the darkness.

I was glad to be spending the evening with Paul. He had the subversive vision of an activist. He harboured aspirations for his people. He used phrases such as 'the long and bitter struggle' and 'a united opposition'. He counselled a change of government as the way to progress and decried the allocation of individual plots of land saying it would destroy the environment. He urged the empowerment of women and talked constantly of the rights of the *wananchi*. 'The people must stop being frightened and intimidated.' Amongst the fatalistic and conservative Maasai, he was a true firebrand.

Paul advocated the introduction of camels to redress the ravages of hordes of goats. He had persuaded Mereso to buy one. 'He won't regret it. In the next drought he will be the only one to have milk. Then everyone else will want a camel too.' The Maasai are connected to their cattle by an umbilical cord of myths and religion. How could you excise them and replace them with camels? But Paul's disembodied voice was fired with conviction.

His perspective of the world dovetailed with mine. There is no celebration without sacrifice. It was an ancient formula. Herbalists, soothsayers, witchdoctors: they all offered up sacrifices to ease the pains of others. The knife plunged into the jugular was attendant upon ritual. Paul was merely viewing an accepted precept through a more pragmatic prism. He was asking the Maasai for commitment and hard work.

Peter was not at home with revolutionary thought. He preferred the established political system even if it was faulty. He was impressed by Mereso because he was strong and big. A leader. When I probed his reaction to Paul, he was reserved. 'He's fine,' he said politely.

Peter listened in silence. Once he offered a rambling and irrelevant discourse on the rise and fall of a Kenyan politician. Paul brought him up short by saying, 'Yes, but that's not what I was asking.' I could tell his patience was being tried.

Migrating flamingo crawed and flapped above the dark clouds. Our talk was accompanied by the nocturnal noises of farts and blubbery stomach gurglings, rich grunts and the faucet sound of urination. From time to time the cattle crowded in close, hanging their fly-bitten heads over us. Then Paul would tell Peter to shoo them away. 'It's like the M1,' he complained.

Peter became more alert. 'You know the M1?'

'It's a big highway with six lanes that connects London to the north of England.'

'You've been to England?'

'No. Never. I'd like to go.'

There was a long pause.

Tell him, Peter. Tell him.

'I have been to England.' He let it drop casually.

'Really?'

'Tell Paul what you did there.'

'I worked on a farm in Buckinghamshire. It was near the M1. It was as big as from here to Engaruka. And I was driven to work every day in the back of a big car. Whoooo-eee, I travelled like a minister.'

By this time our vegetables, boiled over someone's fire, were ready. There were only two spoons in the *boma* so we shared them to eat out of the pot. I had concocted a pretty bland repast: tasteless carrots and crumbly potatoes. We didn't even have salt or pepper. It was the first meal of the day, but I wasn't famished. The less you eat, the less you need. I always felt extremely well in Maasaini. It was illusory though. From past experience, I knew that I was collecting a laboratory of amoebae and worms.

Paul called for a mug of milk, which was brought to him by one of the women. She hovered like a sulky child at the edge of the hide and said something in a complaining voice. I commented she looked tired, but Paul brushed this aside. She was fine. It struck me, yet again, that women were treated like slaves.

It was getting late and Mereso still hadn't returned. He was at yet another meeting. When I mentioned this, Paul enlightened me. Noonkepa had run away to the *boma* of a fellow clan member. She and Mereso had argued and he'd beaten her. It happened quite a lot, he said. Mereso had taken a succession of peace offerings in the way of home-brewed beer to Noonkepa's clan elder. He was negotiating for her return.

So. Mereso was eating humble pie. No victory for the feminists here. Noonkepa was still a chattel. Mereso's actions were driven by what was below his sword belt, not by his brain.

When I stumbled out of a hut early next morning, Mereso was on the cowhide beside Paul. I needed to pee and was struggling to wrench the thorn branches away from the entrance. The two men sat with their legs drawn up in front of them. Their blankets were wrapped round their shoulders and pulled down over their knees. They looked like Buddhas. They were watching me.

'Can you give me a hand?' I called out.

'Of course!' Paul shouted back. He was such a nice man, so helpful.

I am slow to make the transition from the wonderfully rich world of dreams to reality. That's why I expected Paul to stand up, shake his blanket free and walk over. Instead he sent a small boy. He opened the gate for me in two seconds. He was about six.

When, in due course, Peter and I took our leave of everyone, I handed Paul my card. 'That's my English address. If you get there, my home is your home. Come and stay. I know we'll meet again.'

He screwed up his eyes and stretched his arm out in front of him. 'I'm afraid I can't read it. I left my specs behind.'

'One last thing. Has Mereso fixed that business yet?'

He tutted like a schoolmaster. ''Fraid not.'

I grinned. One–nil, Noonkepa.

CHAPTER 28

Matatus are a metaphor for urban Africa: overcrowded, haphazardly maintained and bad for your health. *Matatu* drivers don't subscribe to the principle of cause and effect, even at the most elementary level. They do not, for instance, believe that overtaking on a corner or facing down an oncoming truck might result in a pile-up. Nine people die on Kenyan roads every day; most of them riding *matatus*.

Nevertheless, the taxi was a luxury. The last time we'd visited Engaruka, there had been no public transport. There were two incentives for taking it. The main road lay forty miles to the south at Mto wa Mbu, where it began a snaking ascent to the top of the Rift Valley escarpment. I had planned to walk the entire way. It would take two days and we would have to spend a night in a stranger's *boma*. Peter had accepted this suggestion with equanimity. However, my landscape is littered with discarded intentions. As the time drew near for our return to Arusha and then on to Nairobi, the *matatu* became an increasingly attractive prospect. If we hitched a lift to Silela, the first leg of the journey, we would be able to cover the remaining twenty miles to Mto wa Mbu in one day. Peter said that this option was fine by him too. The other reason for taking the *matatu* was that it would be the only vehicle on the track. This reduced the chances of an accident.

I had worried we might be late. It had taken an hour to walk the five miles back to Engaruka. But when we reached the departure point at the foot of the village, any sense of urgency vanished. There was a lot of activity going on in a lethargic sort of way. The passengers milled about, handing bundles through windows which were then handed back out again. Men shouted at latecomers who sprinted through the dust.

Mary had secured a place in the middle of the back seat. She must have brought her influence to bear as the chairman's wife for, when we arrived, a man was evicted onto the roof and I was shoehorned into his place next to Mary. Peter ended up on the roof too. To my left was a trader from Mt. Meru. His eight-year-old son was sitting on his knee. The boy was going back to school,

The *matatu* was a Land Rover, but it looked like a jalopy even though the headlights were intact and the doors and windows opened and closed. It had a marked list to the left which probably had something to do with the distribution of weight. There were four people in the front seat, five in the seat behind and a forest of heads, including a goat's, in the rear. The touts and several warriors were riding shotgun on the roofrack. Their feet dangled over the windscreen, partially obscuring the hand-painted inscription: Journey to Hell. Allahu Akbar. At a guess, we were twenty-six including the driver.

His name was Aziz and he was Muslim. All I could see of him from my vantage point were his broad shoulders inside a purple T-shirt. When he lent us his goateed profile to harangue the passengers, the back seat was treated to a flared nostril and some extraordinarily long eyelashes. He was a well-built young man in his twenties.

Aziz put his head out the window and shouted up at the sky, '*Songa! Songa! Springs ni weak kidogo!*' His voice was frantic, imploring. There was a shuffling above our heads that sounded like cattle bedding down for the night. The Land Rover heeled and sighed and settled into tentative equilibrium.

I leaned past the trader from Mt. Meru and thrust my camera at one of the bystanders. '*Piga piksha kabla ya kuondoga.*' He took it and, after some encouragement, lifted it to his face then walked backwards a good ten yards before pressing the button. When I had prints made in Nairobi, there it was: a densely populated blue car snapped at a giddy angle that suggests it is diving into the bowels of the earth. Peter has been rudely guillotined at the waist. Below him you can just discern a swatch of blonde hair and a pale arm.

Aziz tied a green and orange bandanna round his head against the dust, gave a wild-eyed look behind him, squared his shoulders and thrust the vehicle into gear.

No sooner were we in motion than a wizened woman in a *rubega* sitting in the front seat eased herself round and nudged me with a large manila envelope. I opened it. There was an X-ray inside. I held it in front of me as best I could given the cramped conditions and perused the grey shadings on the emulsion. She watched attentively for my reaction. 'Very good. Very good,' I said in Maa and handed it back to her. She looked relieved.

The rigours of the journey engendered an easy companionship as the taxi swayed and heaved over the ruts. The passengers were scrupulously considerate. They sat with their hands on their laps, trying not to collapse into their neighbours as we descended into potholes, gullies and ditches. The trader from Mt. Meru told me that he rented a room in Engaruka and went home once a month to visit his wife and family. He said that Aziz rented a room in Engaruka too. He came from another mountain, Monduli.

Mary was clutching her handbag tightly to her stomach. This was the start of a big adventure for her. It was her first visit to Arusha in over ten years. She was going to stock up with supplies for her shop. I was going to help her choose the *rubegas* and tyre sandals and tin mugs that she would sell through the tiny store window. She looked excited. She was contemplating the profit margins.

Wordlessly she wrestled a bead bracelet off her wrist and put it onto mine. Then she gave me a complicit smile. That made me happy. It was further evidence of our deepening friendship.

We came to a steep hill. Aziz shouted at the men on top to climb down, haranguing them about the weak state of the springs. They ran up the incline in the blistering heat, to show off, and Peter was well up there in the front. Aziz waited until they had crested the rise, then revved the engine and set off with his foot flat to the floor. He hurtled over the rocks and soon caught up with the panting warriors. The sight of them excited him further and he shouted 'Get out of the way!' even though they were standing well back. As the vehicle approached he veered wildly to the right, careened over a small crater and rushed at a sharply descending cliff. We caught a lopsided glimpse of the route we had just laboured along before snapping back at ninety degrees in search of the track.

At an irrigation ditch Aziz made us get out and carry large, pockmarked volcanic rocks to build a bridge. The water was less than a foot deep. I wandered off to relieve myself behind a tree. It didn't really hide me, but the sweating passengers were too busy to notice.

'*Mzungu!* We're going!' shouted one of the touts in Swahili. He was wearing a dirty grey jacket, back to front. He looked like a patient in a mental asylum.

I'd had enough of being known as 'the white person'. It was an isolating experience. This was what Peter must have felt like in Somerset. I walked up to the tout and put my face a few inches from his. '*Mwaafrica*, you can call me mamma like the other women.'

The other tout smacked his lips and snickered. 'That taught you some manners. How would you like it if you were called "African" all the time?'

The two boys had been behaving oddly, even for touts. They had a spongy walk and smiled with loose lips. They hung off the Land Rover while it was moving and grinned at Aziz through the windscreen. It was getting to him. He berated them for taking the wrong fares or, worse, forgetting to take any fare at all. 'You have no education, you lousy good-for-nothings!' he shouted out the window. Then he swivelled his bandannaed head around and exclaimed to the world at large, 'They've been smoking *bhangi*. Can't you see their eyes? Lion's eyes!'

Silela is perched on top of a bald hill. There are a handful of wooden buildings, one-room shops which sell single cigarettes, *posho* and sugar or which just have bare wooden shelves and sell nothing at all. There were some women lolling about with water containers at their feet. The water pipe is the reason for Silela's existence. And there were spear-carrying warriors and young men in slacks and shirts with frayed trainers on their feet that showed their toes. Peter and I planned to get out here and walk the rest of the way to Mto wa Mbu. It was only twenty, say twenty-five, miles and it would be fun to stretch our legs and get some fresh air.

The warriors paid no attention to the *matatu*'s arrival, but the boys in Western clothes stared at the descending passengers with blank, cartoon eyes. Aziz was standing by his Land Rover. He had his arms up in the air and was shouting. He looked like a demented prophet. A mass exodus from the taxi was taking place, and no one at Silela was showing any interest in filling up the emptying vehicle. The touts had left him with only ten passengers paying the full fare to Mto wa Mbu. How was he going to cover the cost of petrol? They were stupid, lazy. This was the last day they would work for him. The touts lolled against the car door and smiled their *bhangi* smile.

We said goodbye to Mary. I thought she looked a bit anxious to be left on her own. I told her we would see her in Mto wa Mbu by four, five at the latest.

The strife-torn taxi trundled off, tailed by a spiral of dust. I sat on a rock in a sliver of shade afforded by the tin roof of a *duka*, unscrewed a plastic bottle of water and emptied it down my throat. Peter said he didn't want any. He would wait for tea. He hates drinking water.

In the *hoteli* we were served sweet tea in glasses and four greasy chapatis on a plastic plate. The walls of the dirt-floored room were built with rough offcuts from the forest. The only furniture was the low wooden bench on which we sat. The hotel owner crouched by a fire of coals and grey ashes which smouldered on the ground. It had been set with three stones on which to balance a kettle or a pot. Behind him was a tin *sufuria*. It was filled with an inch or two of murky water in which small indefinable things floated amongst the unwashed glasses. The kitchen.

We had been conversing with him in Kiswahili, but suddenly Peter switched to Maa and dropped his voice. The man answered at length. Peter looked first serious then relieved.

'What's he saying?'

'I was asking directions. There's a shortcut. We turn right when we get to a big acacia tree. He says we can't miss it.' He hesitated.

'And?'

'I was asking if it was safe.'

'Safe' was code for lions.

'And?'

'It is.'

Peter was being protective. I loved him for that.

Outside it was sweltering. It was ten minutes short of noon. Yet even with the sun at its zenith, even when another drought is threatening to leach the land, the Rift Valley is so beautiful it makes you weep with delight. The soft grey surface of its escarpment rose like a canyon wall some miles away on our right. To the left, baobab trees atop a ridge marked the skyline.

The sea of lion-coloured grass was vibrant, alive, strummed by breezes. It whirred and buzzed with insect riffs, hiding unknown dangers. Half a mile ahead an ochred warrior with spear slung over shoulder crossed the plains with a nonchalant, boy-after-a-rabbit stride. Like him, we were walking apace. I felt bullish about our prospects. It was only about twenty miles. Four hours, five at the most, and we would be in Mto wa Mbu.

Peter was in an inquiring mood. He brought up politics, one of his favourite topics. We started with Rabin. He wanted to know which country was most upset by the Israeli leader's assassination and how the opposition had reacted. It was a very interesting situation, he said, because only India assassinated its leaders. He wanted to know about South Africa, too, a subject on which he was less well informed. What was going to happen to de Klerk now that he had quit politics?

I pointed out that de Klerk hadn't retired. He had left the ruling coalition and crossed the floor with his party. But far too often I heard myself saying 'I'm not absolutely certain about this, but I believe . . .' and 'As far as I understand it . . .' I thought I knew what was going on in the world, but as soon as I started talking about it, I wasn't so sure.

Peter walked ahead with his eyes cast down in thought, as he always did when the conversation was serious. He punctuated my explanation with uh huh, uh huh to show that he was taking it all in. From time to time he interjected questions. Would Rabin's death affect the peace process? What was the difference between the ANC and the Nationalists?

Peter's indolent intellect was unpredictable. Much of the time it hibernated. At mealtimes, I would try to draw him into the conversation by asking his opinion, only to discover he hadn't been listening to a word of what was being discussed. But when a subject interested him – politics, soccer, goats – he demonstrated a lively mind.

Today his realm of inquiry was extended to baobabs. He lifted his head back and pointed with his chin to the top of the ridge. 'They are very strange-looking trees.'

'Yeah, sort of mystical.'

'That other one had a hole in it big enough to stand in.' He had earlier disappeared into a gully for 'a long call' behind a baobab. 'Some people have said', he went on, 'that during the Somali war the *shifta* hid inside the trees and by the use of their guns killed people. The passers-by didn't know they were there. It must have been scaring inside.' He screwed his head sideways and back and laughed.

I said, 'If you're going to murder people, I guess claustrophobia is the least of your problems.'

I was getting into my stride, intoxicated by this Promethean world. It was a sunny, Huckleberry Finn feeling. We were travelling light but in my head I was discarding the contents of the knapsack. I made a mental list of the requirements for safari: toothpaste, toothbrush, soap, sun cream, a hat, a knife. No spoon. You can eat with your fingers. A *kikoi* to use as a pillow and towel, dental floss. It's a useful substitute for string. And a good book for when you tire of goats. All the rest, the inessential possessions we cling to, is dross in the bush.

Africa has a liberating effect on me, I am more spontaneous, reckless even – funnier, more relaxed. A great love of my life was enraptured by the sense of freedom I emanate but didn't marry me because he suspected I was untameable. Like a leopard, he said. That was Africa he saw – where hope glides freely over reality. In England I battened down my intuitive side and called the intellect into play. I wore silk shirts and suede shoes and never licked the gravy off my plate.

Recently, I had achieved a certain equilibrium between these two aspects of my personality. I had exposed Africa to my staider side and introduced adolescent Africa into London life. I was happier for it.

That effort to strike a balance between middle-aged Europe, a stranger to him, and the familiar world of Kenya had sparked Peter's madness when he was in England. Peter, who was so patently Maasai, had tried to be like the British. No wonder his ego had imploded. Goethe was right when he said we can't form our children according to our own concepts. We must love them as God gave them to us.

Peter had no idea I was feeling these things, just as his mind process was beyond my reach. He might have been daydreaming about the pistonlike arms of Mamba ya Sumu – Snake Poison – the boxer who intimidated his opponents by shouting: 'I'm going to tear out one of your ribs!' Peter had learned in the *matatu* that Mamba ya Sumu had pulverized Mroso at Mto wa Mbu a few days earlier. Mroso had been the local hero until then.

Or perhaps Peter, like me, was uplifted by the wind-ruffled plains. But he would be oblivious to the aesthetics of it – the play of light and shadow, the scent of seedheads the colour of mustard. He would look at the grass shimmering in the sunlight and think: *There is good grazing here to make the goats fat.*

An hour had passed – no, two – by the time we reached what we had thought was the acacia tree but didn't quite seem to be after all. It was large, but it didn't fit the description. For one thing, the path branching off to the right led into a vast swampy place with shoulder-high grass. All manner of beasts – lions and buffalo, in particular – would hide up in grass that tall. It wasn't the perfectly safe route the hotel owner had been talking about. Hard by the marsh was a herd of cows.

'I wonder why they are at the edge of the grazing.' Peter frowned. 'The boys are drinking from their udders.'

'Doing it secretly?'

'Yes. Look, they have left their spears in the ground. If they do it now, they will give milk in the evening. If they steal the milk at four, the cows will give none.'

'You know all the tricks.' I laughed. The boys were raiding the fridge.

They emerged from behind a sleek rump. Their *shukas* were in tatters. The younger one couldn't have been more than six. His brother was not much older. Peter glanced at the warrior's spear he was carrying. It towered above him. The boy understood the look.

'I am circumcised because my father doesn't have a warrior in the family,' he said defiantly.

It was a tall tale. It didn't bode well for the reliability of his directions. But there was no one else to ask. There were no *bomas* in sight. We hadn't seen another person for over an hour.

The boy said, 'If you go left you will come to the road where the *matatu* goes. But that way is dangerous. There are lions and cheetahs. The animals give us problems. Go right. You will be all right.'

I said, 'Peter, do you remember that warrior we met at Engaruka? The one who'd been bitten in the bum by a lion?'

'Yes.'

'And his left buttock wasn't there? It was all flat?'

'And he fell over when he sat down?'

Usually we laughed at this joke, but instead we fell into a discussion about which was the best path, the left or the right. I wanted to take the one that joined up with the road. We knew for sure that way led to Mto wa Mbu. Peter disagreed. He pointed out that the boys had said it was full of cheetahs and lions. He wanted to go the other way. Through the swamp. Peter was in charge so I fell in with his suggestion.

Peter turned to the smaller boy and asked if he could borrow his *panga*. He took it and began to hack away at a branch of the acacia tree. I could smell the sweet scent of its juices. It was a big branch and he had trouble cutting all the way through. His mouth was scrunched up over his teeth with the effort of it. I began to hum while the boys stood behind Peter, their heads thrown back to watch his exertions.

'Why are you cutting that stick? It won't do you much good if you meet a lion,' said the eldest.

'Are you wishing us bad luck?'

'Oh, no. Have a good safari.'

We walked away as nomads would do. Without looking back. And as nomads do, we walked strongly. Peter rested the stick on his shoulder. From a distance it looked like a spear. I hoped it would fool the lions.

CHAPTER 29

I had walked lion country before at Lesirikan. We'd treated warriors
for lion bites at the clinic. The Samburu related literally blow-by-
blow accounts of encounters with lions. There was the warrior who
had come upon three lions eating his cow. Two had run away. The
third had attacked, leaping at the warrior, head on, and raking his
chest and arms with its claws. He'd thrust his left arm into its
mouth to prevent his head being crushed in its jaws. With his right
arm he'd unsheathed his *simi* and severed its jugular. The lion had
died and the warrior had survived.

That story ended on a positive note. But there was also the bride
who was being walked to her new home by her husband. They had
surprised a sleeping lion on the path and it had mauled the woman
so badly she'd died. Then there were the two men who had been
walking across the plains who stumbled on a sleeping lion. It
had attacked one of them. The other had hamstrung it with his
simi.

Had that man died, too? I couldn't remember. Regardless, the
evidence corroborated one fact: lions were bad-tempered when
suddenly awoken. Just like the Fitzgeralds. The best thing to do
was to make a good deal of noise to warn them of our approach.

The path was narrow so we went single file. I said loudly, 'Peter,
can you sing like you did when you were walking in Sussex? Tara
said they were lovely songs.'

'Oh yes,' he said.

The songs celebrated girls with tight, cricket-ball breasts, and
the thrill of rustling from enemy tribes because all cattle belong
to the Maasai and their god Nkai. They were throbbing dirges
which segued into a higher pitch that swelled from the back of
Peter's throat. As he sang, he stuck his neck forward and jerked his
head back in rhythm to his voice. The warriors did this to emphasize
the luxurious length of their hair. They liked to feel the cat-o'-nine-

tails flick of the tightly twisted braids on their back. Too soon Peter tailed off and fell silent.

'Tell me about when you played football at school. Isn't number nine the key position for scoring goals?'

His mouth became a heart and he said, 'I scored in every game. I was so good, I was wanted on the school team even when I was fifteen. But I was too young. I didn't join the team until the next year when . . .'

I was aware of the rattle and scrape of the grass fronds, the buzz of large insects. These tiny noises were large in the silence heaped around us. We travelled through tall spears of tawny grass beneath a high blue sky. The grass, the sky, the brittle, heatladen air sparkled with an incandescent energy that quickened sight, hearing, the beating of our hearts. We were part of the world around us. There was no recourse, no escape. The sensation was primitive, as if a membrane that had once filtered perception was no longer there.

I looked at the grey earth of the path and saw myriad lines indented in the dust of the black cotton soil. Some were thick and lazy and led to holes in the ground: snakes. Others were squiggly and thin: lizards dragging their long tails behind them. And at some point, as I examined these whiplashes in the dirt, I realized where we were. It wasn't the sea of swamp grass or the Rift Valley wall or the baobabs we had left behind which teased the memory. I recognized the ground itself. I had last seen it at night three years ago, traced by the headlights of the Land Rover we had hired to get to Engaruka. We were in a hunting block used by professional hunters and their megarich clients. Not only that, a hunting block renowned for its magnificent black-maned lions.

I scoured the earth further for signs of anything else that had come this way – the spoor of goats or donkeys, the thin ridged track of a bicycle, the foot-shaped imprint of tyre sandals. Someone had passed along here with two donkeys. And was that the pad of a dog or was it a very small lion? What if I saw lion spoor on the track? It would be better not to know as there was nothing we could do about it. I wasn't frightened. I was alert. Yet ready to be frightened at the slightest rustle in the grass.

I could tell that Peter was apprehensive too by the determined way he'd attacked the acacia tree and because he looked about him with his head lifted high as he talked. But he said nothing of how he felt. He was ensconced in the world of soccer, with its rubbery, dirty-sock smells, its adrenaline and glory.

'We got through the semi-final. That game was very tight. We had to fight hard. A boy on the other team had scored a goal and we hadn't any . . .'

We emerged from the marsh grass and before us in the distance was a ridge crowned by a single baobab. It glinted copper in the sun, and its tangled branches were lifted to the sky. The herdsboys had said that on the far side of the ridge there were *bomas*, but when we crested it, we could see that there was none. Instead there was another plain with another baobab at the end of it. Like the plain and the swamp before it and the plain before that, it was several miles wide.

A herd of zebra cantered across our path, the stallion in the lead, the mares and foals following. The dominant male was stockier than the rest of the herd, his black and white stripes clearly defined. I knew this from my hunting days. The very first animal I'd shot was a zebra stallion. The first round had gone wide and I'd run after it with my 7mm. rifle, dropping to one knee and taking aim when it stopped and turned broadside on to catch my scent. Breathe out. Steady. The wooden stock was heavy. Squeeze. Slowly. Don't rush the trigger. The muzzle reared up and beyond it the zebra rose onto its hind legs, hooves flailing the air. A heart shot. Its rump was scored with thin grey scars. It had, at some point in its life, fought off a lion.

I was Petra's age, younger than Peter, when that zebra had died. I hadn't hunted for nearly twenty years, didn't want to harm living things. The eager girl who had shouldered the 7mm. and placed her hand on the stallion's no longer pulsing neck was someone else, not me. That moment was still achingly clear. Some thread connected the child and the woman. Whenever I looked at Peter, this hopeful knowledge that we evolve, metamorphose into someone else, lay in the recesses of my mind. Another thought pricked at me. I wondered if my shadow was stunting Peter's growth.

There was other game in evidence – Grant's gazelle with tails flicking like a metronome. Peter asked me the difference between Grants and the smaller Thomson's gazelle. Grants are flat-backed with squarish rumps. They are lighter in colour and move with a springy trot. A Tommy's rump is rounded. Its back is gently curved and its coat is darker, slightly reddish. I had learned all this because when you are tracking animals through the bush, you catch only fleeting glimpses of them.

We reached the top of another hill. Yet another plain lay before us with no sign of habitation. Peter was striding out, in good shape. There was a bony ache in my left buttock and upper thigh. Mama Land Rover was beginning to tire.

A mile or two on, I said, 'Why don't we stop for a rest?' It was nearly four o'clock.

We flopped onto the ground in the shade of a tiny acacia, and I produced a grapefruit and tore back its skin with my fingernails. The juice was tangy and refreshing but Peter didn't like it. He called it a bitter orange.

'I heard a hyena,' he said, looking anxious.

Hyenas have teeth like a diamond crusher. Hyenas attack people, bite off their noses. But they shouldn't have been calling in the middle of the day.

'There,' Peter said, cocking his head to one side. The frantic, yipping cries were very close.

'It's only a jackal.' I relaxed then tensed again. 'I think I see something moving in the grass. By the tree. Come on. Let's go.'

The countryside had opened up and, although there was no evidence of them, we sensed that soon we would see huts.

Two white-winged eagles swooped low above us and soared back up into the cerulean sky. The wind in their pinions broke the stillness. This sound and the sudden plunging movement, made me remember the kites on Parliament Hill. When Peter and I had strolled there in the evenings, it had been this quiet. Cyclists, joggers and students playing lazy frisbee were scattered about us. Women with dogs cleaved a brisk path through the long summer grass while London stretched out below them in a distant grey haze. No one spoke. It was peaceful, silent except for the papery rustle of those kites. They darted and twisted, dive-bombed us then climbed towards a pale crescent moon.

It was strange to think I used to walk without looking around me, knowing that I was safe. All about us was untouched Africa with its endless plains and looming massifs of volcanoes. It was eery and unsettling. Even though my head was wreathed in a *kikoi* against the sun, there were drops of perspiration on my temples. I dabbed at them with two fingers. In the distance vultures coasted the thermals. They were smaller than leaves picked up by a gust of autumn wind. Hampstead Heath seemed very far away.

We saw a *boma* in the distance. A man cycled towards us along the path, his toes curled over the pedals. He wore shorts and a battered straw hat. His torso was greased with sweat and black as an axle. Civilization.

Peter was tolerant and protective. He could see I was flagging. When another bicycle approached from the way we had come. He suggested he wave it down and ask if I could have a lift on the crossbar. I shook my head.

In the lee of the escarpment dark smoke spiralled upwards. It came from the fires of charcoal burners. The green shadows of vegetation heralded water and Mto wa Mbu. A low sun sparkled on far tin roofs. Peter stopped to chat to two Maasai women. They pointed out a shortcut which led through palms and irrigation ditches and neatly planted paddies of rice. We waded submerged up to our knees, strangers from the plains in a watery world.

We came to a place of tamped earth that was bright with purple bougainvillaea and rimmed by huts with wooden doors. It felt almost urban. Two men sat on a fallen log listening to a transistor radio. They wore shirts and trousers. One had a cap on his head. They watched us with glassy eyes. As we passed they stood and followed.

I didn't like the covert way they looked at us, but Peter wasted no time in engaging them in conversation. I lagged behind. Peter didn't notice. He was asking them the football scores.

'Peter! Wait! I think I have a thorn in my shoe.'

He stood over me, solicitous, waiting for me to bend down and examine my foot. The men had slowed down. They lingered under a palm.

'Don't get too close to those guys. I don't like the look of them,' I said quietly.

'They're very friendly,' he protested, 'I trust them.'

'That's the problem. You trust everyone. Let them go on.'

The sun turned bronze and brushed the lip of the escarpment. I had thought we were on the perimeter of the town, but the maze of palms and mud huts didn't seem to end. Then suddenly there was a thick hedge with a mud-brick bungalow on the other side and a grassy football pitch where boys ran barefoot. Buildings crowded in on the path and it filled with men and women strolling to take the evening air. A woman rode past on a bicycle. She had curlers in her hair and wore lipstick. It was a shocking, brazen sight.

Peter stopped and pulled me to one side. He had become concerned. He touched my arm and said, 'Will you sleep well tonight?'

'Like a log.'

'But there will be many men in town like them.'

'Like who?'

'Those men we met.'

I gave him a fond look. 'I'm not worried about the men *here*. I was worried about those other men because there was no one else around.'

We breasted a corner and were in the main street. There were bicycles and pedestrians, children dragging each other along by the hand. Men lounged outside the tea houses and were a still point in the hustle and bustle. A Landcruiser whistled by packed with tourists. They were thinking of supper and didn't notice the two weary travellers.

Mary was sitting on the verandah of the Red Banana lodging house. She gave a small smile when she saw us and some of her anxiety seemed to fall away. I ordered three Cokes from the bar and pulled up a chair beside her. It was nearly dark.

'We're late. The road was too long.'

'Before, everyone took that road. But they never walked there unarmed. We were talking about you in the *matatu*.'

'The lions could have attacked us,' Peter said.

'And the leopards. They're worse than lions,' Mary added.

'If I had a curse on me, a lion would have got me.' Peter said it in a bold way to mask his relief. He knew that men who had curses on them were eaten by lions or bitten by snakes. Sometimes he wondered if someone had secretly placed a curse on him. The thought made him uneasy.

'Curses are more dangerous than lions,' Mary pronounced.

I could see where this was heading. A long discussion about spells and witchcraft. There were more urgent matters at hand. The metallic smell of charred meat was wafting through the air.

'Is anyone hungry?'

'M. A., do you mind if I order a leg of goat?'

'A whole leg? You'll never finish it.' I looked at Peter's eager face and, even as I said it, I knew that he would.

'If I can't, I can take it with me on the bus tomorrow.'

Mary pulled her *kanga* down over her feet against the mosquitoes and grimaced. These travellers. They had no manners.

CHAPTER 30

There is darkness made companionable by a dusting of stars. There is moon-bathed darkness which is another form of light because it reflects a sun that happens to be somewhere else. There is the nursery darkness of a hut soothed by the snuffles of sleeping goats and children. And there is darkness so impenetrably black you can't tell which way is up and which way is down.

The polymorphous nature of the dark is one of the reasons I always travel with a torch. When I wake up in the middle of the night, I can examine what is caught in its pencil beam – an armature of woven boughs, tufts of grass, a wall – and establish whether I'm in a *boma*, the great outdoors or a room. This exercise in orientation is reassuring. When you're on the move it's easy to forget where you are.

I slid my hand over the rough cotton sheet until it came to rest against something hard and unyielding. A wall. I repeated the exercise with the other hand and felt cool metal. A bed frame. My fingers continued downwards until they touched another hard, unyielding surface. The cement floor. They tiptoed across it and closed round a smooth cylinder. The torch.

I pointed it downwards and switched it on. A swaddled form lay in the opposite bed. No need to disturb Mary. Although, frankly, there wasn't a turtle's chance in a mudslide she was still asleep.

I retrieved the key – lying next to the torch – knotted my *kikoi* and walked across the room. A few heaves and jerks later I was loose and on the prowl. I was in search of the perpetrator of the racket that had woken me up – a cauldron of tinny guitars and wailing voices.

It is well known that rural folk are not nocturnal. In the absence of movies and opera and ballet, not to mention television, books and electricity, they go to bed early and stay there until the sun is about to come up. So why had someone chosen to play music, full blast, at an hour so indecently early that even the cocks weren't ready to crow?

There were no telltale slivers of lantern light beneath the doors of the other five bedrooms giving onto the courtyard. The wicker and hide chairs under the bougainvillaea, occupied by beer-drinking roisterers until the outrageous hour of 9:30 p.m., stood empty. No one was pottering about in the wire-meshed cubicle where I had last seen the barmaid grilling a goat haunch. The caterwauling persisted. An insomniac neighbour perhaps. I strode over to the door that led to the street. I rattled the handle and the door sighed on its hinges. The Red Banana was a fortress. We were locked in.

I could tell by her silence that Mary was awake. She heaved restlessly.

'What's the time?' I asked in Swahili.

She moaned and said in a strangled voice, 'Ten hours.'

Swahili time is calculated according to the sun. Seven o'clock, one hour after dawn or dusk, is one o'clock. Eight o'clock is two o'clock and ten o'clock is four in the morning.

We were catching the six o'clock bus to Arusha. It was too early to dress and pack and too late to sink back into sleep. I lay on my back with my arm flung above my head and speculated on what motivated Peter.

I couldn't figure out why he hadn't said anything when he had discovered that Nanyokie was married. We had talked about her so many times over the years. Why had he never mentioned that she was already engaged? I sensed that Peter was as confounded by my reaction as I was by him. After my outburst on Enchani Pus Plain, he was on his guard and watched me with shuttered eyes. It was strange how one seemingly small incident could shift the footing of a relationship. I had taken it for granted that we were mutually supportive. We had an unspoken pact to look out for each other. I felt this trust had been betrayed.

How to explain it? I debated which was at the root of the confusion: culture or ego. I was tethered to the same old dilemma. Maasai versus Lekerian. The white lies, the complaints that his goat herd was too small, the scheming to extract small amounts of money from me, this I understood. It was the spoilt child riding roughshod over the gentle, caring man. But there was more to it than that.

Since I had returned to Kenya, his behaviour had become increasingly mystifying. In his letters he had written he was looking forward so much to my arrival. He hadn't said so, but I knew that he had wanted me to sleep a night at his place in Ongata Rongai. Yet he had never mentioned it. I hadn't even been invited in for a cup of tea. I wondered if it was lack of thought or something more substantial – mistrust.

In the absence of understanding, I instinctively resorted to the two commodities which were in short supply in Peter's life. Love and discipline. Discipline and love. It was a constant refrain. There was no other way to transcend the misconceptions.

Sometime between five and six, scuffling and scrapings filtered through the wall by my head. They were followed by the greasy smell of paraffin. Peter was lighting his lantern.

Mary groaned and stirred and sat up on the side of the bed. Slowly, petulantly she began to gather her things about her and stuff them into a woven basket. Her plaited hair was tousled. There were sleep creases on her cheek. It made her look blowzy and intimate. She watched with bleary eyes as I slipped on a pair of sandals. 'Can I wear those?'

'No.'

'You have your shoes,' she protested.

My trainers were still damp from the rice paddies. They reeked like a skunk so I had tied them up in a plastic bag.

'These are going on the roof of the bus. They stink.'

Mary was so funny. She had no qualms about asking for what she wanted. It was a childlike quality, rather appealing. At least you knew where you stood.

The bus was painted with the stars and stripes of the American flag. Squawking chickens were being heaved onto the roof. A bicycle had been tied onto the front fender. Passengers clambered into seats. They sat in silence, looking tired, listless.

Mary and I had managed to get two seats in the front row behind the driver. She sat with her handbag clasped to her. Her hair was combed now, her bright *kangas* neatly arranged. My *kikoi* and shirt

313

looked as if I had been wearing them for days. Which I had. Already a few drops of perspiration had appeared on my forehead. I wore no make-up, looked faded, dusty.

Peter sat behind us. He was dressed for town in a pink shirt and his loose-fitting, Lego-blue pants. They were the sort of trousers that French train conductors wear. He stared at saffron rice paddies, men on bicycles and three herdsboys sitting on a midden of wrecked cars as they rushed past the window.

It had been a good safari, but I was pleased at the thought of being back that evening at the friends' house I was using as a base. Peter and I would have connected directly with the minibus that shuttled between Arusha and Nairobi except that we had agreed to spend the morning with Mary, shopping for her *duka*.

I'd done some market research at Mto wa Mbu. Well, a long chat with a Somali trader whose shop was across the road from the Red Banana. He'd reassured me that mugs and bowls and *rubegas* and tyre sandals were just what was needed for a commercial venture at Engaruka. I'd fetched Mary from the hotel and taken her back to chat to him. He knew her and had played up to her avaricious bent. 'Big profit. Big profit,' he'd said with oily conviction. Mary's eyes had gleamed.

He'd told her which wholesale shops gave the best price for goods in bulk. He used them himself, he'd said. 'Go to the petrol station and a bit further on you'll see it in a side street. The other one is near the old cinema.' The directions had seemed vague, but Mary had listened intently, nodding her head. I'd not paid much attention. It was her shopping trip, not mine.

The bus stopped and started, stopped and started, gathering up children in clean school uniforms and women hefting unwieldy bundles. Soon every seat was taken and the residue of passengers who continued to crowd in stood in the aisle. But unless you turned round to look at the sea of brown heads, you would have thought the bus was empty. No one talked.

The bus tout sat down on the metal hump covering the gear box and rested his sweaty back against my legs. He fed the driver biscuits and cigarettes. Whenever the ruts in the road deepened to gullies, the driver veered off into the bush, knuckles wrapped around the shimmying steering wheel.

The talk at the Red Banana bar the previous evening had been of an ugly occurrence two days earlier outside an army base not far from Arusha. There had been a bar brawl between three soldiers and some civilians in the village opposite the barrack gates. One of the soldiers had tried to drag away a bar girl. She had refused. A gun had been drawn and some knives. The drunk soldiers had stormed off and returned with reinforcements. They had poured petrol over the bar and set it alight. The bar and two houses had been razed to the ground in the ensuing blaze.

Mto wa Mbu residents had learned of the incident when they had tuned in to the news on their radios. It had since been fleshed out by travellers and embroidered in the eating houses.

As we approached the barracks, a frisson of anticipation coursed through the bus. At moments like this, you expect to see wailing women sitting on the ground, a few hastily retrieved possessions scattered about them. Instead everyone was going about their business as normal. You wouldn't have known of the tragedy if it hadn't been for the charred skeletons of the buildings. I got the impression they were still smouldering but couldn't be sure because the bus didn't slow down. The passengers turned their heads to look and turned away again.

Africans accept intimidation unless they have a gun in their hands and can intimidate in turn. They are ruled by fear. One look at their art over the centuries, and you know that it has always been so. All those leering masks and menacing figures carved out of dark wood. I felt angry for the villagers, sickened by what I saw. But there was nothing I could do about it except try to instil in Peter that scenes such as this were a violation of humanity.

'That's awful. Those poor people.' Peter and Mary said nothing.

We entered Arusha and the bus depot. The bus squeezed in amongst other buses laden with people and chickens and bicycles, and wheezed to a halt. Pedestrians clogged the back streets. They walked in the middle of the road to avoid the garbage-filled ditches at the side. Mary strode business-like through the throng while I trailed in her wake. Peter lagged behind. He was dreamy, in a world apart.

I dithered at each corner, bemused by the hustle and bustle. But Mary didn't hesitate to stop strangers and ask directions. She was in full sail. No one took any notice of me. I didn't attract startled looks or cries of '*Mzungu!*' I thought, *This is what it's like to be an African. I am one of them.*

The *rubega* shop was in a row of others just like it a few high steps up from the street. The owner's wife, a middle-aged Indian whose hair trailed in a single plait down her back, was serving. Behind her were shelved walls stacked with *rubegas*. They were fresh and neat. Like hotel laundry.

Mary pointed with an outstretched arm and watched eagerly as the Indian spread one after another on the broad wooden counter. There were deep purple *rubegas*, plaids of red and black, blue ones with thick white borders. Mary turned to us, 'Do you like this one?' and back to the woman. 'Bring that one. There. No. That one above it.'

The shopkeeper fetched and carried and expelled little snorts of air through her nostrils as she laid the cloth on the counter for Mary's perusal. She stood with her arms spread wide, palms down on the counter, and stared over our heads.

A gradual selection process was taking place. Slowly, steadily, the pile rose. Mary asked the price – it came to tens of thousands of shillings – and accepted it without demur. This didn't bode well for her future as an entrepreneur. I had always thought shop-owners haggled, whittling away at the value of each item when buying and loading it back on when selling. Never mind, Mary would learn. It wasn't my business. And I was tired after the previous day's walk across the plains.

Mary arranged the *rubegas* in a pile and said she would pay for them when she came back later to collect them. She was heading for enamelware which, the Somali trader had said, was to be found near the cinema on the main street.

I trailed behind her, unhappily aware I was tramping the territory of two worlds – the greater African one and the smaller orbit of the settler community of hunters, farmers and safari operators. The whites knew me as Mary Anne, the *Sunday Times* correspondent. While they embraced eccentricity, assimilation with the locals was a touch beyond the pale. I prayed I wouldn't bump into anyone I knew.

The shop was an Aladdin's cave of dishes, pots, pans and arcane utensils designed to turn food into shapes other than nature gave it. There were little spoons for making melon balls, egg slicers, garlic crushers, aluminum trays for coddling eggs *en masse*. Only Westerners care what food looks like. Africans are simply concerned with whether there is enough of it.

The owner was a rotund Indian in his thirties. He asked me what I needed, and I pointed to Mary. 'She's the customer.' The opulent surroundings had put a dampener on her enthusiasm. She looked ill at ease but stoically pointed at enamel plates and bowls and mugs, guiding their journey from shelf to counter with her eyes. The Indian's interest was rapidly fading, sustained only by the hope that I might be bankrolling Mary. Then another customer came into the shop and he slid away.

The new customer was a white man. He had a pair of sunglasses in his hand with which he was pointing at large, shiny contraptions. Lots of them. The Indian smiled in an unctuous way and said, 'Of course, Robin. No problem. If you want a bigger one, we can have it made for you. Chop chop. I'll make you a good price.'

The big fish took precedence over the minnows. I had seen it happen hundreds of times before, knew that it was the way things operated here, but couldn't help being irritated by the Indian's manner. I felt an irrational dislike for the safari operator too. Who did he think he was with his trousers pressed into razor-sharp creases? I was worried that he would recognize me and at the same time annoyed that he hadn't. Like Mary and Peter, I was invisible.

Meanwhile the swells and drifts of crockery on the counter were consolidating into a veritable mountain. Mary summoned down a few more white bowls with red roses on them. The neat stacks now eclipsed the assistant to his hairline.

Mary looked at me and murmured, 'How many mugs do you want to buy me?'

My heart plummeted.

I was born on this continent, have lived here most of my life. I should have seen it coming. Pashet had set me up. I was supposed to play the *deus ex machina* to Mary's retail trade.

'We've got to talk.' I hustled her out of the shop and into the doorway that led to the flats above. A faint smell of urine wafted up from the rubble at our feet. Mary stood with her back to the door.

'Have you got any money on you at all?'

She stiffened and her eyes became stones. She shook her head.

'Look, I'm sorry. There's been a very bad mistake. I have no money either. I said to Pashet I couldn't pay for this. It's not like before. I haven't got a job.' I lifted my hands up, palms towards her. They were pressing the air as I talked. 'I can't,' I said lamely and added, 'I'm really sorry.'

Mary's shoulders sagged as if something inside had been punctured. She said nothing. She didn't need to. The sight of her was reprimand enough.

The remains of the day unfolded like a banal nightmare that spun around my rapidly dwindling cash. We hired a taxi, bought two tickets for the shuttle bus, drove to a friend's house to return the water container I had borrowed. All the while I was carefully calculating what was needed for the taxi fare and Mary's trip back home.

At the *rubega* shop I sent Peter in with a handful of crumpled notes on instructions to buy what he could. He climbed back into the car with a parcel that was pitifully thin. Mary was sitting beside me on the back seat. She was a volcanic presence.

I handed her the package. 'These are for you.' She ignored me so I put it on the seat between us. 'It's something for the shop. I think there's six in there. Aren't there, Peter? Well, anyway, it's a start.'

Meanwhile the taxi driver, with whom I'd agreed a fixed price, was becoming fractious. I'd been stringing him along mercilessly by adding unscheduled stops to the itinerary. When I asked him to detour via the bus depot, he braked and pulled over. He swung his head round. 'What are you trying to do to me?'

'Nothing, nothing. It's okay. She can walk there,' I demurred. I knew when I was beaten.

Mary got out of the car with slow, heavy movements. I remember thrusting some coins into her hand and saying, 'Take it. For food. It's all I've got. Peter and I can eat this evening.' Then I put my hands on her shoulders and looked straight into her eyes. 'I'm very sorry . . . We're still friends, aren't we?'

She shrugged me off wordlessly and turned away. I watched crestfallen as she walked down the street. I had thought those intimate evenings when we had sat around the kitchen fire and discussed plans for her shop had been the foundations of friendship. But for her I was nothing more than a mobile bank that came to town on occasional, unscheduled visits. The last words she'd said were, 'How many mugs do you want to buy me?' Mary had checked out when she realized the credit had dried up.

Peter touched my arm. 'You were wrong to do that to Mary. You should have sat down and talked to Pashet and explained you weren't going to pay for the *duka*.'

'I did talk to Pashet. My mistake was wrong expectations, I guess. Come on, let's go find our bus. I'm tired and hungry and I want a hot bath and a meal with my *wazungu* friends in Nairobi.'

CHAPTER 31

The Rift Valley was shifting and swaying as if wafted by a current at the bottom of the sea. Thorn trees trembled in a golden haze, and the riverbed shimmied across the plains. Only the smudged volcanoes were still – grey triangles hemming the horizon.

'School should be out now. Let's pick up Tumpeni before we go to see Nnee.'

Peter nodded in agreement and we continued down the road, past the turn-off to the *boma* and on towards Ol Tepesi. As we approached the sparkling tin-roofed shacks, a figure emerged from a dancing spiral of refracted light. It was Nalotu-esha. We stopped and she bent to the window of the car and spoke to Peter in Maa.

He turned to me. 'Tumpeni's at home today. He's sick.'

'What with?'

'Malaria.'

'Poor little chap.'

'He's had it for two weeks.'

'We should take him to the dispensary. Get some chloroquine.'

'He has already been treated by Mebikie.'

'What with?'

'Herbs and milk.'

'But he's still sick?'

'Yes,' said Peter, untroubled.

'He's so skinny. If he's had a fever that long he must be very weak by now.'

The Maasai attitude towards illness could be frustrating. They were fatalistic and superstitious, subscribing to spells and potions. They considered Western medicine a retreat of last resort but, once dragged off to the doctor, placed total faith in the recuperative powers of a hypodermic syringe. Kipenget, who that morning had complained with hoarse whisperings that she had nails in her ribs, would never have gone to the Catholic-run clinic at Kiserian if I had not taken her. The nuns had said it was pneumonia.

I knew that Peter put great store by Mebikie's healing powers and, distressed as I was, I wanted to be diplomatic. I hoped that by nudging the conversation along a certain course, Peter would suggest that we take Tumpeni to a doctor. But he was silent.

'So the herbs haven't cured the malaria.'

'Yes.'

'Do you think it would be a good idea if somebody had a look at him?'

Peter reflected on this. 'Okay,' he said.

I parked beside the road and waited while Peter walked down the dirt track that led to the *boma*. I was looking after Mike's house while he and his wife Evelyn were away. Mike had given me permission to use his car, but I didn't want to scrape it on the rocks.

After half an hour or so Peter returned with Nnee and Tumpeni. She had dressed him in his school shorts and shirt and was carrying him piggyback, with his arms wrapped around her neck and his head lolling on her shoulder. He looked pitiful and my heart thudded with dismay. My anxiety was reflected in Nnee's strained face. Tumpeni's eyes were shut, but he opened them when Nnee greeted me and whispered, '*Jambo*, Mary Anne.'

We put Nnee in the back seat with Tumpeni beside her. He cuddled up to her, his head resting against her bosom. Nnee's spine was straight as a plumb line as she stared straight ahead, but Tumpeni was crumpled and limp. She fluttered her elbows to loosen her *shuka* and scooped the material over his head to protect him from the bright light. She said something to Peter in Maa.

'Nnee wants to know where we're sleeping tonight. She has not changed her clothes for town.'

'Don't worry. We'll be back here soon. If we hurry, we can get to the clinic at the church before it closes.'

This did little to reassure Nnee for when I glanced at her in the rear-view mirror, her face was flat and expressionless. It was impossible to tell whether her unease was triggered by Tumpeni's illness or the prospect of heading into the unknown. We drove in silence. I was too worried about Tumpeni to pretend that everything was all right.

The sun fell behind a distant mountain and dusk crept over rocks and trees. A saloon car came up behind us and hovered dangerously close to the rear bumper. Every so often it pulled out and tried to pass, but the dips and bends followed fast one on the other as the road snaked over the tumbled scarps and round dark boulders that crabbed the thorn trees.

Peter kept on turning around to stare at the driver and passenger, both men. 'I have an empty bottle. I can crash it on their faces like I had the stick to fight against the lions,' he remarked.

Thugs were known to stake out this lonely road, ambushing travellers and hijacking their vehicles. In other circumstances, I might have found the car's proximity menacing. Not today. I could only think of Tumpeni.

It was late by the time we arrived at Kiserian, and the clinic had already closed for the night. When I knocked on the door, it was opened a crack to reveal a white veil framing a pinched face. The sister's expression softened when she saw who it was. She stood back and opened the door wide enough to let us in. As Mr Wagaki said, you could never be too careful these days.

Another sister sat at a table, head bent over a file card she had taken from a shoebox. She acknowledged our arrival with a businesslike nod and went back to writing up her patient notes. Both nuns were Maasai. They looked exhausted, as if they had been interrupted in the midst of heaving a long sigh. They muttered something to each other, and the first sister motioned to a bench in the middle of the room.

We sat in a row with our hands in our laps. Nnee looked stoic, her gaze unfocused. But Tumpeni had brightened, his eyes several apertures wider than before. He was staring at the AIDS poster hanging by the table where the sister worked with calm concentration. He had never before sat in the back seat of a real car. He had never been driven over a tarmac road which whipped through the undergrowth like a black mamba. Kiserian with its handful of mud alleys and its church made of stone was the first town he had been to. Now here he was in the largest room he had ever seen, about to be examined by a real doctor.

The nun bent over Tumpeni, her veil falling forward over her shoulders. She pulled down his lower eyelids, pressed a spatula onto his tongue and peered down his throat. She placed gentle fingers on the glands beneath his jaw. Then she straightened up.

'He needs an X-ray. We don't have one here. You must take him to Nasaroni.'

Nnee pulled Tumpeni to her with a protective arm. She looked comforted by this suggestion. I turned to Peter and raised my eyebrows. 'Nasaroni?'

'He is a doctor. That is where we go when we are sick.'

The sister ushered us out into the darkness. She stood framed in the doorway and said, 'You must be tired. Twice in one day. Thank you for looking after our people.'

I nodded and smiled. She didn't understand. Tumpeni and Kipenget were family.

Nasaroni's clinic was by the marketplace, wedged into a row of one-storey cinder-block buildings. It was on the point of closing. We stepped over an open drain which was black with sewage and hurried inside. A young woman was seated behind a wooden desk in the narrow passage which served as the anteroom to the surgery. She would have turned us away if I hadn't insisted the case was urgent. Peter, Nnee and Tumpeni sat down to wait on the bench against the wall. I asked if I could use the *choo*.

The woman led me outside and down a dank passageway which ran between the buildings. The ground was damp and the walls smelt of urine. We sidled past buckets of brownish water in which floated empty bottles and syringes. Tomorrow they would be used again on the next batch of patients. I ducked to avoid a washing-line from which three pairs of disposable surgical gloves had been hung to dry. The limp fingers looked obscene, like used condoms. She unlocked a listing door, gestured to a hole set in the cement floor and left. The cubicle was covered in excrement.

By the time I got back, Nnee, Peter and Tumpeni were in the doctor's minuscule surgery, squeezed onto a little bench in front of his desk. Nasaroni seemed to sag inside his dirty white coat, and when he turned to address me, I saw that his eyes were bloodshot. I disliked his tetchy manner and the way he kept on demanding, 'Do you catch me?' He explained that he had treated Tumpeni for tonsillitis two weeks earlier. The drugs he had given him obviously hadn't cleared it up so he must come back tomorrow for an X-ray. Meanwhile, he was going to give Tumpeni an injection to bring down his temperature. 'Do you catch me?'

'Yes, I catch you. What Tumpeni's mother may not have told you is that his temperature has already come down a lot since we left his home so he won't need an injection. He's much cooler than he was. I think he'll sleep well tonight.' I glanced at Peter for his reaction, but he was staring into space. 'I apologize for keeping you here so late. We should let you get home. We'll come back tomorrow for the X-ray.' He may not have believed me, but it was a face-saver.

When we got back into the car, Nnee tried to make Tumpeni lie down. He refused. He wasn't going to miss out on anything, even if he did feel sick.

'Where are we going?' Nnee asked.

'Nairobi. The hospital.'

Peter leaned across and said in a low voice, 'Thank you, M. A. I really appreciate this.'

The night was clear. A silver moon hung in the sky. Lights from Ongata Rongai's red-tiled houses pricked the groves of acacias. We passed the turn-off to Peter's place and soon after that plunged into suburbia. I glanced into the rear-view mirror. Tumpeni's eyes were large and white in his dark face. He looked like a bushbaby, a wild creature alert to everything around him.

'You okay?'

'Stop driving, Mary Anne. I want to go to sleep.'

'We're nearly there.'

'There are too many lights. They are dangerous.'

I looked about me at the streets I had driven for over twenty years and saw them as a Maasai boy would see them. Blinding headlights, the dark shapes of pedestrians in the road, bicycles weaving amongst the cars. Chaos. 'It's all right. We're almost at the hospital.'

Peter said he knew a shortcut. We twisted and turned along deserted streets past high fences and gates with signs that said

Mbwa Kali, Fierce Dog. Three children trudged ahead with their satchels on their backs. The eldest was about twelve. I felt the stirrings of unease. It was late to be walking home from school on their own. Nnee watched them too and mumbled something.

'What did she say, Peter?'

'Those children shouldn't be out at this time of night.'

By now I had no idea where we were and decided to retrace our route. Tumpeni scolded his brother in a clear voice. 'Why are you getting Mary Anne lost when she has to take me to the hospital?'

When we finally reached the casualty ward, it was seething. Harried doctors and nurses passed on squeaking shoes and vanished into curtained cubicles. A Chinese man was explaining in halting English that he had been in a car crash and his driver was dying. The nurse was telling him he couldn't be treated until he paid a deposit. In the waiting room the silent patients looked as despondent as sheep in a storm. I felt their unblinking gaze upon us when we entered. Did they too think I was helping their people?

Eventually, Tumpeni was attended to by an efficient, unruffled doctor. He said that Tumpeni had enlarged tonsils and prescribed pediatric antibiotic to clear the infection and bring down his temperature. We bought a bottle of it at an all-night chemist in town and left Peter there to catch a *matatu* home. By the time the car crunched down Mike's gravelled driveway it was well after nine o'clock.

Nnee and Tumpeni, whose temperature had indeed fallen, were subdued. Neither had been in a *mzungu* house before. We went into the kitchen for mugs of sweet tea with bread. I spread a slice with peanut butter and gave it to Tumpeni. He bit into it gingerly and, when he thought I wasn't looking, spat it out into Nnee's handkerchief. I spread another with honey and awaited his reaction. 'It is very sweet, but I will eat it.'

Then I led the way to my bedroom. Tumpeni followed, one hand clutching the banisters, the other pressed against the wall. The slow way he mounted each step, legs at an awkward angle, reminded me of a bird with a broken wing. He had never seen stairs before.

Nnee and Tumpeni were restive in bed, shifting and sighing in their half-awake state. Sleep eluded them just as it does with *wazungu* the first time they spend the night on a bed of cowhide and boughs. Nnee had pulled the sheet up over their noses so only their eyes peered out from the bedclothes. Tumpeni was nestled close to her, hard by her side with his head tucked under her arm.

'Tumpeni?' I whispered.

'Mmmmm?'

'Tomorrow I'll buy you a lunch box. You can carry your food to school and you won't have to eat corn.'

'Thank you, Mary Anne.'

'Tumpeni . . .'

'Mmmm?'

'You can tell them at school you're a Bintou Nairobi.'

CHAPTER 32

Time was running short. I had been away from home for over two months, much longer than I had anticipated. Work was going well for Tara in Brighton, and Petra was doing fine at university in Liverpool. Still, I missed them. Besides, I was running out of money. I needed to get back to London and hustle some more magazine assignments. I'd booked a return flight. Only two days remained before my departure.

As always when I left Kenya, I felt as if there were many things left undone. I worried about how Kipenget and Isaac would fare in my absence. There had been no news of Tumpeni, whom I had returned to the *boma* more than two weeks ago. Peter still hadn't invited me for a cup of tea at his place. This bright and sunny Monday had been put aside to tie up loose ends. It was Peter's day off. I planned to collect him from his place in Ongata Rongai then drive to his *boma* so that I could say goodbye to his family.

It started inauspiciously in Peter's rented room. There was a bed, a chair and table, a few plates and mugs piled next to a small paraffin stove. The Los Angeles jacket which he had worn to the raves in England hung on a nail in the wall. Peter was sitting on the pink-and-white flowered counterpane. Joseph was there, too, wearing his macintosh. He had his knees tucked under the table, pen in hand, and was in the midst of writing a letter. I could sense resentment at the interruption.

'Let's go,' said Peter.

'As it's our last day together, why don't we chat for a bit first?'

'All right. We can sit by the side of the road.'

'Actually, I was thinking of talking here. It's rather hot outside.'

Peter looked uncomfortable and glanced across at his friend. 'We would disturb Joseph. He's working.'

'Joseph, would we bother you if we stayed?'

'I have some business outside. I'll be back in an hour,' he said. He rose to his feet and shook my hand before leaving.

'Well,' I said brightly to fill the silence, 'mind if I sit down?'

Peter motioned to Joseph's chair and, once we began chatting, the tension fell away. There was still much about his life before we met which puzzled me. I wanted to banish the lacunae which hung over his childhood. By doing that, I hoped, I might at last come to understand him. I asked questions, and Peter answered them. In this way we poked and prodded at the past. Peter spoke of being a herdsboy in the *boma* and of having no bed, no books and no phone box. He said that he and the other boys followed the goats and cows in the hills with nothing to eat or drink all day.

'I felt I had to be in two worlds – at school and herding the goats. But at times I felt my life was finished because I saw no hope of coming back to school. My uncle wanted me to look after the herds.'

I looked blank. 'But you *were* at school.'

'That's when you made a strong request to pay the school fees because you wanted me to be in school. I had dropped out of school for a full year before that.'

'Why?'

'My uncle didn't want me to go to school so he sent me back home to herd the goats.'

'Your father's brother?'

'I was not calling him my father. I was calling him my uncle.'

'You mean Mebikie.'

Peter nodded. The further I delved into Peter's truth, the more complex it became.

'Mebikie's the one who didn't want you to go to school,' I continued.

'Yes. He wanted me to stay at home. I called him my uncle because my mum was his sister.'

'You mean your aunt was his sister.'

'Yes, Naserian. I thought she was from Samburu.'

'She *was* from Samburu.'

'But he's not from Samburu.'

'No, that's true. He's Maasai like you. I guess Naserian was his sister but in an extended family sort of way.'

'Not *tumbo moja*.'

'Right. Not *tumbo moja*.' I sighed, 'Well, that's sort of made things a bit clearer.' It was a situation which had no parallel in Western society. No wonder Peter had trouble expressing it. The chronology of his life remained elusive, but one new fact had emerged. It was obvious Paul had asked me to sponsor Peter not because he was an orphan but because Mebikie had refused to pay the school fees.

Soon after that we set off in the car. I'd hired a brand new four-wheel-drive Suzuki. This time there were going to be no breakdowns. We stopped at a *duka* and bought packets of tea, sugar and *posho*. One each for Nnee, Kipenget and Isaac. Peter tossed the plastic shopping bag onto the back seat and we continued on our way. The sun sparkling on the tops of the thorn trees reflected our mood. Nothing was going to go wrong on our last day together. We crested a rise in the plains. Kiserian's flat roofs lay below us. It was market day, and a mass of people flowed between the squat buildings.

As the car rolled down the hill, it became sluggish then juddered to a halt. I put my foot flat on the accelerator and revved. The car jolted slowly forward and stopped again. The petrol wasn't feeding through from the tank to the engine.

'I don't believe this. Peter . . .'

'What?'

'This heap isn't going to get us anywhere.'

He was not perturbed. 'What are you going to do?'

'Leave it at Kiserian. We'll hitch.'

The Suzuki heaved and sighed up the dirt road which led to the church. I parked it under a pepper tree, where I hoped it would be safe. If it was left by the side of the road, it would be stripped by the time we got back. When I knocked on the door of the clinic to tell the nuns what had happened, they gave me a cheery smile.

After waiting by the main road for an hour or so, Peter managed to persuade a truck driver to let us have a ride. We clambered up into the cab. We were in luck. He was going all the way to Ol Tepesi. He was about Peter's age and pulled the steering wheel from left to right to left with calm assurance. We hurtled closer to the Ngong Hills, at times leaving the road to avoid oncoming traffic. Peter was untroubled by our zigzag progress but my nerve failed well before reaching the lip of the escarpment. When we reached Kipenget's *boma*, I insisted we get out. She was at market, Meriape said. He was at home because he and the other *matatu* driver were on strike for higher wages. They'd chosen market day as there would be a lot of people at Kiserian who wanted transport back home. That way, the strike would be noticed, he explained. He gave us a look that was defiant and proud.

We sat companionably on the ground, and as we discussed Meriape's chances of success, it reinforced his determination not to give in. Soon Lepapa arrived from school. He threw down his satchel and stretched out on his stomach facing us, his chin propped in his hands. Behind his head the Rift Valley stretched for hundreds of miles, marked by shadow and light. Its majesty excluded all else, and my irritation over the car quickly ebbed away. Out here time was of no importance. I felt good and I could see that Peter was happy too. The plan was to catch the Magadi bus which passed every afternoon at two o'clock. Or thereabouts.

'I can hear it coming,' Peter said, suddenly alert. 'It will only stop for us if we stand at the corner.' The corner, where the road made an abrupt right-hand turn to follow the curve of the Ngongs, was a good 200 yards away.

'We'd better run for it,' I said and got to my feet. I slung my bag over my shoulder and fished out a packet of tea, a packet of sugar and one of *posho* from the shopping bag. I proffered them to Peter. 'These are Nnee's.'

He made no attempt to take them. 'I cannot carry those.'

I gestured impatiently with the sugar. 'Come on. We've got to hurry. We'll miss the bus.'

He looked at the packets as if they were a trap that would spring shut round his hand. 'I cannot carry Nnee's food like that.'

'Why on earth not?'

'I need a plastic bag.'

I dropped the packet of sugar at his feet. The brown paper split at the seam and a few white grains trickled onto the grass. 'If you don't want your mother to have the food, that's up to you. I'm going to catch the bus.'

I presumed Peter would pick up the packets and follow. Yet after walking some yards, when I turned round to look, he was still standing in the middle of the road. His shoulders were hunched forward, his head thrust out. His face, like mine, was masked by anger.

'Cool down, M. A.! Be reasonable,' he shouted.

'No! I'm tired of being reasonable.'

'Why are you so angry?'

'I'm the one who always does everything. You never help. I hire the car and drive it and sort it out when it breaks down. Buy the food for your family. All you have to do is carry it a few yards and you won't even do that. You don't even offer me a cup of tea when I come to pick you up. And if I want to talk to you, I'm supposed to sit in the dirt by the side of the road. Well, I've had enough.'

I turned on my heels. Peter could take the food or leave it, stay where he was or come. It was up to him. I reached the corner and kept on walking. I'd signed off as his mother.

These days my presence seemed to transform Peter's sunny, open nature into brooding resentment. Our relationship perpetually teetered on the brink of conflict. I had stumbled and toiled to regain equilibrium and in the process prostrated my sense of self before his quivering dissatisfaction. Now my patience had run out. How petty to lose my temper over a bag of sugar. Yet the outburst was a release. It felt good to say what I felt, behave – like Peter – without thought for consequence.

Far in the distance, twenty-five miles or more, was Nairobi, dwindled by perspective to the size of my hand. Between me and this remote city lay an infinite and empty expanse of green. Peter had been wrong about the bus. Nothing moved on the plains. I veered onto a footpath, a shortcut between a long, lazy loop in the road. The mangle of emotions had unmoored reality. I strode on. There was no objective. No plan. Nothing mattered.

'*Eeee! Mama ya Wasijana!*' The cry carried easily on the still air. I grinned and headed towards the waving figure.

We sat by the road on the earth verge, our feet planted on the tarmac. I patted her swollen belly. 'Well, little mother, you haven't got long now. You don't know what you're in for. Children. They'll give you a headache just like you did to Kipenget.'

She threw back her head and squeezed her eyes shut, giggling. 'When the baby is big enough, I will give it to Kipenget to look after while I go back to school.'

'Then you must send an *aya* too. Your mother needs a rest. You have a rich husband. You can afford it.'

'I will,' she said and laughed again.

On my previous visit to Kenya, Segenun, Kipenget's second daughter, had been at the top of her class in her last year at school. Since then she had become the wife of a man who lived in a one-room stone house with real windows and doors. The marriage had sidelined an ambition to become a doctor or a nurse. As we chatted, my frustration evaporated. Her optimism was infectious.

A young boy came running down the slope of the hill and stopped a hundred yards short of where we sat. It was Lepapa. Segenun shouted at him and he shouted back.

'Why are you here?'

'Peter sent me to see what Mary Anne is doing.'

'Tell him he should come himself if he wants to know she's all right.'

'Don't bother,' I yelled. 'Join us. We're having fun.'

Lepapa ignored this. He ran up and up and disappeared over the horizon. It looked as if he had flown into the sky. Then out of that same blue void came a white vehicle, listing at an angle and descending the hill no faster than Lepapa had. It drew to a halt beside us. I ducked my head to the level of the window.

'I thought you were on strike, Meriape.'

'Get in, I'm taking you to Kiserian.'

Fifteen years ago I used to drive with my friends through this stretch of countryside. We would gaze about us with a lordly eye, on the lookout for animals and a shady picnic spot. The scenery was beautiful, the Maasai picturesque. We were *wazungu* on safari, getting out into the bush.

This place was not that place. The mud huts, the straggly patches of maze, the grazing herds and the robed herders who importuned

332

the *wazungu* to stop and buy the beadwork they held aloft, had been fleshed out into a community of people whom I knew by name and who knew me. I shared a history with Oldonyati.

When we reached Kiserian, Meriape said, 'You must not be on your own. I will find Mama.' He dredged Kipenget out from the crowded marketplace and she came with me to the phone box to call the hire-car company. Then we sat on a culvert by the side of the road and waited for the mechanic. By this time the children were walking home from school. They streamed through the mud and bunched up in a knot beside us, their gaze curious and fearful.

Kipenget regarded them with irritation. 'Why are you looking at my sister? Have you never seen a white person before? Get a move on!' They paid her no heed so she gave a contemptuous grunt and swivelled her back to them.

She sat leaning forward with her elbows resting on her knees. She wanted to know if I had heard about the *majeen* at the secondary school. People could get land and cars from the *majeen*. Did I think she should try it? I looked blank. She lowered her voice, 'The students get high marks in their exams because of the *majeen*. They come at night and throw the furniture around and make the students scream.'

'Ah, yes. Genies. Don't count on getting land from them. They're difficult to talk to.'

Witchcraft hysteria was sweeping the country. The previous week a mob had tried to lynch an old woman accused of introducing demons into a primary school. They had said she was a witch and had accused her of the deaths of twenty pupils. Frightened parents had already withdrawn 300 students from the school. The woman had been rescued by the local district commissioner before the outraged crowd could hang her.

Poor Kipenget. She was clutching at straws. She knew she would be working until she was in the grave.

I got home safely, but Peter didn't phone the next day to find out if I had managed to fix the car. Nor did he phone the day after that, even though a friend had intervened and urged him to ring me. Peter had said, 'It's best to leave Mary Anne alone when she's like that.'

On the third day, the day I was leaving for London, I went to see Peter at the Ostrich Park. Neither of us referred to the fiasco of Nnee's packets of food and the bus. Instead we talked to each other in a way that was polite but guarded. I asked after Tumpeni and he said that he was well but still had a fever. This worried me, but it was too late to do anything about it. I made Peter promise he would visit him again the following week and take him to the doctor if he still wasn't well.

'Explain his whole case history. Tell him what Tumpeni had.'

'What was wrong with him?'

'Tonsillitis,' I said flatly.

We said goodbye without touching.

I drove on to Kipenget's *boma*. It was early evening, and the Ngongs were shaded by a subdued grey light. She was standing by the house amidst the chickens and rubbish and the beans she had spread out on the ground to dry. She tried to say hello but bubbles of wetness broke from her mouth like someone who is drowning. Her sorrow took my breath away as surely as if I'd been punched in the stomach. I took her in my arms and held her tight. Then I grasped her long, graceful fingers and led her inside to a stool by the fire. She was sobbing so hard she couldn't speak. When eventually she did, it was a breathless outpouring of Maa.

Lepapa's voice came from the shadows. 'Mama says you have been a mother to her all these years. You gave her a cow and took her to the doctor when she didn't want any more children. You fenced our *shamba* so we could grow maize. Whenever she needed you, you were there. You are a part of us.'

Kipenget gave another sob, wiped her nose with the back of her hand, and pulled an old leather bag towards her. The shadows leapt away from her face as she leaned forward to produce a bracelet of red and white and blue beads. She took my fingers and worked it over my hand with fierce determination. 'Live with us. You looked after me when you had a house. Now I will look after you.'

'I can't. My house is in England.'

'I will be alone without you. What am I going to do?'

There was no adequate answer for this. I stared at the bracelet and our tears that fell on it. Then I said, 'Where is Isaac?'

'He is herding the cows. These days he is sleeping in his house on the bed you gave him. He has put up the gutters and there is water now. He asked me to say goodbye.'

There was a commotion outside and Meriape stood framed by the doorway, his dark glasses pushed up onto his forehead. I rose and we embraced and kissed.

'The strike?'

He smiled ruefully, 'We didn't get any more money so I keep on working. I can't stay. My passengers are waiting on the road.'

'Look after Mama while I'm away.'

'We'll see you again when it pleases God. I will miss you.' He turned and strode away.

It was time to lighten the moment so I said to Lepapa, 'I suppose you lost your plastic bag to Peter. Did he use it to take the food to Nnee?'

'No,' said Lepapa. 'After you left, a man gave him a lift to Nairobi. He didn't go to see Nnee.'

'So he passed me in Kiserian while I was waiting to be rescued?'

Lepapa shrugged. 'I don't know.'

'Kipenget, I must go. This is for food.' I pressed the notes into her hand. 'And these clothes are for you. This is my favourite dress. Think of me when you wear it.'

She nodded and another bubble escaped her mouth. We walked up the slope in silence. I held her, kissed her wet mouth. Before getting into the car I bent down and fumbled with my shoes.

'Here, yours are falling apart.'

I looked back only once. For a long moment I saw Kipenget's crumpled brown face as she stood by the road, a solitary figure in the encroaching darkness. Then I turned the corner where, every afternoon, the Magadi bus picked up its passengers, and pressed my bare foot down on the accelerator.

I wrote to Peter from England but he did not reply. It seemed the fault line between our cultures had become an irreparable crack. Then, five months later, I received a letter.

I miss you and the girls a great deal. I love Petra and I badly miss her. When cool, she is just too cool in her room like a nun. I miss Tara's great care and wisdom and wonderful adventures of Brighton. If I focus my mind back to England it is like going to dreamland. It is like an activity in fairy tales.

M. A., I know that you do love me deeply. In my heart, my mind, my soul and spirit I love you a great deal too. As I have been growing up, I have been naughty to you and good just like other children are to their parents. It must have been very difficult for you raising us all without a job at times. In your heart I know that you were proud of having a big family and you needed the best for everybody. You did offer us everything. As one of your children, I am very proud of you. You have taken me a long way. It is through your encouragement, love and care that steered me this far.

When we had that little understanding as we were near Kipenget's home, I could not see why we had to behave like that. Till now, I still believe that I am wrong or probably you were wrong too. To forget this episode, we need to think of the future and look forward to being ourselves. If our love is like the sun that rises, the wind that blows, the sea and the ocean, it will forever be there.

The letter dispelled our fantasies of each other: the Maasai mother and the Western son. I had behaved as many mothers do and tried too hard to change him. He, as any child, had rebelled and returned, in his way, in his time.

This adoption that wasn't an adoption had been a strange coming together of two people. I, the mother who was not his mother and never would be. He, the orphan who was not an orphan. I wondered if we had unconsciously decided to assume these roles to assuage convention, make it easier for nurturing to take place. Piecing together the jigsaw of Peter's tale, as he had related it in dribs and drabs over the years, I realized he must have always felt he had a mother. His aunt Naserian was replaced by his real mother Nnee. And at times maybe he had even thought of me as a mother. Most children need one to help them grow up. Others want more. That's fine. Whatever it takes to get there.

I found Peter's fathers more difficult to come to terms with.

Mebikie, Nnee's husband, had wanted to kill Peter because he was not his biological son. When Peter was a small child, Naserian's lover, the herder at Naivasha, had walked out on woman and boy. Many years later, following my expulsion from Kenya, Mike Eldon had taken over as guardian, providing a home, sound career advice and financial support. And finally Peter's anonymous biological father had presented himself – the man who swiped at his ears when he was angry, Nnee's lover of a quarter of a century back. There had been no commitment there either save an empty promise to give Peter a cow. With the exception of Mike, none of this pool of fathers had shown much interest in their collective son.

My last real conversation with Peter, the one that had taken place in his room at Ongata Rongai two days before I flew back to London, had underscored how ineffective his paternal role models had been. When Peter had related how he'd been attending school until his 'uncle' Mebikie had refused to pay the fees, another truth had been revealed. The orphan story, encouraged by Mebikie, was a bait to attract a sponsor for Peter. The timing had been fortuitous for Peter when Paul the headmaster had summoned me to his office to discuss Isaac's disgraceful behaviour. I was playing the mobile bank again. I had a right to be angry but I wasn't.

To have given because Peter was an orphan would have been an act of charity. I paid Peter's school fees so that this particular boy – who never seemed to have enough pencils and notebooks, who played a mean number nine on the soccer pitch, who wanted so badly to be loved and adored – would have the tools to make something of his life. Yes, I was guilty of attaching strings of hope to the gift. I'd had visions of a leader amongst men who would change the course of Kenyan history. But finally I'd come to accept that it was wrong to relive my values through Peter. He was not a political man or even a particularly venturesome one. During his time with us in England, my aspirations for him had gradually been realigned. I hoped Peter would eventually acknowledge his own worth without having first to see it reflected in another's eyes. I hoped he would always be truthful, compassionate and honest with friend and stranger alike. I hoped his marriage would be a love-match and that he would always be able to support his children on the money he earned. I hoped these things for him because I loved him, not because he was my sometime son. I also knew that these thoughts had nothing to do with culture. The parental blueprint is universal, appropriate to African and European alike.

I lift my head and look onto the rooftops of London, veiled in a winter mist. I see Peter's dark face. His expression is relaxed and happy, neither shuttered nor resentful. My son has spoken with an open heart and, without casting blame, laid before me forgiveness. I have lived my life following my own path. I have come to accept that he must do the same.

A man's deeds are greater than the facts of his birth. It is a Maasai saying.

GLOSSARY

*= Kiswahili
Sheng is the name for Kiswahili slang

asaroi – cow's blood mixed with curdled milk (Maa)
ashe oleng – thank you very much (Maa)
ayah – nanny *
bhanghi – marijuana *
Bintou Yookay – someone who has been to England (Sheng)
boma – Maasai encampment *
ceilidh – Scots folk dancing (Gaelic)
chai – tea *
chapati – flat, circular bread introduced from India *
chini – lower, below *
choo – lavatory *
Chunga mwizi – Watch out for thieves *
dawa – medicine *
debe – large container *
duka – shop *
emala – gourd (Maa)
emanyata – a large circle of ceremonial mud huts (Maa)
emonyorit – a woman's marriage chain worn around the ears (Maa)
emorata – circumcision (Maa)
enchani pus – blue tree (Maa)
engipaata – dance of the warriors before a cattle raid (Maa)
entawuo – the heifer a man pays for a bride from his own clan (Maa)
esumeita – a tree root that has medicinal properties (Maa)
eunoto – the ceremony that marks the end of warriorhood (Maa)
ganja – marijuana (Sheng)
gogo – grandmother (Maa)
habari – how are you *
habari ya siku nyingi – what news of many days, as in: long time no see *
hakuna – none *
Hamjambo wananchi! Sikiliza maneno yangu – Greetings people! Listen to
    my words *
Hana akili – He's not smart *
hoteli – eating house *
iko – he/she/ it is there (used as both statement and question) *
Ilaiser – the name of Kipenget's clan (Maa)
Illoorridaa injikat – the people who confine their farts (refers to white men,
    who wear trousers rather than loosefitting robes) (Maa)

339

Ilukumae – the name of Peter's clan (Maa)
Irkipali – the name of Peter's age group (Maa)
isurutia – a married woman's scrolled earrings (Maa)
jambo – hello *
juu – upper, above *
kali – fierce *
kanga – patterned sarong worn by women *
karibu, karibuni – welcome (sing., pl.) *
kayamba – musical instrument made of six-inch hollow reeds tied together
    and filled with seeds *
kikoi – sarong worn by men *
Kiserian inkera? – How are the children? (Maa)
kushuk – cloth worn as turban or sarong (Tigrinya)
laisungu – a white person (Maa)
lakira – star (Maa)
Imura – penis (Maa)
Imurani – warrior (Maa)
loikop – murder (Maa)
lokop naibor – the white Samburu (Samburu)
lorika – stool (Maa)
Maasaini – Maasailand *
majeen – genies *
mama ya wasijana wawili – mother of two girls *
mamba ya sumu – snake poison *
mambo ya wazee – men's talk (Maa)
manyanga – goodlooking taxi or girl (Sheng)
matatu – taxi *
maziwa lala – curdled milk *
mbwa – dog *
memsahib – madam as a form of address, usually referring to a white woman *
miti – stick *
Mimi natoka London – I come from London *
Mimi ni bodyguard yake – I am her bodyguard * (and English)
mroso – rough (Sheng)
mto wa mbu – mosquito river *
muratina – a strong beer brewed from honey *
Mwaafrica – African person *
mzungu, wazungu – white person, people *
Neserian inkishu? – How are the cattle? (Maa)
Nkai – God (Maa)
nkai nanyokie – the red god (Maa)
nkai narok – the black god (Maa)
nyama choma – roast meat *
olamal – group of people attending a traditional ceremony (Maa)
ol doinyo – mountain (Maa)
ole – son of (Maa)
oloirujuruj – the drizzling season (Maa)

Oloolaiser – the Maasai name for the Ngong Hills (Maa)

oloorruka – hump (Maa)

olpirron – firestick elders, the age group that disciplines warriors (Maa)

ol tepesi – thorn tree *

ongata rongai – narrow plain (Maa)

oringesherr – the ceremony following *eunoto* that marks the transition from warrior to junior elder (Maa)

osutua lai – my umbilical cord, a common term of endearment (Maa)

ou – come (Maa)

paan – Indian delicacy of lime paste and crushed areca nut wrapped in betel leaf (Hindustani)

paashe – heifer (Maa)

panga – curved, broad-bladed knife *

pee elak Irkololik enkeene – the time of the untying of the knot of the Irkololik, referring to when the Irkololik age group ceased to be warriors (Maa)

Piga piksha kabla ya kuondoga – take a picture before leaving *

Poleni safari – loosely translated: you must have had a terrible journey, but it's good to see you *

posho – maizemeal *

rubega – red, purple and indigo cloths worn by the Maasai *

rungu – club *

safi – clean, good *

serenget – savannah (Maa)

shamba – plot of cultivated land *

shauri ya wanawake – women's business*

shifta – Somali bandit *

shuka – length of cloth worn by the Maasai *

simi – broad-bladed fighting sword *

sobua – stick (Maa)

songa – move over *

sopa, ipa – hello (Maa)

Springs ni weak kidogo – The springs are a bit weak * (and English)

sufuria – cooking pot *

sukuma wiki – a type of chard *

tabula rasa – blank slate (Latin)

tambac – tobacco *

tumbo moja – literally, one stomach, used in polygamous communities to establish if siblings have the same mother *

twiga – giraffe *

uji – maizemeal gruel *

Wahindi – Indians *

wananchi – people, usually used to refer to the man in the street *

wazee – elders, old men *

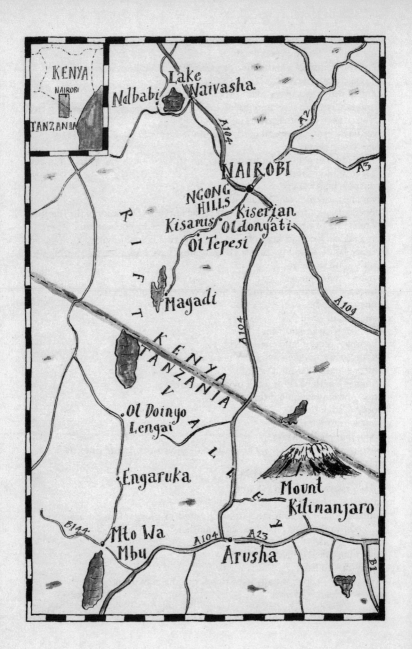